亲历日本文化

My Experiences and Musings of Japanese Culture

（汉英对照）

(美)托德·杰伊·伦纳德 著
赵琦 高李义 刘悟明 编译

北京师范大学出版集团
BEIJING NORMAL UNIVERSITY PUBLISHING GROUP
安徽大学出版社

图书在版编目（CIP）数据

亲历日本文化：汉英对照 ／（美）托德·杰伊·伦纳德著；赵琦，高李义，刘悟明编译．—合肥：安徽大学出版社，2021.5
ISBN 978-7-5664-2217-0

Ⅰ．①亲⋯ Ⅱ．①托⋯ ②赵⋯ ③高⋯ ④刘⋯ Ⅲ．①文化史－日本－汉、英 Ⅳ．① K313.03

中国版本图书馆 CIP 数据核字（2021）第 070400 号

亲历日本文化（汉英对照）
Qinli Riben Wenhua

（美）托德·杰伊·伦纳德 著
赵 琦 高李义 刘悟明 编译

出版发行：	北京师范大学出版集团 安徽大学出版社 （安徽省合肥市肥西路 3 号 邮编 230039） www.bnupg.com.cn www.ahupress.com.cn
印　刷：	安徽省人民印刷有限公司
经　销：	全国新华书店
开　本：	170mm×240mm
印　张：	14.25
字　数：	330 千字
版　次：	2021 年 5 月第 1 版
印　次：	2021 年 5 月第 1 次印刷
定　价：	47.00 元

ISBN 978-7-5664-2217-0

策划编辑：	李　梅　李　雪	责任印制：	赵明炎
责任编辑：	李　雪	装帧设计：	李　雪　李　军
责任校对：	高婷婷	美术编辑：	李　军

版权所有　侵权必究

反盗版、侵权举报电话：0551-65106311
外埠邮购电话：0551-65107716
本书如有印装质量问题，请与印制管理部联系调换。
印制管理部电话：0551-65106311

译序
Translator's Preface

  有关日本文化的书籍，国内外已经出版了不少，本书的独特之处就在于，它发端于作者给家乡美国印第安纳州一家报刊《谢尔比维尔报》的栏目 Hoosier in Japan《印第安纳州人在日本》撰写的文章，这些文章简述了作者在日本工作30多年来亲历的日本文化。他曾利用学术休假在美国威斯康辛州州立大学进行学术研究工作，其时适逢我在该大学任教，有幸阅读作者的相关栏目文章，觉得耳目一新。作者以其独特的视角，时间的沉淀和更平民化的旅日生活经历对日本文化真实再现，可读性很强。

  我曾将作者的部分文章作为学生翻译练习的素材，学生既能欣赏地道优美的英语，又能在翻译实践中提高翻译能力，一举两得，受益匪浅。于是我萌生了将相关文章翻译成中文以飨中国读者的想法，使他们能在全面了解日本文化的同时，提高英语鉴赏水平和翻译能力。征得作者同意后，我们遴选汇编了具有代表性的文章并翻译成中文，内容涉及国民性、教育、社会、生活、风俗、节日和旅游。通过这些方面，读者可以对日本有全方位的认识，体味作者对日本的了解和敬仰，以及在克服文化差异融入日本社会之后，对日本及其国民寄予的真情实感。

  翻译是把一种语言准确而完整地转换成另一种语言的过程。翻译活动包含两个重要的环节：正确的理解和恰当的表达，后者必须以前者为前提。在翻译过程中为了尽可能准确地让读者感受到译文的科学性、趣味性和可读性，译者曾多次与作者就文章的中心思想、写作的意图、措辞的准确性等问题往来函电；就有关日本习俗、节日、词汇的表达等向南宁师范大学的日本外教和日语老师请教和求证。

一方面，译者希望本译著能对英语翻译工作者、英语教师、翻译专业的学生及广大英语学习者都有所裨益，尤其是能让学生在翻译学习阶段，了解翻译的实际要求，从一开始就少走弯路，掌握正确的翻译方法；另一方面，希望本书能为读者提供一扇全方位了解真实日本文化的窗户。

本书的编译由赵琦（南宁师范大学）、高李义（南宁师范大学毕业生）、刘悟明（加拿大卡尔加里大学）完成。本书从提出项目建议到最终完稿，自始至终得到了南宁师范大学外国语学院领导和同人的关心和支持，尤其是日语专业的梁丽娟等几位同事，在编译修改过程中及时提供了非常中肯、极富洞见的建议，使本书更具有可读性和真实性，并尽可能把错误率降到最低。对此，译者表示由衷的感谢。

由于成书时间比较仓促，加上译者的学养不高，能力有限，书中不妥之处乃至错漏谬误，恳请广大读者、各位专家同仁批评指正。

赵 琦

2021 年 4 月 12 日

Author's Preface

There have been so many books written on Japan over the years that there possibly could not be anything new to add to the plethora of literature already out there…or at least one would think so. Historians, sociologists, experts and scholars have written voluminously on Japan, its history, society, people, and culture covering just about every aspect of all things Japanese. The dilemma, though, is that Japan—like all cultures—is ever changing and shifting. Like an ocean that ebbs and flows continuously, so does Japanese culture and society. There will always be something new to add to the existing literature on Japan because it will always be metamorphosing, while tenaciously holding on to certain aspects that have endured for eons. Hence, future Japanologists and Japanophiles must not worry that there will come a time when there is nothing new to report or comment upon with regards to this enigmatic and fascinating culture.

This book you are holding in your hands is a compilation of personal observations and experiences that are uniquely my own, so it is impossible that there is any other publication "just like it". Granted, there are certain facets of Japanese culture and society that include customs, traditions and celebrations that are for the most part "matter-of-fact", but these can take on a completely different meaning and significance when interpreted independently through one's own encounters and knowledge based on personal observations and experiences.

This volume is actually a translation of two previous books, *Letters Home—*

Musings of an Expatriate Living in Japan (iUniverse, 2003) and *An Indiana Hoosier in Lord Tsugaru's Court: Musings of an American Expatriate Living in Rural Japan* (iUniverse, 2009). Both had their genesis in a column I wrote for my hometown newspaper, *The Shelbyville News*, Shelbyville, Indiana. The original series was called "Letters Home—A Hoosier in Japan" and dealt with my impressions and experiences of living in rural Japan.

The column proved to be a huge hit in my hometown and attracted quite a following. Perhaps the reason why it was so popular amongst the readership was because many people were intrigued by Japan but did not know much about its culture, customs, and traditions. In addition, the writing style—like personal letters—appealed to many people because the articles covered topics related to my everyday-life in Japan, as well as to Japanese history, politics, education, and social issues—but through my eyes and cultural filter. I suppose by reading and learning about Japan by virtue of my perspective, the readers were able to connect personally with what I experienced, which seemed more credible and authentic coming from a person who had the same small-town roots. For the same reason, Japanese people who read the English versions of this book encouraged me to have these books translated into Japanese so more Japanese can learn about their own culture through my eyes and my interpretation of cultural cues I have experienced throughout my tenure in Japan.

All over the United States, as well as in my hometown, Japanese people are a part of the community—some marry Americans and relocate to the US; others come to work in both Japanese and US owned industries; while still others come to study, visit, or just get to know individual Americans through educational programs and sister-city exchanges. Likewise, all over Japan, communities have growing foreign populations and more and more Japanese people are coming into daily contact with foreigners who now call Japan "home".

The positive feedback generated from all of these groups of people, coupled with the success of the English versions of the book, I set out to rewrite and edit some of the more amusing and provocative articles which appeared in both books. The result is this book—a series of letter-essays relating my impressions and experiences of being a foreigner living in rural Japan. The content of each essay consists of information that has been borrowed primarily from my own personal observations and encounters while living in Japan, and from factual information about the various aspects of Japanese society and culture—differing attitudes, customs, and traditions—as I witnessed, experienced, and finally interpreted them.

Therefore, the perceptions and recollections contained herein are my own, so I certainly do not speak for every foreigner living in Japan—nor would I want to as everyone who comes to Japan, and those who eventually choose to call it home, have a different interpretation and reaction to the same situation. These are mine and mine alone.

As a general point of reference, to compare and contrast cross-cultural differences, I do often refer to the United States and my experience being born and raised in the Midwest throughout my essays. This is in no way meant to disenfranchise other foreigners or to give the impression of being "American-centered". Simply, it is what I am and what I know best; it is a compilation of writings about an American teacher from the state of Indiana who lives and works in the countryside of Japan.

I arrived in Japan in 1989 and lived in Hirosaki-shi, Aomori-ken for 20 years. In 2010, I relocated to Kyushu and I now call Munakata-shi, Fukuoka-ken home; this is where I live, teach, and write now. Each place has its own distinct traditions, customs, and even dialects of the Japanese language.

I first relocated to Japan in July of 1989, and what was intended to be a one year stint has turned into over thirty. Amazingly, this occurred quite effortlessly prompting me to ask myself, "Where did the years go?" It has been an amazing journey, indeed, and one that I cherish deeply. I am quite aware how privileged I am to have been able to live and work in this amazing culture, meeting a variety of wonderful people, and being able to grow on a personal and cultural level. Interestingly, I never planned to live here for so long, it just happened.

In 1989, after finishing a graduate program in history, I was offered an opportunity to live and work in Hirosaki, Japan as an Assistant Language Teacher (ALT) on the Japan Exchange and Teaching (JET) Program(me). For two and one-half years I taught English alongside a Japanese Teacher of English (JTE) in junior high schools all over the Tsugaru region of Aomori. It was during this tenure as a "one-shot" teacher traveling around the countryside to visit rural schools that I was offered an associate professorship at a local university in the Faculty of Liberal Arts, where I taught Cross-Cultural Understanding, Comparative Studies, History, and naturally, English until 2010. I relocated to Kyushu in order to accept a position at a national university where I am a full-professor and I teach both undergraduates and graduate students Cross-Cultural Understanding and English in the Faculty of Education.

My first introduction to Japan was as an elementary school child when a Japanese art teacher taught classes at my school. I had heard about Japan from TV programs, magazines, and books (there was a huge "Japan-boom" for some years after the Tokyo Olympics took place in 1964). This teacher, though, really intrigued me. She left her home and family—everything that she knew and was familiar and dear to her—to come to my little town to teach American kids art. Her accent, mannerisms, and style of dress fascinated me.

This fascination continued throughout my life and as a 17-year-old high school student, I finally had an opportunity to experience Japan first-hand. I spent the summer of 1979 as a Youth for Understanding Exchange (YFU) student living in a suburb of Tokyo. This experience quite literally changed my life. I had been bitten by the Japan bug and was chronically smitten by its people, culture, traditions, and history. That same summer, the son of the family I stayed with came back to the United States with me and lived with my family for a year. This further cemented my relationship with Japan and by the end of his year in Indiana, my entire family and circle of friends were "Japanophiles".

As an undergraduate student at Purdue University, I settled for studying Japanese history because in the early 1980s few Japanese language programs existed. I did have an opportunity to return to Japan for a summer as a participant on the 35th Japan-America Student Conference (JASC). After this last trip to Japan, however, I would not return to Japan for a number of years. I did have an opportunity to study at Universidad Complutense in Madrid, Spain, for a year during my junior year abroad. Later, after I finished my graduate work at Purdue University, I studied at the Universidad de Costa Rica in San José, Costa Rica as a Rotary Scholar where I was an ambassador of goodwill for Rotary International's Graduate Scholar Program as a postgraduate student in history. Each of these places, although unique and interesting, never fully substituted my sincere desire to return to Japan.

Fast forward more than 30 years, and as I embark upon my fourth decade in Japan, I realize that I have lived over half my life in Japan. Little did I know, as I sat in that Japanese art teacher's class as a little boy, how much Japan would become an integral part of my personal and professional life. I, the same as my art teacher, made the decision to leave all that I knew and loved in order to teach Japanese children in a country far away from my roots and home. My yearning for cross-cultural understanding has indeed turned into a lifetime vocation.

Prof. Todd Jay Leonard

April. 2021

Contents

1　第一部分　日本国民性　Japanese National Character

  2　矜持谦恭　|　4　The Fine Art of "Reserve"

  6　关注细节　|　8　Attention to Details

  11　坚忍精神　|　12　The Idea of Perseverance

  14　文化与国民　|　16　Culture and People

20　第二部分　日本教育　Japanese Education

  21　教育　|　22　Education

  25　学生的就餐修养　|　26　Students Serve Lunch for Their Peers

  28　育儿之道　|　29　Child Rearing

  31　幼儿早教　|　33　Early Childhood Education

37　第三部分　日本社会　Japanese Social Issues

38　安全　｜　40　A Safe Country

42　老龄化　｜　45　"Top-heavy" Japan

48　移民　｜　51　Immigration

56　流浪汉　｜　58　Homeless People

60　离婚　｜　62　Divorce

65　收养　｜　69　Adoption

75　宠物　｜　77　Pet

81　第四部分　日本生活　Japanese Life

82　房屋　｜　84　Homes

86　泡浴　｜　89　Bath

92　马桶　｜　95　Toilets

99　垃圾回收　｜　101　Recycling Garbage

104　发廊　｜　107　Hair Salons

110　包裹服务　｜　112　Parcel Service

114　宠物　｜　116　Pampered Pooches

119 第五部分　日本风俗　Japanese Custom

　　120　茶道　｜　122　The Way of Tea

　　125　相扑　｜　128　Sumo Wrestling

　　132　邻里协会　｜　134　Neighborhood Association

　　136　小费文化　｜　139　Tipping

　　142　送礼文化　｜　146　Gift Giving

　　151　婚礼　｜　155　Weddings

　　160　葬礼　｜　163　Funeral Rituals

167 第六部分　日本节日　Japanese Holidays

　　168　新年　｜　169　New Year's Day

　　172　女孩节和男孩节　｜　174　Girls' Day and Boys' Day

　　176　7-5-3　｜　177　7-5-3

　　179　成人礼　｜　181　Coming of Age Ceremony

　　183　睡魔节和盂兰盆节　｜　184　Neputa Festival and Obon Season

187　第七部分　日本旅游　Japanese Tourism

188　公共交通　｜　190　Public Transportation

193　出租车行业　｜　195　Taxi

198　抵达与入住　｜　200　Arrival and Hotels

203　在东京游览　｜　204　Touring Tokyo

206　在东京就餐与购物　｜　208　Restaurants and Shopping in Tokyo

210　观赏樱花　｜　212　Cherry Blossoms Viewing

第一部分
日本国民性

Part 1
Japanese National Character

矜持谦恭

这些年来,我已经慢慢习惯了日本文化中令人十分费解的一面——"遠慮"。

关于"遠慮",最贴切的解释是"矜持谦恭",意思是,当别人为你送上饮食、礼物或提供座位时,谦恭有礼的反应应该是沉默不语并向对方表示敬意。尤其是女性,最初拒绝接受对方的好意才算是有礼貌的表现。

我首次领会这一跨文化概念是我初到日本之时。当时,我邀请了一群上了年纪的女士来家里参加美式餐宴。

我煞费苦心地准备好一切,甚至额外买了一些"座布团"(放在地上的坐垫),以便人人都有一个舒服的地方就坐。如今,我家的布置十分西方化,但在日本生活初期,我遵循着十分传统的日本生活方式,家里不摆放家具也不铺地毯,只有一张矮桌供大家围坐,地面铺着榻榻米(草席地板)。

这些女士到达后,我理所当然地给她们每人一个坐垫,请她们坐下。6位女士都接过了我给的坐垫,之后却小心翼翼地把垫子放在地上,继而跪在垫子旁边,而不是坐在垫子上。

她们当时的举动确实令我大为不解,压根无法理解她们为什么不坐在这些崭新的坐垫上。是觉得坐垫脏吗?难道是我在文化上有什么失礼之处而不自知?

随着夜晚的时间一点点地过去,每一位女士也一点点地把身子挪向坐垫。当晚聚会结束时,她们都踏踏实实地坐在了垫子上(有些人甚至不是保持正式的"正坐"姿势,而是将腿置于身体一侧)。我觉得她们此刻才算最终放松下来并尽享愉快的时光。

就这样,我在无意之中见识了"遠慮"——日本人表示克制的艺术。要是她们之中有人一开始就接受我给的坐垫并立刻坐上去,而不是事先犹豫并按照被认可的社交礼节等上一段时间,在场的其他人会认为她们举止粗鲁,没有淑女风范。

日本文化和礼仪在许多方面都十分注重礼节和行为举止,一个外国人要弄清楚孰是孰非,有时的确很难。当然,每个日本人从小就接受这方面的教育,因此他们十分清楚自己在社会中的角色,并依此行事。

不合规矩之举很容易冒犯日本人。我的一位日本朋友曾邀请一位同事及其太太到家里吃饭。主人是单身,客人的太太因此成了在场唯一的女性。按照日本习俗,在单身主人家做客吃饭的客人中如果有女性,饭后,她应该主动提出清理厨房,这一请求可能会被主人婉拒,但却是合乎礼节的一种表现。

这位女士不仅没有主动帮忙清理,反而索要烟灰缸,还是当时唯一抽烟的人。当然,朋友当时什么也没说,强装高兴的样子,但后来,我听到的都是关于朋友同事的太太举止如何粗鲁的牢骚抱怨,在朋友看来,她没有表现出应有的克制或"遠慮"。

另一种相当古怪的"遠慮"是礼貌地拒绝礼物。我出差在外的时候,隔壁邻居常会帮我打扫院中的走道,浇花,并照看我的房子及财物。

因此,不管我去哪儿出差,都觉得必须为她带回一件纪念品,以感谢她的善意和帮助。然而,每次她都要按日本古老的习俗恭敬地推辞一番。

我首先送上礼物,她则礼貌地拒绝;之后,我坚持送她礼物,并解释说她给予了我莫大的帮助,我对此深表感激,她则再次拒绝,并礼貌地来回摆手;我第三次将礼物双手奉上,一边深深鞠躬一边说"本当どうぞ"(意为请您务必收下),然后我就等着。第三次总是奏效的,因为她接受了礼物,并一个劲儿地感谢我,说让我出差时为家里牵肠挂肚,还那么麻烦地带礼物给她,令她深感歉意。

瞧见了吧,如果她二话不说就接受礼物便是粗鲁无礼的表现,因为那会显得她不够克制。而从美国人的文化视角来看,拒绝别人给的礼物(哪怕是礼貌地拒绝)、提供的座位或饮食,都是粗鲁的行为。即便是讨厌的食物,至少得尝一口,以示对食物感兴趣及感谢对方。这就是我美国文化背景的体现。在日本人看来,立刻接受别人给的东西太过直接。一开始拒绝接受,表明你谦卑,不想给对方添麻烦。

我已经习惯这方面的日本文化,不管我送什么,预料到日本人一开始都会礼貌地推辞或拒绝,之后才最终收下。但从文化角度出发,日本人可以接受在一定时限内推让礼物。对我而言,尽管在日本生活了这么多年,但有人送我礼物时,我还是倾向于立刻收下。我认为老话说得对:你可以离开美国,但你身上的美国烙印不会消失。

The Fine Art of "Reserve"

There is a very puzzling aspect of Japanese culture which I have slowly become accustomed to over the years called "enryo".

Enryo can best be translated as "reserve" or the idea that it is courteous to be reticent and to show deference when offered something to eat, drink, a gift or a place to sit down. It is considered polite initially to refuse such offers, especially by women.

My first experience with this cross-cultural concept happened when I first arrived in Japan. I had invited a group of older ladies to my home for an American-style dinner party.

I had painstakingly prepared everything and even purchased extra zabuton (floor cushions) so everyone would have a comfortable place to sit. Today, my home is quite westernized, but in my early years of living in Japan I lived a very traditional Japanese life-style with no furniture or carpet. I had a low table that people sat around, and my floors were covered with tatami (straw mat flooring).

When the ladies arrived, I of course gave them each a cushion and asked them to take a seat. Each of the 6 ladies accepted the cushion, but then gingerly laid it on the floor and then proceeded to kneel beside the cushion, not using it to sit on.

Hmmm, this was indeed puzzling behavior to me in those days. I was thoroughly confused as to why they refused to sit on these brand-spanking new zabuton. Did they think they were dirty? Was there a cultural faux pas I had committed without realizing it?

Gradually, as the night progressed each lady inched her way on to the cushion. By the end of the evening they were all firmly seated on the cushions (some even sitting with their legs to the side instead of the formal "seiza" or kneeling position). I felt they were finally relaxed and were enjoying themselves.

I had unwittingly witnessed "enryo", the Japanese art of showing reserve. It would have been perceived by the others in attendance as being rude and unladylike had anyone of them quickly accepted my offer of a cushion, and immediately proceeded to sit on it without first hesitating and waiting a socially acceptable amount of time before doing so.

So much of Japanese culture and etiquette focuses on proper protocol and behavior that it is sometimes hard for an outsider to know what is correct and what is not. Of course, every Japanese person from early childhood has been trained in this knowledge and is keenly aware of his or her place within the social structure.

Japanese are very easily offended if a breach of protocol occurs. I remember a Japanese friend of mine who had invited a colleague and his wife for dinner. The host was single, so the only woman there was the guest's wife. After dinner, it is customary that if a woman is among the guests visiting a single man's home for dinner, that she offers to help clean up the kitchen. The offer maybe refused, but it is proper to do so as a gesture.

This woman not only failed to offer to help with the cleanup, but she asked for an ashtray and was the only person who was smoking. Of course, my friend said nothing at the time and put on a "happy" face, but later I got a near full about how rude his colleague's wife had behaved. She failed to demonstrate proper reserve or "enryo" in his estimation.

Another type of "enryo" that is actually rather quaint is the polite refusal of gifts. Often when I am away on trips, my next door neighbor will sweep my walk, water my flowers, and generally keep an eye on my house and property.

I feel obliged, then, to bring her back a memento from wherever I have been as a thank you for her kindness and help. Each time, though, we go through an ancient Japanese ritual of deference.

I first offer the gift—she politely refuses. I then insist, explaining how helpful she has been and how appreciative I am—she refuses again, waving her hand back and forth politely. The third time I offer the gift, I do so with both hands, my head bowed low and say "honto dozo" (really, please take it), and wait. The third time is always the charm, because she then accepts it, thanking me profusely and apologizing that she has made me worry during my trip and for being so much trouble.

See, it would have been rude for her to accept it immediately because it would make her appear to be unreserved. From my American cultural perspective, it would be rude to refuse (even politely) a gift, a chair to sit down on, food, or a drink that is offered or served to me. Even if it is something that I hated, I would at least taste it in order to show some interest and appreciation for the offering.

This is my American cultural background shining through. A Japanese person may interpret immediate acceptance of an offering as being too forward. By first refusing, it portrays humility and the desire not to be any trouble to the person offering.

I am used to this aspect of Japanese culture, and expect people first to defer or refuse politely, then eventually accept whatever it is I am offering. But in a time-frame that is culturally acceptable to them. I do, however, still tend to accept an offering immediately even after living here for so many years. I guess the old adage is true: you can take the boy out of America, but you can't take the America out of the boy.

关注细节

每当家乡的朋友造访日本，他们对这个国家及其国民的最初印象之一就是日本人对细节的关注，这种对细节异乎寻常的关注使日本人的生活惬意了许多。

无论是火车站身着整齐制服的清洁工，还是餐厅和咖啡厅在顾客进门时递给他们的热毛巾（用来清洁面部和擦手），抑或是女性在用完厕纸后，小心翼翼地将卷筒最上层的厕纸向下折叠成三角形（使厕纸对下一位取用者而言更美观），都足以说明日本是一个讲究细节的国家。

我可以举更多的例子，因为这些经常发生的小事在日本实在是数不胜数。正是这些小事，使我经历的任何事情都美好了很多。日本人的彬彬有礼人尽皆知，这种特质融入到了日本社会和日常生活的方方面面。

事实上，日本如此关注细节的现象在我看来十分有趣，这大多根源于一种普遍的礼节意识——试图使各种场合对他人而言更舒适、更便利。

我已步入中年，因此，对于在细节上便利我们这些年长者的行为，我颇感喜悦。公共场所（如邮局、政府机构、医院、银行等）都放有供老人处理业务使用的小物件。这些让平淡生活更加美妙的额外努力，表明了日本老年人受尊敬的程度之高。

例如，在许多这类场所中，摆放在醒目位置的是供办理业务者借用的一系列眼镜——以防有人忘记带自己的眼镜，或因顾及自己的形象而不愿意在公共场所佩戴眼镜。一般而言，这些眼镜按镜框的颜色分为三类：鲜红色、黄色以及蓝色。每副眼镜都清楚标明了适用对象的年龄段：分别供"40岁""50岁""60岁"及更年长的老人使用。

虽然眼镜的度数并不完全适合所标定年龄段中的每一位使用者，但接近岁数与该年龄段相仿者的平均视力。在必要的时候，这些眼镜可以暂时满足使用者阅读文件上极小的文字和签名的需要。

幸运的是，我从来不需要借用这些眼镜，因为我一直都戴自己的眼镜。我确实看到顾客们在办理业务、阅读小号字和填写表格时频繁地取用这些镜。

由于某种原因，日本的眼镜店数量众多。我敢说，单单在我居住的城市，就有超过100家眼镜专卖店。这些眼镜店关注细节的一个体现是，它们会为大众提供一台电子清洁仪，行色匆匆的路人可以用它来清洗自己的眼镜。

很多眼镜店门外会摆放一张桌子，桌上放一台声波振动器。声波振动器能够用液体彻底清洗镜片和镜框。眼镜店还会提供用于擦干眼镜的纸巾以及可以让大家确保把眼镜戴正的可调式镜子。

说到镜子，日本的许多公共场合设有边缘贴有广告的镜子，供人们路过时打扮或打量自己。这一细节有两个作用，一是免费为大众服务，二是可以让企业向驻足使用镜子的人宣传自家的产品。

许多公司采用的另一种广告形式，让员工在火车站和汽车站外面分发小包纸巾。路人很容易立即把只有一张纸的广告扔掉，但像纸巾这样有用的东西，日本人更有可能会把它们放进包里或口袋里以便稍后使用。人们每次使用这些纸巾，都会注意到上面的广告。

用这种方式做广告十分聪明，这一讲究细节的做法深受那些突然需要纸巾的人的欢迎。在日本的许多公众场合很容易找到厕所，但这些厕所往往不提供厕纸。这些地方通常设有纸巾贩卖机，紧急情况下，人们可以从贩售里买到纸巾。然而，大多数人往往会携带在大街上别人递给他们的免费包装纸巾，如此一来，拿到包装纸巾的人最后更有可能会使用这些纸巾。

实际上，一些服务型企业常常通过给顾客送有用或需要的礼物进行广告宣传。一些公司会在炎炎夏日给上下班途中的人分发扇子。这些扇子同样是实用的东西，能缓解暑热，因此人们会一直收着以备他用。

我认为，日本人的这种做法和美国房地产公司分发附有各种必要联系方式的冰箱贴，或美国保险公司分发笔身醒目位置印有公司标志的钢笔的做法没什么两样。只是这些讲究细节的行为在日本更流行、更普遍。

我同样赞赏日本人关注细节的另一种做法：路人如果捡到别人丢失的东

西，如钥匙、掉在地上的毛巾等，会把它们放到显眼的地方（如高处），以便失主回来寻找时更容易发现。如果有"失物招领处"，好心人就会把这些物品交去，以便失主认领。

这样的态度同样源于礼貌，而这种彬彬有礼的行为是日本人精神和文化中不可撼动的一部分，是促进日本文化和社会这台大机器正常运转的润滑剂。

种种关注细节的事在日本十分普遍，这也使这里的生活显得更加文明。我当然欣赏个人和企业在日常生活中所做的额外付出。他们让我知道在某个地方，有人正在思考让普通之事变得极不普通的新方法，只为有助于提高我们的生活质量。

Attention to Details

When friends from home visit here, the Japanese "attention to details" is one of the first things they notice about Japan and the Japanese: a wonderful respect for the finer points and niceties that help to make daily life that much more pleasant.

Whether it is the nicely uniformed janitorial workers at train stations or the hot towel customers are offered when entering many restaurants and coffee shops (to refresh their faces and wipe their hands) or the way women gingerly tuck under and fold into a triangular shape the top layer of toilet paper on the roll after using it (to make it more attractive for the next person who reaches for it), Japan is a detail-oriented country.

I could go on and on, because there are so many little things that are done regularly in Japan to make whatever experience you are having just that much nicer. Politeness is a well-known trademark of the Japanese, which transfers to all facets of society and daily life.

In fact, most of the attention to details I find so intriguing here are rooted in this pervasive sense of politeness as an attempt to make the occasion or situation more comfortable and convenient for others.

Now that I am clearly middle-aged, I am amused at some attention to details that are designed to make life simpler and easier for those of us who are getting older. In public spaces (such as post offices, government offices, hospitals and banks), items are offered for the aged to utilize while transacting their business. These additional efforts to make a mundane experience more refined show the level of respect that older people in Japan are afforded.

For instance, in many of these establishments, displayed prominently is a selection of prescription eyewear to borrow while conducting the business at hand—in case people either forgot to bring their own or are too vain to wear glasses in public.

Normally, there are three types that come in bright red, yellow and blue frames. Each one is distinctly marked with the intended age of the user: For people in their "40s" "50s" "60s" and older.

Although the prescription isn't exact for every person that falls within the prescribed age group, it is approximated to the average eyesight of a person around that age. In a pinch, the eyeglasses will suffice momentarily for reading the fine print on a document or seeing to sign one's name.

Fortunately, I have never had to resort to using these, as I wear my own glasses all the time. I do see customers frequently reaching for the glasses to use when trying to conduct business, read small print or fill out a form.

For some reason, eyeglass stores in Japan are very plentiful. In my city alone, I'll bet there are more than 100 shops specializing in eyewear. One attention to detail that these shops offer to the general public is an electronic cleaning machine that passersby use to clean their eyeglasses while on the run.

Outside many of these stores, a table is set up with a sonic-vibrating contraption that uses liquid to clean the lenses and frames completely. Tissues are provided to dry the glasses, as well as an adjustable mirror to make sure they are on straight.

Speaking of mirrors, many public places in Japan display mirrors with small advertising on the edges for people to primp and peer at themselves when passing by. This attention to detail serves two purposes: It provides a free service for the general public, while allowing a company to advertise to those people who stop to use it.

Another form of advertising many companies employ is placing staff outside train and bus stations to pass out packets of tissue. It is rather easy for a passerby to immediately throw away a mere piece of paper, but something as useful as tissue is more likely to be placed in a bag or pocket for later use. Each time it is used, the advertisement is noticed.

This is a very clever way to advertise and an attention to detail that is greatly appreciated by people who suddenly find they need tissue. In many public spaces, toilets are readily easy to find, but often these do not provide toilet paper. Usually tissue vending machines are provided so one can purchase a package of tissue in an emergency. However, most people tend to carry the free tissue packets handed to them on the street. This makes it all the more likely that someone given a tissue package will use it eventually.

Actually, a number of service-oriented businesses regularly use a form of advertising that involves a free gift that is useful or needed by the consumer. In the summer, some companies pass out hand fans to commuters in the heat of the day. Again, it is something practical that helps to alleviate the heat, so the person will keep it for another occasion.

I suppose this is not so different from an American real-estate office passing out refrigerator magnets with all the necessary contact information included, or an insurance company that offers pens with the company logo prominently displayed on the side. It just seems so much more prevalent and available in Japan.

Another attention to detail I appreciate here is how passersby who find lost items, such as keys or a dropped handkerchief, will pick it up and place it in a prominent place (high off the ground) so it can be found easily if the person who lost it returns. If a "lost and found" office is available, a Good Samaritan will often return the item so the person who lost it can retrieve it.

Again, this attitude goes back to politeness, and this polite behavior that is such an unshakable part of the Japanese psyche and culture is the oil that keeps the cultural and social machine in good running condition.

The attention to details that is so common in Japan makes daily life here seem more civilized. I certainly appreciate all the extras that people and companies do on a regular basis. It just makes for a better quality of life, knowing that someone, somewhere is thinking up yet other new ways to make the ordinary quite extraordinary.

坚忍精神

日本人具有"我慢"（耐心与坚忍）精神。人们用"我慢"一词鼓舞面对艰巨任务或问题的人，或激励运动员们拼尽全力做到最好。这个词在日本应用十分广泛，即使是漫不经心的游客也会注意到它，想知道它的意思。

在日本中学的晨会上，所有学生都站立在指定的位置，全神贯注地听演讲者讲话——不管演讲可能是多么枯燥乏味。

学生们在这些集会中表现出了异乎寻常的尊重、耐心和自律。这种自制力同样体现在会议、演讲、讲座以及长时间的演出过程中。这一切都可以归功于日本人所具有的"我慢"精神——耐心忍受不愉快境遇的能力。这也是日本儿童从很小的时候就开始学习的能力。

我经常试着想象美国的年轻人在类似的情况下会作何反应。我觉得，很多人会唉声叹气，不耐烦地翻白眼，坐立不安。我曾目睹日本学生连续听同龄人演讲长达3个小时，几名演讲者之间没有间歇，几乎连喘气的机会都没有。

遇到这种情况，美国学生恐怕不会乖乖就范，而教师则会花费大部分的时间试图让他们安静地坐在座位上。除非演讲的主题既吸引人又有趣味，否则美国年轻人专注听讲的时间不会超过几分钟。而日本学生似乎能够兴致满满地听完演讲中最枯燥的部分。

关于日本人的"坚忍"和美国人的"浮躁"，我有一个难忘的例子。那是我在谢尔比维尔高中读书的时候，一名叫Jun的日本交换生在我们家寄宿了一年时间。

为了观看另一个朋友在教堂唱诗班的独唱表演，我和Jun，连同我们的几个同学，在圣诞节前后前往教堂参加一次特别的烛光礼拜。朋友的表演在礼拜的前期就结束了，我们正准备离开，却被困在了教堂长椅的中间，无法脱身。当时有一个特别冗长的布道，所以我们被困在座位上一个多小时，没有办法逃脱。

不用说，没过多久，我和我的美国朋友们就开始坐立不安了。我们既烦躁又无聊，翻着白眼，低声抱怨这里的座位有多硬、天气有多热又有多冷，我们简直要彻底发疯了。

我碰巧瞥了一眼Jun，他纹丝不动地坐着，背脊笔挺，双手合十，全神贯注于讲坛上牧师的布道。与之相反，我则因为无聊透顶几乎快要断气了。

布道结束后回到家,母亲还没睡,在忙着。母亲问Jun觉得晚上的礼拜如何,他实事求是地回答说:"很无聊,但没办法。"啊哈!他也觉得很无聊,但令我难以置信的是,他竟然可以泰然自若地坐着,丝毫显露不出无聊的感觉。

我当时不太理解他的行为,但我现在确实明白了,因为我不得不学会"我慢"精神,以使某些情况变得可以忍受。日本人认为,有些情况是个人无法控制的,只能忍受。他们认为,与这些情况抗争是没有用的,因为有时接受和忍耐不愉快的遭遇,直到熬过去才是更好的选择。

幸运的是,自高中时代以来,我已经成熟了很多。长大成人的我现在意识到,我们美国人也有一种"我慢"精神,也许在程度上不能与日本人相提并论,但它确实存在。

生活中,很多时候我会遇到这样的情况,忍受是更好的选择,因为这完全是无计可施的事情。由于我在日本生活了很长一段时间,我对日本的"我慢"精神有了更深刻的理解,同时也愈发认识到自己身上的"我慢"精神。

我一直在磨砺自己的"我慢"精神,我想会一直如此。我真希望在儿时就已经学会了日本人"我慢"精神的精髓。如果我们为了和谐,给美国的孩子潜移默化地传授忍耐和宽容的艺术,这不太讨喜的"我慢"精神一定能够经久不衰。毕竟,我们大多数人都在花费大量的时间和精力和那些"无计可施"的事情缠斗,并为此烦恼。

The Idea of Perseverance

Japanese people have "gaman" (patience and perseverance). This term is used to cheer people on when faced with a difficult task or problem, or to encourage athletes to do their best. It is a term that is so widely used in Japan that even a casual visitor will notice it and wonder what it means.

On the junior high school's morning assembly, all of the students stood at attention in their assigned spots, concentrating intently on the speaker at the podium—no matter how boring or uninteresting it may have been.

The respect, patience and personal discipline students demonstrate during these gatherings are remarkable. This restraint is also exhibited by Japanese students at meetings, speeches, lectures and long performances. This can all be attributed to having "gaman", the ability to endure patiently an unpleasant situation. And it is something that Japanese children learn from a very early age.

I often try to imagine how American young people would behave in similar situations. I have a feeling that there would be a lot of sighing, eyes rolling and fidgeting going on. I have seen Japanese students listen to their peers giving speeches for three hours straight with no breaks in between speakers, with little to no elbow room.

I am afraid that American students would rebel and the teachers would spend most of their time trying to keep them quiet and in their seats. Unless the subject matter is riveting, fun or entertaining, then it is difficult to keep American young people engaged for more than a few minutes. Their Japanese counterparts seemingly remain undaunted through the driest of ceremonies.

One memorable example I have of Japanese "gaman" and American "impatience" was when I was a high school student at Shelbyville Senior High. My family hosted a Japanese exchange student, Jun, for a year home stay.

Jun and I, along with several of our classmates went to a special service around Christmas to watch another friend sing a solo in the church choir. Early on in the service they had the special performance that we wanted to ready to go...but we were stuck in the middle of the pew and couldn't leave. There was an exceptionally long sermon, so we were stuck in our seats for over for an hour, with no way to escape.

Needless to say, it wasn't long before my American friends and I were restless, fidgety and bored. We were rolling our eyes and complaining in whispers about how hard the seats were, how hot it was, and how cold it was. We were just downright mad.

I happened to glance over at Jun and he was sitting perfectly still, folded with his full and undivided attention directed toward the pastor in the pulpit. I, on the other hand was barely surviving, almost dead from boredom.

After it was over, we arrived home where my mother was still up and about. She asked Jun how he enjoyed the evening's church service and he replied rather matter-of-factly, "it was very boring but it couldn't be helped." Aha! He was bored too, but I couldn't believe how he could sit so stoically without even a hint of ennui.

His actions didn't make much sense to me then, but I certainly understand them now as I have had to learn to acquire "gaman" to make certain situations bearable. Japanese people believe that some situations are beyond one's control and just have to be endured. They maintain that there is no use in fighting them because it is sometimes better to accept and endure the unpleasantness until it passes.

Fortunately, I have matured a great deal since my high school years and I now realize as an adult that we Americans too, have a kind of "gaman". Perhaps it isn't on the same level as Japanese "gaman", but it is there nonetheless.

There have been many times in my life that I have been in situations where, yes, it is better to endure something because it just can't be helped. Now that I have lived in Japan for an extended period, I have become more attuned to Japanese "gaman" and more conscious of my own form of "gaman".

I am constantly honing it and always will, I suppose. I only wish I had learned the idea of Japanese "gaman" as a child. A little "gaman" would certainly go along way if we were to instill in our children in America the art of endurance and tolerance for the sake of harmony. As it is now, most of us spend a lot of time and energy stewing over and fighting things that really can't be helped.

文化与国民

不管在哪，都会有好人，也总会有一些不那么好的人，这是很自然的事，日本也不例外。每种文化都有其积极的特征，也有不尽如人意的现实状况。

例如，美国人众所周知的特征是既友好又乐于助人。人们普遍认为，日本是一个十分注重礼节的国家，将集体利益置于个人利益之上，致力于保持社会的稳定。

正如料想的那样，这些例子过于简单，可能显得老套，真实情况并非完全如此。很多美国人其实一点都不友好，很少为他人考虑；同样的，也有很多日本人举止粗鲁，自私自利。把一个群体中的所有成员归为一类是很危险的，因为在任何一种文化里，人与人之间都存在差异，良莠不齐。

然而，一些人为了表明一种观点，讲述一个故事或试图比较细微的差异而非关注绝大部分相似之处，确实会对某个国家及其国民进行这样或那样的笼统概括。个人对群体的看法是很不可靠的，因为这一看法会受到观察者自身文化态度、观念和经历的影响，而这些影响因素塑造和界定了个体及其性格的核心特征。

1979年，在准备前往日本做交换生前，我参加了一场情况说明会。会上，指导老师让我们谨记千万不要用自己的眼光看待异国文化，而是应该换一种角度，从东道国民众的视角加以审视。他说，当我们离开美国前往日本体验当地的文化、食物、风俗和生活方式时，我们必须摘掉我们自己的文化太阳镜。

我对他的话印象尤为深刻，以至在40多年后的今天仍记忆犹新，就好似发生在昨日。作为某一特定文化团体或族群的一员，我们人类往往只关注与其他群体间的文化差异，而忽略了种族背景各异的不同群体所共有的诸多相似之处。

我有幸在北美洲、中美洲、欧洲和亚洲居住过。尽管这些地方地理位置不同，但每一种文化的核心特征在很多方面却如此相似，这让我十分惊讶。当然，在这些地方，许多信仰、礼仪、风俗和传统差异极大，但绝大部分基本需要、渴求、欲望和希冀——"文化上的人性"，都是大体相同的。在所有文化中，行为背后的意图往往都是相同的。无论是庆祝一个人出生、成年以及结婚的仪式，还是葬礼——在这些仪式、风俗和传统背后都有着相同的目的。

所以，当我说我赞赏日本这个民族时，当然，我是指赞赏日本民族人性的大多数层面，也包括对其文化遗产的敬仰和欣赏，正是这些文化遗产成就了今天的日本人。

我喜欢日本文化的所有元素吗？不，不是的。正如我不能全盘接受包括美国文化在内的其他任何一个文化群体的所有方面。跨文化交流时，无论我们多么努力，总是难以卸下这样或那样的文化包袱。母国文化是一个人本质中不可或缺的一部分，因此，人们很难与伴随一生的文化理念、态度和信仰割裂开来。

最近，一个朋友向我讲述了一件趣事。她的一个亲戚去夏威夷度假后，一直抱怨日本游客的举止多么的不文明：他们推来挤去，大声说话，根本不在乎周围人的感受，等等。起初，听到她抱怨所有的日本游客行为都很粗鲁时，我十分诧异，因为她所描述的许多情况与我对日本人的了解相去甚远。

此事让我大感意外的原因还在于，如今的日本游客个个通情达理、见多识广和彬彬有礼，懂得体谅照顾别人。至少，这一直是我的看法。

我突然意识到，或许朋友的亲戚把这些行为粗鲁的人误认为是日本人了，只因他们都是亚洲人。一些美国人往往错误地认为，所有亚洲人都来自同一个地方，有着相同的文化倾向。这就好比美国和加拿大这两个国家的文化相似，人们因此把美国人和加拿大人混为一谈。或许是因为在美国的部分地区更容易见到日本人，而且他们经常去夏威夷度假，这些行为不雅的人因此被认为是日本人。

20世纪50年代，第二次世界大战结束之后，美国人破天荒地开始出国旅游。当时人们用"丑陋的美国人"这个绰号来形容讨人厌的、乱哄哄的、文化意识迟钝的美国游客。然而，一晃半个多世纪过去了，跨国旅游不再像过去那样是件稀罕事。多年来，美国人更加积极主动地融入并适应陌生地区的风土人情，并广泛游历，"丑陋的美国人"这一恶名也因此烟消云散。

日本人同样如此。20世纪60~70年代，当日本首次成为工业化的富裕国家，从未离开过这个东瀛岛国的日本游客被认为是粗鲁的和不会体谅人的。现如今，出国旅游的日本人不计其数，这种休闲方式已经成为日本人生活中的惯例，不再像近40年前那样是件稀罕事。

正如此前"丑陋的美国人"以及上世纪60~70年代步其后尘的日本人，这些没什么经验的旅行者终将适应国际旅游，自然也会学会进行国际旅行时所需的恰当礼仪。

这让我思考"粗鲁"的真正含义是什么。当然，每个人都有自己的看法。因为，从文化角度上讲，那个在夏威夷旅游的美国妇女认为粗鲁的行为，在她所遇到的游客的本国文化里可能是很自然的事。从他们自己的语言和文化立场看，他们的行为很可能是完全可以接受的，合乎常理的。

有句老话说得好，"入乡随俗"，但是我认为，我们对于来美国旅游的外国游客应该包容一些，因为在旅游方面，他们或许不像我们那么有经验。不要忘了，曾几何时，我们也是世人的笑柄，因为我们按照自认为合适的文化规范和观念行事时，却被贴上了"丑陋的美国人"的标签。

Culture and People

Of course, there are nice people and some not so nice people everywhere. Japan is no exception. Every culture has its positive attributes and not so great realities.

For instance, a well-known trademark of Americans is friendliness with a sense of wanting to help one's fellow human being. Japanese people are widely considered to be a nation of very polite people, putting the "group" needs above one's individual needs, helping to keep society moving smoothly.

As expected, these examples are too simplistic, perhaps stereotypical, to be entirely accurate. Many Americans aren't at all friendly and have little regard for the needs of others, and an equal number of Japanese are impolite and self-centered. Lumping an entire group of people into one category is quite dangerous because differences—both positive and negative—do exist within any culture.

However, a number of people do make certain sweeping generalizations about a country and its people in order to make a point, tell a story or try to compare the minor differences rather than concentrating on the overwhelming amount of similarities. Making personal observations about a group of people is tricky, because it is filtered through one's own cultural attitudes, ideas and experiences which have served to mold and define core characteristics of one's being and personality.

In 1979, I remember an orientation session I attended as I prepared to go to Japan as an exchange student. The facilitator was trying to impress upon us the importance of seeing another culture not through our own eyes but from an alternative perspective—through the eyes of the host culture's inhabitants. He said that as we depart for Japan to experience its culture, food, customs, way of living and lifestyle, we needed to take off our own cultural sunglasses.

His words impressed me so much that after more than 40 years, I still remember it as if it were yesterday. Too often, as a member of a specific cultural or ethnic group, we humans tend to focus on the cultural differences with the other groups without taking into account all the many similarities that various groups of people from different ethnic backgrounds share and have in common.

I have had the great fortune to live in North America, Central America, Europe and Asia. Although each place differed geographically, it was amazing to me how similar so many aspects of each culture's core characteristics were. Of course, many beliefs, rituals, customs and traditions were quite different, but the most basic of needs, desires, wants and hopes were the same—the human aspect or the "humanity of culture". The intent behind the act is often the same in every culture—be it life's rituals surrounding the birth of a new baby, transition into adulthood, marriage or funeral rites—all have commonalities in the purpose behind the ritual, custom or tradition.

So when I say I admire the Japanese as a people, it is, of course, on the most human of levels, but it is also with a sense of respect and appreciation for their cultural heritage that has served to make them who they are today.

Do I like everything about Japanese culture? No, just like I can't accept every aspect of any other cultural group, including my own. No matter how hard one tries, it is difficult not to carry some sort of cultural baggage when crossing cultures. One's own culture is such an integral part of a person's essence, and being that it is hard not to separate oneself from a lifetime of cultural ideas, attitudes and beliefs.

Recently a friend recounted to me a story about a relative who traveled to Hawaii. She said the woman complained about how rude all the Japanese tourists were behaving, pushing and shoving, talking loudly, without regard to the others around them, etc. First, this surprised me that all the Japanese tourists were being rude, because many of the things she described seemed so out of character according to my experience with Japanese people. Second, it really surprised me, because today Japanese are quite savvy and well-seasoned travelers, being courteous and aware of others around them. At least, this has always been my observation.

Then it occurred to me that perhaps the person mistook the tourists as being Japanese just because they were Asian. Erroneously, some Americans tend to think all Asians hail from the same place and have the same cultural tendencies. It would be the same as putting Americans and Canadians in one category as being culturally one and the same. Perhaps since Japanese are more common in some parts of the country, and are frequent travelers to Hawaii, it was assumed the people were Japanese.

In the 1950s, when Americans first started to travel abroad, the moniker "ugly American" was used to describe obnoxious, loud and culturally insensitive American travelers. Fast forward more than a half-century later, however, and we find that international travel is not as uncommon as it once was. Americans have adapted over the years by blending in more readily to unfamiliar places and have experienced a wide variety of travel, making the label incorrect.

The same is true of the Japanese. In the 1960s and 1970s, when Japan was first becoming an industrialized and rich nation, tourists who never had ventured from the borders of this island nation were perceived as being rude and inconsiderate. Today, so many Japanese travel internationally that it is a routine part of their lives and not extraordinary like it was some 40 years ago.

Just like the "ugly Americans" before and their successors, the Japanese of the 60s and 70s, these newbie travelers eventually will acclimate themselves to international travel, and the appropriate etiquette associated with such travel will naturally become a part of who they are.

This leads me to ponder what "rudeness" actually is. It is certainly in the eye of the beholder, because perhaps culturally, what seemed like rudeness to the American woman in Hawaii was a natural part of the cultural being of the people she encountered. On their own linguistic and cultural turf, their behavior is probably quite acceptable and the norm.

True, "when in Rome, do as the Romans do", but I think we need to cut some slack to foreign visitors who venture to our country as tourists, perhaps they are not as seasoned in traveling as we are, and keep in mind that not so long ago we were the laughingstock of the world, being labeled as "ugly Americans" when in fact we were behaving according to our cultural norms and ideas of what was culturally appropriate.

第二部分
日本教育

Part 2
Japanese Education

教育

第二部分 日本教育

日本的教育在很多方面和大多数西方国家的教育存在巨大差异，而其中大部分差异基本上又是日本文化和西方文化之间差异的体现。这种在文化、传统和风俗上的差异，体现了各国教育制度中许多不同而有趣的方面。

在任何一个国家，授课只是初高中教师教书育人工作的一半而已，另一半则是教导学生如何遵循礼节以在社会中生存，这同样是至关重要的。

在中学的这几年正是学生们成长发展的阶段。其间，他们必须学会如何成为社会中积极向上且有价值的一员；如何举止得体，为社会所认可，以便在成人后终要踏入现实的社会后能游刃有余。

无论在美国还是在日本，情况都是如此，教育的最终目标是让学生为自己所要扮演的社会角色做好准备，但实现教育目标的方式和方法却各不相同，两国教育者有着相同的期望并都为实现这些目标而努力。

日本学生所受的教育基本上使他们成了"被动"学习者，只会吸收基于事实的信息。与之相反，美国学生则大多是"主动"学习者，他们学会了关注学习材料本身，或创造性地提出解决方案，并对所给信息进行批判性的分析。

这种差异或许解释了为什么日本教育以学生高度自律和课堂气氛严肃而著称，而美国学生不仅课堂气氛放松而且不会如此专注于学业。

但这样的看法并不完全正确。事实上，日本的课堂也会因为学生大吵大闹而混乱不堪；而美国的学生在课堂上也会非常专心、守纪和安静。

两国的文化差异有助于解释这一现象。日本崇尚团体协作和共同努力并将其视作行为准则，这里的学生在被叫起来回答问题时，常常会根据其他同学的回答得出结论，以此形成一个集体性的结论。最终的结果是，学生们异口同声对回答问题的学生低声说出问题的答案。该学生在其他同学就问题的答案达成一致后，她/他才会说出这一答案。

在西方教师看来，日本课堂上的这种"集体"协作是混乱无序的表现。在美国，这种行为会被视为作弊，学生们会因不合时宜的发言和提供答案给被叫起来回答问题的学生而受到惩罚。

而在日本，这种小声告知答案的习惯则是非常合乎准则的行为，深深地融进了基于社交礼节的传统之中。这一以风俗为导向的做法深深地根植于日本社会和社交规范。现今的学生通过效仿父母、兄弟姐妹和老师的行为学会了这种集体共识。

分享信息(在这个案例中是提供答案)给集体中的一员,对日本人来说是很自然的反应。如果事先没有得到同学们明确的提示,日本学生对于这个答案就会犹豫不决。毕竟,如果所说的答案是错误的,那会十分尴尬;而如果是正确的,又会显得学生自吹自擂、自命不凡。窘迫和自夸是日本人试图避免和贬抑的状况。

通常情况下,日本的学生不会主动回答问题,除非被老师特意叫到或随机点名。即使被点名的学生知道问题的答案,她/他也不会立刻说出答案,其原因有三:一是希望通过犹豫不决来表现谦虚和顺从,二是害怕表现突出,三是等着周围的学生认可他/她的答案。

从文化和社会角度而言,这些"小技巧"在回答直截了当的问题时是可以接受的礼貌行为,它们深入到了学生生活的方方面面。这些技巧将在他们随后的生活中大有裨益,那时候,他们需要在职业生涯中按照约定俗成的潜规则行事。

认为日本学生没有表达自我观点的自由,甚至他们根本没有自己的观点,这是不公平的。因为,这等于说,美国的教育无视集体主义和事实性的知识。在这两个国家的执教经历告诉我,美日两国的传统以及作为各自文化缩影的教育制度是不同的,因此,万万不能以一种文化的标准去评价另一种文化的价值。

教育年轻一代是所有国家的重要任务,尽管每个国家采取的方式各不相同。

Education

Education in Japan is markedly different in many respects to education in most western countries. For the most part, the differences are largely symptomatic of the distinction between Japanese culture and western cultures. This diversity in culture traditions and customs serve to reveal many different and interesting aspects of their respective countries' educational systems.

In any country, teaching students academics is only half of the overall teaching load that faces teachers in lower and upper secondary schools. Instructing students on how to live in a society based on propriety is of equal and crucial importance.

It is during these developing years that students must learn how to conduct themselves as active, valued members of society. They must learn how to exhibit proper, socially acceptable behavior in order to function effectively in their "real world" where they will eventually be forced to go.

This is true in both the United States and Japan, but the methods and manners involved to achieve these goals are quite reserved. The ultimate desire, however is to prepare students for their roles in society; the expectation of educate in both countries, and their efforts to achieve these goals, are very much the same.

Japanese students are basically taught to be "passive learners", absorbing information that is mainly "factual" in basis. To the contrary, students in the US are mostly "active" learners, being taught to concentrate on the "creative" solutions or aspect of the material and to analyze critically the information given to them.

This difference is perhaps why Japanese students have the reputation of being highly disciplined students with a very formal atmosphere in the classroom while US students are generally regarded as having an informal environment and been less dedicated to their studies.

The perception is not entirely accurate. In fact, a Japanese classroom can appear to be very disorderly with boisterous and loud behavior while the American counterpart can be very attentive, structured and quiet.

Cultural differences help to explain why this so—in Japan where a group effort is encouraged and is considered the norm, a student who is called upon to give an answer will often elicit responses from other students in order to come to a "group" conclusion. The end result being a chorus of answers being shouted in hushed tones to the student being asked questions. After getting a consensus, she or he then reports the answer.

In the eyes of a Western teacher observing Japanese classroom, this "group" effort appears to be disruptive and disorderly. In the United States, this behavior would be considered to be cheating and the students would be reprimanded for speaking out of turn, and for giving the answer to a student being asked a question.

This Japanese custom of whispering answers is actually very ordered behavior, steeped in tradition that is based on proper social manners. This custom-oriented practice has roots running very deep in Japanese society and social order; "group" concurrence was learned by today's students through modeling behavior of their parents, siblings and teachers.

Sharing information (in this case, giving answers) to a number of the group is very natural response for a Japanese person. A Japanese student would be very hesitated to offer an answer that was not first cleared with a sampling of her/his colleagues. After all it would be very embarrassing if the answer were to be wrong and very boastful or vainglorious if it were correct. Embarrassment and boastfulness are two traits that Japanese people first try to avoid and then attempt to play down.

Generally Japanese students display the tendency not to offer answers or solutions voluntarily, but only when specifically singled out by the teacher or called upon randomly. Even if the student knows the answer, she or he may not offer the answer rapidly when called upon for several reasons: in order to demonstrate humility and difference by hesitating; for fear of standing out and/or; and to wait for the other students around him or her to concur on an answer.

These ploys are the polite, culturally and socially acceptable ways of responding to the direct questions which permeate every facet of a student's life. These skills will serve them well later in life when they will be expected to behave according to an unspoken and unwritten code in their professional lives.

It is unfair to say that Japanese children are not allowed to express their own opinions—or worse, they have no personal opinions—as it is to say that US education ignores group membership and the need for factual knowledge. One thing that I have learned from teaching in both cultures is that both traditions, as well as the educational systems which are microcosms of the cultures, are different and is vitally important not to judge the merit of one culture by the other culture's standards.

Educating young minds is the principle goal of each nation, even though each country approaches this goal in a uniquely different fashion.

学生的就餐修养

30多年前,很多学校还没有可供学生享用午餐的正规食堂。当我第一次来日本时,我在一所初中教英语。作为教学安排的一部分,我有时会去一些小学参观。

每天上午11点左右,一辆卡车会将大锅的食物运送到学校。每班会轮流安排学生下楼取回本班的饭菜。之后,学生们会把课桌摆成几组,另外几个学生则会穿上白大褂,戴上白帽子,以流水线作业的方式给同学们分食物,其他同学则拿着托盘和碗筷,排队领取同学分发给他们的食物。

当大家都拿到食物后,值日班长就站起来说"頂きます"(在英语里找不到合适的词组来翻译,但类似法语 Bon appetit,表示可以开始吃了)。大家吃完后,值日班长会站起来说"ご馳走様でした",这是用餐结束后说的话,大意是感恩有这餐饭吃。

然后,每个学生会把自己的托盘和碗筷放到一辆手推车上,当天值日的同学会收集所有的餐具,并用手推车推到门前,以便食品公司来收集。那些餐具会得到专业的清洗,待第二天午餐时使用。

每个星期轮换值日的学生。这样,所有学生都有机会参与午餐的服务工作。这样的供餐形式不仅为学校省去了建设食堂和雇佣食堂工作人员的高昂费用,也教会了学生团队合作的重要性。

如今,学校也开始现代化了,开始在学校大食堂为学生供餐,但以前学生做的许多工作,包括领取和分发食物,以及餐后的清洗等,仍由他们自己完成。

另人惊讶的是,日本的学校一般没有清洁工打扫卫生。每天学校放学前,全体学生从上到下打扫学校的卫生。学校给每个学生都分配一项特定的任务——清扫楼道、打扫厕所、倒垃圾——做能想象得到的各种杂活,以便让学校保持井然有序、干净和整洁。

日本学生欢快地忙于分配到的任务,好像这就是他们日常生活的一部分。没人对此抱怨牢骚,至少表面上如此,因为大家本就该参与其中,帮着打扫卫生。年龄小一些的学生分到的是容易些的活,而大一点的学生则做更繁重的活。

也许是因为亲身参与这些活动,日本学生更加珍惜每天为保持学校清洁以及为全校分发食物等付出的劳动。当然,日本学生极少乱扔垃圾或损坏公物,毕竟,也是由他们自己来收拾垃圾。

Students Serve Lunch for Their Peers

When I first came to Japan over 30 years ago, I taught English in a junior high school. I sometimes visited elementary schools as part of my teaching schedule. In those days, many schools didn't have a formal cafeteria where students would eat their lunches.

Each day, at about 11 o'clock in the morning, a truck would deliver big pots of food; each class had a rotating schedule of students who would go down to retrieve their class's food and dishes to bring back to the classroom. The students would then arrange their desks into small groups, and several other students would don white coats and hats to serve each student in an assembly line. The other students would lineup with trays, chopsticks and bowls to receive their lunch that was served by their classmates.

When everyone had their food, the class leader for the day would stand up and say "itadakimasu" (there is no good English translation for this phrase, but it's like saying "Bon appetit"). This signaled that it was time to begin eating. When everyone had finished, the leader would stand and say "gochisosamadeshita", a phrase which is said after a meal. It basically means "thank you for the meal".

Each student then placed his/her tray, bowls, and chopsticks on a cart; the students who were assigned to work the lunch for that day gathered all of the pots and pans and wheeled all of it back down to the door, where it was picked up by the food company. The dishes, pots and utensils would be professionally washed and then made ready for the next day's lunch.

Every week, each set of duties changed, allowing all students to participate equally with the lunch service. This system saved the school the considerable cost of creating an expensive cafeteria or hiring an on-site staff to prepare and cleanup after each lunch service, and taught students the importance of working as a group.

Today, as schools have begun to modernize, they are beginning to adopt the big cafeteria, but many of the same duties and obligations involving the retrieval and serving of the food, as well as the after-lunch cleaning duties, are still performed by the students.

This might surprise you, but in Japan, there are generally no janitors in the schools to keep them clean. Each day, before the school day ends, the entire school body descends upon the school like a small army of ants to clean it from top to bottom. Each student is assigned a specific duty—sweeping the hallway, cleaning the toilets, emptying the trashcans—every conceivable chore that needs to be done to keep the school orderly, clean and neat.

Japanese students cheerfully go about doing their assigned chores, as it is just a part of their normal daily school life. No one complains, at least outwardly, because everyone is expected to participate and to help out. The smaller children are given tasks that they can do more easily, leaving the harder jobs to the older students.

This might surprise you, but in Japan, there are generally no janitors in the schools to keep them clean. Each day, before the school day ends, the entire school body descends upon the school to clean it from top to bottom. Each student is assigned a specific duty—sweeping the hallway, cleaning the toilets, emptying the trashcans—every conceivable chore that needs to be done to keep the school orderly, clean and neat.

Japanese students cheerfully go about doing their assigned chores, as it is just a part of their normal daily school life. No one complains, at least outwardly, because everyone is expected to participate and to help out. The smaller children are given tasks that they can do more easily, leaving the harder jobs to the older students.

Perhaps by cleaning the school and serving the food to their peers at lunch, Japanese students become more appreciative of the effort it takes to keep a school clean and to serve lunch to an entire school every day. Certainly, Japanese students are much less likely to throw trash or garbage on the floor or to damage property. After all they will be the ones who will have to clean up the mess.

育儿之道

刚到日本时，我发现了一件非常有趣的事，却令我大为困惑。一天晚上，当我步行回我住的公寓时，路过一个邻居家，看见屋外有一个孩子正一边哭泣一边拼命地敲门。

我停下脚步，想看看发生了什么事，能否能帮上忙。就在此时，我注意到孩子的母亲正透过窗子窥视着他。那个男孩八九岁，喊着："お母さん……入れてください！"（妈妈，让我进去！）

又过了好一会，母亲还是对孩子的请求置之不理，最后才打开门让他进屋。刚才发生了什么？眼前发生的这一幕让我大惑不解，甚至让我对这位母亲的育儿方式感到担忧。

当天晚上，一日本朋友来家里做客，我向他讲述了之前发生的整件事。他的第一反应是钦佩："她是一位好母亲，因为她在教她的孩子成为更好的人……"

不用说，朋友的反应让我更加不解。朋友接着问我，美国人如何惩罚调皮捣蛋的孩子。我向他解释说，方法有很多，有的很温和，有的则严厉些。

有时候，我们用严厉的责骂来纠正孩子们的行为，比如不给零花钱或让他们待在自己的房间里。听到惩戒方式的最后一点时，我的朋友说："所以，基本上是一样的，对吧？""不，我们不会把孩子锁在屋外。"我反驳道。他说："不，你们让孩子待在他们自己的房间，这等于将他们锁在了屋里。"

这是一个非常合理的观点：美日两国家长用以纠正孩子不端行为的方法没有太大的区别，只是具体操作上有所差别。最终结果都是为了惩戒孩子的不良行为，并教育孩子以后不要再重复这种行为。毕竟，孩子学会明辨是非，将来成为一个对社会有益的人，这才是最重要的。

我对美日两国父母在孩子教养方式上的这种差异极感兴趣——这是两种看似截然相反的做法，但其实质又非常相似。我们可以认为这些方法同样合乎逻辑，但又彼此不同。看待惩罚的方式基于文化的考量，但惩罚的预期结果实际上是一样的。

例如，美国孩子会很乐意被关在屋外作为惩罚——这样孩子会自由地奔跑和玩耍,陶醉于独立和自由之中,他们无法忍受因被迫待在自己房间里而产生的孤独感;相反,日本孩子则更愿意待在她/他能够得到安全感和集体温暖的地方(此例中是家庭)。两种惩罚方式都迫使孩子远离他们更愿意去的地方,不管是室内还是室外。

总的来说,在我看来,在美国,我们对年龄小一些的孩子更严格。在父母认为什么是不恰当的行为方面,日本孩子所拥有的弹性空间比美国孩子大得多。

在日本,旁人基本上不理会一个孩子在公共场合的不端行为;要是在美国,一个孩子要是行为不端,很可能会被当着别人的面严厉训斥一通,性质恶劣的还要被打屁股。

有一次,几个日本朋友带着孩子来我家做客。当我走进客厅,震惊地发现其中3个蹒跚学步的孩子竟在沙发和椅子上蹦蹦跳跳。他们的妈妈则坐在旁边聊天,似乎没意识她们的孩子究竟在做什么。因此,我当即建议大家都到外面的院子里。

不可否认,我的房子并不适合孩子玩耍;近日,另一位朋友带着她的孩子来我家,她儿子说:"这房子里的东西容易碎。"家里有太多旅行中收集的吸引人的手工艺品,引得那些天生好奇的小家伙们忍不住要去触摸和玩弄。

尽管日本和美国在管教孩子方面有不同的手段,但两国的父母都在为同样的结果而努力——那就是培养健康、适应力强、从经验中学习如何在社会上表现得体的孩子。

Child Rearing

I observed something very interesting when I first arrived in Japan that puzzled me greatly. One night, when I was walking home to my apartment, I passed a neighbor's house where there was a child crying and pounding frantically on the door.

I paused to see what was going on and to see if there was anything I could do to help. At this point in the incident I noticed his mother peering out of the window at him. The boy who was 8 or 9 years old, was yelling "Okaasan...iretekudasai!"

(Mother, let me in!)

She ignored his pleas for a few moments, and then finally opened the door to let him in. What just happened? This whole scene that transpired before my eyes left me bewildered, confused and even worried about the child rearing habits of this mother.

That same evening a Japanese friend came to visit me and I recounted the entire episode to him. His first response was one of admiration: "She is a good mother because she is teaching him to be a better person..."

Well, needless to say I was further confused at his reasoning behind leaving a child outside as punishment. My friend then asked me how Americans punish children for misbehaving. I explained to him that there is a variety of methods, some very mild and some more severe.

Sometimes we correct children's behavior with a firm scolding to withholding allowance money or sending them to their room. On this last point my friend said, "So, basically the same way, right?" "No! We don't lock children outside of the house." I countered. He said, "No, you lock them inside, by sending them to their room."

Hmmm, he had a very valid point. There really isn't much difference in the "method", only in the "means". The end result of both approaches is to discipline the child for bad behavior, and to teach the child not to repeat the behavior in the future. After all, the important thing is that the child learns right from wrong in order to be a productive member of society.

This difference in child-rearing and parental discipline fascinated me—it was the opposite way of doing it, yet at the same time it was very similar. The methods could be regarded as equally logical, but different. The way of viewing the punishment was based on cultural considerations, but the intended outcome of the punishment was virtually the same.

For instance, an American child would love to be sent outside of the house for punishment—the child would run and play freely, reveling in his/her independence and freedom. A Japanese child on the other hand would prefer inside where s/he is afforded the security and warmth of the group (in this case the family).

Perhaps the American child finds the forced solitude of his/her room unbearable. Both punishments exclude the child inside...or outside.

In general, it seems to me that in America we tend to be stricter with children from an earlier age. Japanese children have a lot more flexibility as to what is considered inappropriate behavior by their parents than their American counterparts do.

In Japan, a small child who misbehaves in public is largely ignored by bystanders; American child who acts in the same manner would probably receive a stern talking to and when I was a child, a light smack on the behind (if really bad), right in front of the bystanders.

Once when I had some Japanese people over with their children I was shocked to walk into my living room and see three of the toddlers jumping on my sofa and chairs. The mothers were sitting nearby chatting, seemingly unaware of what their children doing. I quickly suggested we all go outside on the patio.

Admittedly, my house is not "kid friendly"; another friend who has a very well-behaved child visited recently and her son said, "This house is really breakable." There are just too many tempting artifacts from my trips to touch and handle for little ones who are naturally curious and inquisitive.

Although Japan and the United States have different methods and means for disciplining children, parents from both countries strive for the same results—healthy, well-adjusted children who are learning from experience how to behave properly and appropriately in society.

幼儿早教

幼儿早教是个十分有趣的话题,但必须承认,我对此知之甚少,因为我自己没有孩子。于是我向一位好友求助,在日本,她的孩子有过四次"幼儿早教"的经历。

在日本,幼儿早教基本上有两种学制。从出生到6岁的儿童可以入读属于"日托中心"类别的"保育園"(托儿所)。

设立这类学校的主要目的是保障儿童的福利,并由福利部依据《儿童福利法》进行管理。托儿所重视给予幼儿身心上的关爱。

不同的是,"幼稚園"(幼儿园)面向3~6岁的儿童,由教育部根据1947年颁布的《学校教育法》进行管理,旨在教育儿童。

托儿所学制对在职家长来说十分方便，因为其可支配的时间相当灵活，也比幼儿园体系长很多。幼儿园一般允许幼儿每天在里面待6个小时，而托儿所则可根据家长的日程安排，允许孩子每天早来晚回。

每个孩子上幼儿园的学费是固定的，只是上公立学校或私立学校的学费有差别。托儿所的学费则根据学生家长的收入水平来收取，让收入较低的家庭能够享受和较富裕的家庭一样的地位。

在日本的普通托儿所，我个人认为有一件事十分有趣，就是几乎所有托儿所都有写日志（日记）的习惯，详细记录孩子一天之中所做的重要事情，大事小事都有。

这种日志是由家长和教师共同撰写的。日志每天都放进书包里，在家校之间传递。每天下午午休期间，教师会浏览家长前一天晚上写好的日志，然后接着写下孩子当天的表现，供家长晚上阅读。

这种日志制度是家长和教师共同了解孩子家校生活的绝佳方式。日志内容一般包含孩子日常生活：所吃的食物、睡眠习惯、语言发展、玩耍及与其他孩子互动的情况。

以下摘录的是朋友孩子的老师写的关于她孩子智史的两篇日志：

  4月26日

    今天早上，桃子班（1~2岁孩子的班级）的小樱躺在地上大哭，智史见状马上走过去牵起她的手轻声安慰。他越来越像大哥哥了，不是么？之后，在外面的操场上，他把几辆玩具卡车推到一个角落，在那儿建起了一个停车场。在停车场旁边，他把沙子一铲铲地装进卡车，堆得满满的，他看起来像个十足的工人！

  5月15日

    今天，我们在外面玩了一整天。我们一起去散步，智史看到鲤鱼旗欣喜不已。他把鲤鱼旗拿给我，嘴里不停地说"鱼"。我们摘花，捉昆虫，尽享自然之美。之后，我们把大纸板当成滑板滑下草坡，智史很喜欢这样滑下去，滑了一次又一次。下午，当我们收拾打扫时，智史积极帮忙，一直在收拾，直到完成为止。

一般说来，日志只记录孩子在生活中的积极方面，家长和老师都记录有关孩子好的方面。有趣的是，朋友告诉我，如果一个孩子在学校被另一个孩子咬了，老师会口头告知被咬孩子的父母，并进行解释和致歉，而不会告诉咬人的孩子的父母。

这个时候，如果孩子的父母详细询问孩子的情况，比如说："小路在家里常常咬他的妹妹，他在学校也会咬人吗？"大部分日本老师这时都会尽量委婉地给予积极的回答，"哦，偶尔会，但只是在别人惹怒他的时候才会。"

这已经足以让家长了解情况,并决定在家怎样教育孩子。

这背后的意思是,孩子终究是孩子,这极可能是他们成长的必经阶段,所以最好不要对孩子的一些不良行为太过在意。

我朋友告诉我,她发现,在她儿子的托儿所里,老师们都使用她所谓的"同伴约束"鼓励孩子们介入到其他孩子的争吵当中去,充当小调解员。

当然,如果孩子吵架吵得无法控制时,老师会出面调停。但老师也可能站在不远处观察,然后对另一个孩子说:"快看那呀,我不知道他们到底在吵什么呢。"这个孩子通常会自告奋勇地前去探察情况,劝那两个吵架的小孩停止争吵。

一般来讲,日本人比美国人更能宽容小孩子的吵闹行为,他们很少对孩子订立条条框框,让孩子们充分享受自由并按照自己的意愿行事。

然而,一旦他们到了一定年龄,就面临许多社会压力,人们希望他们能够规规矩矩地行事。等进了初中,他们就已经被培养成听话孝顺、恭敬有礼的小大人了。对于这个年龄的孩子来说,不容他们有任何不端行为,因为同伴很快就会让任性的学生安分守己。有些很严重的实例就起源于不合群的孩子受到欺凌。这诚然是很残忍的事件。他们还是孩子,本该过着无忧无虑、幸福快乐的生活。

Early Childhood Education

Early childhood education is a very interesting topic and one that I admittedly know little about, since I don't have any children of my own. So, I enlisted the help of a good friend who has experienced "early childhood education" in Japan four times with her children.

There are basically two systems that are used in Japan with regard to early childhood education. From birth to age 6, children can be enrolled into a "hoikuen" (nursery), which is classified as a "daycare center".

These are primarily geared toward the "welfare" of the child and are regulated by the Ministry of Welfare under the Child Welfare Law. The emphasis of "hoikuen" is to take care of the child physically and mentally.

In contrast, the "youchien" (kindergarten) system, for children ages 3 to 6, is regulated by the Ministry of Education under the School Education Law of 1947. These schools are geared toward the education of children.

The "hoikuen" system is very convenient for working parents, because the hours it can be utilized are quite flexible and much longer than the "youchien" system. A typical kindergarten allows children to stay up to six hours in a day, where as a "hoikuen" will allow children to come early and stay late each day, depending on the parents' schedule.

The "youchien" fee for a child is fixed, and the price depends upon whether it is public or private. The "hoikuen" fee is based on the income of the parents, allowing lower-income families to have equal footing with more well-to-do families.

One aspect I personally found very interesting regarding the average nursery school in Japan is the practice of keeping a daily diary ("nikki") that details the highlights of the child's day, from extraordinary to mundane events.

The "nikki" features daily entries by both the parents and the teachers. The diary itself travels back and forth from home to school in the child's bag each day. Every afternoon during nap time, the teachers read what the parents wrote the night before, and then write about the child's day thus far for the parents to read later that evening.

This diary system is an excellent way to keep parents and teachers abreast of the child's school and home life. A typical entry includes details about the child's daily routine: foods eaten, sleep habits, language development, playtime and interactions with other children.

The following excerpts are two "nikki" entries written by the teacher for my friend's child, Satoshi:

> April 26
>
> "This morning, Sakura-chan in Momo Class (1~2 years old) was lying on the floor crying. As soon as Satoshi saw her, he went over, held her hand and spoke gently to her. He really is becoming a big brother, isn't he? Later, out on the playground, he was pushing the trucks over to one corner, where he made a car park (parking lot). Next to that, he was shoveling sand into a toy truck until it was piled high. He looked like a real workman!"

May 15

"Today we played outside all day. We went for a walk, and Satoshi was happy to see the 'koi−nobori' (banners shaped like fish). He showed them to me and kept saying 'fish'. After picking flowers, looking for insects and enjoying lots of nature, we used big sheets of cardboard to slide down the grass hill. Satoshi really enjoyed it, sliding down again and again. When we were tidying up this afternoon, Satoshi was really helpful, working right up until we finished."

Generally, the diary tends to focus only on the positive aspects of the child's life, with both parents and teachers including favorable content about the child. Interestingly, I was told by my friend, that—for example—if one's child is bitten by another child at school, the teacher will verbally inform the parent of the child bitten to explain and apologize about what happened. The parents of the child who did the biting may never be told.

Now, if a parent specifically inquires about their child, for example, "Little Koji has been biting his sister at home. Does he do it here?" The Japanese teacher most likely will still try to give the situation a positive spin by replying, "Well, occasionally, but only when provoked."

This is enough information, however, for the parent to know the situation and then decide how to deal with it at home.

The idea behind this is that children will be children, it is most likely a phase the child is going through and it is best not to bring too much attention to the bad behavior.

My friend related to me that she has witnessed what she labeled "peer discipline" being used by teachers at her son's nursery school. Children are encouraged to intervene in other children's disputes as minimediators.

Of course, the teacher would intervene if the dispute was really out of hand, but the teacher may watch from a distance and mention to another child, "Look over there. I wonder what they are going on about?" The child often will volunteer to go over and check out what is happening, mediating the disagreement by encouraging the other two to stop their fussing.

In general, child rearing in Japan allows for more raucous behavior by small children to be tolerated than what Americans normally find acceptable. Discipline is rarely done, allowing small children a lot of freedom to act and behave as they wish.

However, once they reach a certain age, societal pressure kicks in and children are expected to walk a straight and narrow line. By the time they are in junior high school, they have been transformed into obedient and respectful little individuals. There is little wiggle room from around this age for any bad behavior; peers will quickly put wayward students in their place. In severe cases, students who don't fit in socially are bullied. This is a sad reality, indeed, considering how carefree and happy-go-lucky their lives most likely were when they were small children.

第三部分
日本社会

Part 3
Japanese Social Issues

安全

总的来说，和许多其他国家相比，日本是一个安全的国家。和全球其他大城市相比，世界上最大城市之一的东京十分安全。

比如，当我独自一人走在昏暗的东京街头，从不会因为深夜行走在陌生的区域而紧张或不安。但是，一旦到了美国，我就会提高警惕，就算是在我熟悉的地方，我也会对周围的人更加警觉。

前不久，我和一位美国朋友正走在东京的一条狭窄街道上，这时一群留着粉红色和绿色尖刺状头发的青少年大摇大摆地向我们走来，他们身着饰有可怕的骷髅图案的皮夹克，佩戴着时尚的粗链子。

我们俩谁都不害怕，甚至根本没在意他们。我们只说，要是在纽约或是洛杉矶，一帮如此打扮的小伙子走上前来，我们都会高度警惕，密切关注对方的一举一动。

不管是对日本国民还是外国游客而言，在日本旅行或居住的安全感是这个国家最宝贵的财富之一。在日本，几乎没听说有针对外国人的犯罪活动，这也使日本成了深受人们欢迎，尤其是受女性青睐的旅游目的地。

日本的低犯罪率可能归功于佛教和本土神道教教义中的儒家思想。纵观日本历史，宣扬非暴力的神道教和佛教信仰一直是其宗教和道德教育的基石。

在德川幕府时期（1603~1868），日本武士曾以铁腕手段负责维护和平。据说，他们甚至可以当场处决言行无礼等轻微违规或违法的人，而这些行为在现代社会是不会受到惩罚的。

这一历史传统使日本演变成总体上诚信守法的现代社会。初到日本时，我在十字路口必须小心翼翼，因为我有时候会在没有车辆的情况下闯红灯过马路。而日本的行人则恰恰相反，他们会一直等到绿灯亮起才过马路。我不想造成不良影响，所以现在我也会这样做。

这里的司机却有时会闯红灯，那是因为本该转绿的红灯会多亮几秒钟，以便让落在后面尚未走到马路的对面的行人通过人行道。闯红灯在美国是绝对不可以的，这些司机会因为闯红灯收到许多罚单。在日本人们接受这样的事，而且每个人都这么做。

日本人因将人们遗忘在火车上的物品归还失主而闻名。我曾偶尔将一个包或一把伞（或二者）落在出租车、巴士或是火车上，多亏了好心人将东西交给失物招领处或司机，每次我都能拿回我遗失的东西。

我一直提醒我的日本学生在国外旅行时要小心谨慎，因为他们从不担心骗子和小偷会利用他们初次旅行时的天真烂漫而占他们的便宜。

在日本，日本人总是在上火车后，将自己的包或公文包往座位旁边的置物架上一丢，便迅速睡着了。到站后，他们会猛地起身，拿上自己的东西，向车门走去。他们在坐火车时似乎全程都在睡觉（或者至少在装睡）。

在纽约地铁列车上可不能这样做，要不然，当你醒来时，你的包很可能已经不见了。因此，在学生出发前，我尽量给他们一些简单但明智的旅行建议。

日本的火车站或机场有空座位供游客在临出发前购物、使用公用电话或上厕所时放包，日本游客对此习以为常。但是，在其他国家，这样的做法并不明智，因为有些人会将别人的包拿走。同时，由于大家都对恐怖主义感到恐惧，一些人可能会对一个无人看管、孤零零地放置在公告场所座椅上的包产生怀疑。

我还提醒日本学生在国外时不要冒险在夜晚或独自一人前往陌生的地方。探索新的地方固然有趣和刺激，但是游客必须当心，要对目的地做充分了解，并到人多的地方去。这是去日本以外的大多数国家旅行时，必须面对的现实。

但这并不是说日本不存在犯罪，因为事实并非如此。在日本犯罪现象较为罕见，而当某人遭到攻击，甚至被杀害，就会成为全国的新闻头条。近年来，越来越多的儿童遭到绑架并常常被杀害，这一趋势着实令人忧心。

过去几年来，日本青少年犯罪率正以惊人的速度增长。曾经闻所未闻的青少年犯罪，现在却变得越来越频繁，屡屡见诸报端。在美国，这种滔天罪行几乎司空见惯，人们对发生的这类案件已经麻木了。这类事件在日本还是少有的，只要媒体一报道出来，整个国家都恐慌不已。

日本政府以及教育工作者都在努力弄明白是什么造成了这一令人不安的现象。像许多工业化和富裕的第一世界国家一样，日本在处事态度、生活水平、文化等方面发生的巨大变化，已使日本社会无法通过培养学生的正义感和明辨是非的社会良知来理解这些变化。

很不幸的是，这种情况曾经发生在美国，而我担心日本正在重蹈覆辙。

A Safe Country

Japan is a safe country. Generally speaking, this statement is true when comparing Japan to most other countries. Tokyo, one of the world's largest cities, is quite safe when compared to other big cities around the planet.

For instance, when walking down a dark street in Tokyo alone, I never feel anxious or uneasy about walking late at night in an unfamiliar area. However, as soon as I get to the United States, I have my guard up. I am much more aware of others around me, even in places I know well.

Not long ago, an American friend and I were walking down a narrow street in Tokyo when a group of leather-clad teens—with punked-out pink and green spiked hair, dressed menacingly with skulls and crossbones on their jackets, adorned with chunky chains as fashion accessories—came strutting toward us.

Neither of us flinched or even paid them any mind at all except to comment that if we had been in New York or Los Angeles and a gang of boys approached dressed in a similar fashion, we both would have been on high alert, vigilantly eyeing their every move.

This sense of security when traveling or living in Japan is one of its greatest assets for not only Japanese people but for foreign visitors as well. Crimes against foreigners are virtually unheard of here, making Japan a popular travel destination, especially for women.

The low crime rate in Japan may be attributed to its Confucian ideals found in Buddhism and in its own indigenous religion of Shinto. Throughout Japanese history, Shinto and Buddhist beliefs advocating nonviolence have been a cornerstone of its religious and "moral" education.

During the Tokugawa Shogunate (1603~1868), samurai warriors were in charge of keeping the peace and did so with iron hands. Reportedly, they were even permitted to execute people on the spot for minor infractions such as impoliteness or breaking the law—things that people in modern society routinely do with impunity.

This history and tradition has translated into a modern society that is largely honest and law-abiding. When I first arrived in Japan, I had to watch myself at crosswalks because I would sometimes cross when it was red if there were no cars in sight; Japanese people, on the other hand, will stand and wait until the walk sign lights up. I don't want to be a bad influence, so I now wait until the light turns before crossing.

Drivers here, though, do run red lights as sometimes. The opposite light stays red for a couple of extra seconds to allow the stragglers to get through before the other light turns green. This is a definite no-no in the United States. Many a ticket has been issued to such drivers for running a red light. In Japan, it is expected, and everyone does it.

Japan is notorious for having mislaid or forgotten items on trains returned to the person who lost them. I have left the occasional bag or odd umbrella (or both) in a taxi or on a bus or train; each time I was able to get my belongings back because some good samaritan took the item to the lost-and-found office or gave it to the driver.

I always warn my students who are visiting a foreign country to be vigilant and careful because they are not used to worrying about scam artists, conmen, or thieves who might take advantage of their naivete as first-time travelers.

Routinely in Japan, Japanese people will board a train, place their bag or briefcase on a shelf above their seat, and promptly fall asleep. When they reach the station where they want to get off, they jump up and grab their belongings, then head out the door. The whole time they are riding on the train, they appear to be asleep (or at least playing possum).

You cannot do this on a New York subway train. Your bag most likely won't be there when you wake up. So, I try to give my students some simple, but smart travel tips before they leave.

In Japan, it is common for Japanese travelers to find an empty seat at a train station or in an airport to leave their bags while they do some last-minute shopping, use a public phone or go to the toilet. Again, this is unwise in other countries, because someone will probably see the bag and take it. Also, with terrorism on everyone's mind, others may be suspicious of an unattended bag sitting alone on a seat in a public place.

I also caution my Japanese students not to venture into unknown areas at night or alone when abroad. It is fun and adventurous to explore new places, but they have to be smart about it, research the area and go to places where there are a lot of people around. This is the reality of traveling abroad in most places other than Japan.

This is not to say, however, that Japan is "crime-free", because it's not. It is rarer here, and when someone is attacked, or worse, murdered, it makes national headlines. A disturbing trend that has been occurring more frequently is crimes against children who are abducted and often killed.

Youth-generated crime has increased at an alarming rate in the last several years. Once unheard of, it is now becoming more and more frequent. This rash of violent crimes committed by children against children has been in the news more frequently in recent years here. Similar heinous crimes against children in America are almost commonplace, to the point where people are desensitized to it when it does happen. In Japan, it is still rare enough that the media is right on it and it causes the nation collectively to gasp in horror.

The authorities here, as well as educators, are trying to understand why this disturbing trend is happening. Like most first-world countries that are industrialized and wealthy, the rapid transformation of Japan regarding its social attitudes, standard of living and culture has outpaced the ability of society to digest the changes in a way that teaches its youth a sense of propriety, giving them a social conscience to know right from wrong.

Sadly, it happened in the United States, and I fear it is happening in Japan.

日本目前正在经历人口不断减少的严重危机。这一正在发生的人口巨变将会在未来对日本造成持续而深远的影响。

不幸的是，这一令人不安的趋势似乎并没有好转的迹象，反倒进一步恶化，让日本的领导人和学者们感到无所适从。这是日本历史上前所未有的危机。

在日本现代历史上，新生儿的数量首次低于死亡人口数量，这意味着日本的人口正朝着"老多少寡"型结构发展，老年人口的数量正在超过新生儿的数量。

专家们预测，未来几年，日本很有可能会减少数万人口，而当如今的这一代婴儿成年时，会锐减数十万。这种情况就发生在全球人口寿命最长的国家之一的日本。

如果日本不能即刻采取强有力的措施改变在老年人口快速增长的同时新生人口数量骤降的窘境，未来就可能出现严重的社会和经济灾难。由于人口老龄化，未来缴纳医保和退休金的人数越来越少，目前的医保资金和退休金将面临耗尽的危险。随着越来越多的日本人寿命达到80多岁、90多岁甚至100多岁，照料这些人的重担便落到了今天的年轻一代劳动力身上。

使这一形势愈发紧迫的是，2007年到2009年，大批在第二次世界大战结束后的"婴儿潮"时期出生的日本人（他们曾经靠令人景仰的职业精神和养育的众多子女支持着日本的社保体系）现在已经到了法定退休年龄。

过去，由于死亡人口数量高于新生儿数量，缴纳医保和退休金的人数大于领取这些费用的人数，医疗体系因而得以顺利运行。那么，又是什么原因导致日本人口迅速减少呢？

人口骤减的原因可能有很多，从女性选择在育龄阶段追求自身事业发展和工作的自由意识，到将子女从嗷嗷待哺抚养至经济上独立所需的高昂成本，不一而足。

至于日本夫妻为什么选择少生孩子甚至压根不要孩子，其中的确切原因我们不得而知。但可以肯定的是，这一现象出现已经不是一天两天了。显然，在这一趋势能够得到解决或扭转的时候，日本政府却无所作为。

目前受冲击最严重的当属苦苦挣扎的日本农村地区，当地的小学正逐渐关闭；年轻的医生选择到与照顾老年人相关的部门工作，以致孕妇找妇产科大夫就诊都十分困难。

与此同时，大量的农村青年背井离乡到城市谋求发展机遇，在没有新鲜血液注入的情况下，农村地区依靠日渐衰老的居民继续从事曾经作为日本农村支柱产业的农业、家庭店铺及作坊维持下去。

日本一直以来都是一个勤俭节约的国家，这一传统使得日本人可以享受愉快甚至无忧无虑的退休生活。但近些年来，这种情况也因为20世纪80年代末日本泡沫经济的崩盘以及年轻一代纷纷涌向大城市而发生了改变。

在过去，日本的年轻人经常会在到城市工作一段时间后返回家乡。但是，近年来这一趋势已经改变，他们中很多人不再返乡照顾年老的父母。

现在，日本的老年人正越来越多地依靠储蓄支付日常开销、医疗及其他与老龄相关的费用。而这些开支在过去大多是不必要的，因为家里的长子及其家人通常会留在原籍照顾他们。随着越来越多的家庭独立生活，这一态势在过去大概10年里发生了很大变化。

我预测日本在未来几年会发生三件事。

一、税收，尤其是消费税将会大幅提高。

在我刚到日本生活时，这里根本没有消费税，商品的标价就是顾客需要支付的价格。

20世纪80年代末泡沫经济的崩溃迫使日本政府开始征收少量的消费税，而后又将其提高到5%；而这一税率已经翻倍至10%的水平，我估计将来甚至很有可能会更高。

二、人们用以支付社会医疗保险的费用也将增加。

日本的医疗体制要求每一位职工都参保缴费，而用人单位也会替员工缴纳同样金额的费用。我很喜欢日本的社会医疗体制。我在日本任何诊所和医院只需出示医保卡就可以马上得到治疗，且每次就诊只是收取象征性的费用，这笔费用累加起来很可能抵消老年人的医疗支出。由于人口"老多少寡"，根本没有足够多的年轻人缴纳医保费用以保证巨额医疗费的支出。

日本目前实行的医疗服务势必会迎来全面改革。日本人已经习惯了动不动就因为感冒或胃痛之类的小毛病去看医生。

日本的医院和医生往往就一些小病痛给病人过度开药或者让其进行费用高昂的各项检查，医院这样做可以从政府收回各项诊疗费，而正是当前的医疗体制让医院有机可乘。

目前，在日本接受手术或介入式治疗的病人通常会住院长达一个月。反观美国，保险公司则要求病人尽早出院，有时甚至是在手术当天就让病人出院。

日本现行的医疗体系必须进行改革，使其依靠更低的成本实现更高的效率和更强的偿付能力。考虑到与子女一起生活的老年人越来越少，从而使社会医疗体系承担起了这些人的基础医疗需要的现状，应该叫停过度治疗现象以节约资金，保障更严重疾病的治疗。

很多老年人每天都去看医生或者上医院，他们只是将其视作看望朋友或与之闲聊的一种社交性聚会。这些老年人一大早就到医院排队占位，顺便看看朋友。他们这种做法妨碍了医疗机构为那些真正需要治病的人提供医疗服务，这对业已紧张的医疗体系而言确实是一个负担。

三、法定退休年龄的提高。

因为退休人员寿命越来越长，生活质量通常要比以前好很多，过了60至65岁还可继续工作。

幸运的是，很多日本老年人愿意也乐于继续工作。随着人们的寿命达到90多岁，在60岁退休就意味着要度过30多年的退休生活。

人口数量下降使日本许多学院和大学的形势严峻。招收足够的学生已经是一个挑战。并且在未来,随着包括我所执教的学校在内的高等教育院校试图通过调整专业,尽一切可能使大学得以顺利运转,各校间招生的竞争将变得更加激烈。

最终,日本将不得不向更多愿意在此定居工作的外来移民敞开大门。要真是如此的话,日本的面貌就将会发生剧变。二三十年后,日本的人口构成很可能变得多元化,而非当前的单一民族结构。

事实上,这种情况正在发生。

"Top-heavy" Japan

Japan is currently experiencing a very serious crisis: a declining population. The rapid demographic changes that are occurring will have far-reaching and long-lasting repercussions on this country that will be felt for generations to come.

Unfortunately, there seems to be no reversal in sight of this troubling trend, which is further serving to perplex Japan's leaders and academicians. It is a crisis that is unprecedented in the history of Japan.

For the first time in modern times, the number of babies born are fewer than people dying, meaning that the population is edging toward a configuration that makes it "top-heavy". The number of aged citizens is outpacing the number of babies being born.

Experts are predicting that the declining number, which most likely will be in the tens of thousands in the next few years, will jump sharply into the hundreds of thousands by the time today's babies are adults. This is in a country that has one of the highest life expectancies in the world.

A briskly growing "graying" population, coupled with the sharp decrease in births, signals social and economic disaster in the future if drastic steps to remedy the situation are not taken immediately. The socialized health system, as well as pensions for retirees, is at risk as the aging population drains the current funds with fewer future contributors on the horizon. As more and more Japanese continue to live well into their 80s, 90s and even 100s, the cost to care for these people will be put on the shoulders of today's young workers.

Adding to the immediacy of the situation is the fact that beginning in 2007, and continuing through 2009, the bulk of the World War II Japanese baby-boom generation (who helped to fuel the system through their admirable work-ethic and prolific production of children) reached the mandatory retirement age for Japanese workers.

In the past, this system functioned smoothly because the number of deaths outpaced the number of new births, keeping the system "bottom-heavy". Why is Japan's population declining so rapidly?

There are a number of probable causes...from a sense of freedom afforded women to pursue careers and to work during their child-bearing years, to the high cost of raising a child from cradle until they are financially independent.

There is no clear-cut reason as to why Japanese couples are opting to have less children (or none at all), but for sure it has been occurring for quite a while; the government certainly dropped the ball in trying to troubleshoot or reverse the trend at a time when it could have been corrected.

Hardest hit now are rural communities who are struggling to survive. Elementary schools are closing. Expectant mothers have a difficult time finding obstetricians because young doctors are opting to pursue residencies in fields that cater to the elderly. As well, young people are leaving in droves for the bright lights of the big cities. These communities are left to make do with an aging citizenry, with no influx of young blood in sight, to carry on with the farming or "mom and pop" type of shops and businesses that in the past were mainstays in rural Japan.

Traditionally, Japan has always been a "saving" nation that allowed retirees to enjoy a happy and somewhat carefree retirement. This has also changed in recent years due to the economic collapse of the bubble economy of the late 1980s and the migration of children to the big cities.

In the past, children often returned to their hometowns after working a while in urban areas, but recently the trend has changed, and many are not returning to care for their aged parents.

Today, the elderly in Japan are spending more and more of their savings on daily living, health care and other age-related expenses that in the past was largely unnecessary because the oldest son and his family often cared for his parents in the ancestral home. With more and more families living apart from one another, this dynamic has changed tremendously in the past decade or so.

I predict three things will occur in Japan in the next few years.

(1) A sharp increase in taxes, especially sales tax.

When I first came to Japan to live, there was no sales tax at all. The price on the product was the price you paid.

The "bubble" debacle of the late 80s forced the government to implement a moderate sales tax initially, which was increased to 5%. This has doubled to 10%, I predict it will be raised even higher in the future.

(2) A raise in the amount of money people pay for socialized health care.

The system here requires each worker to pay into the system and this amount is matched by the employer. I love the socialized health care system because I can show my card at any clinic or hospital in Japan and receive immediate treatment. The cost per visit is nominal, but this will most likely rise to offset the total cost of health care for the elderly. With the "top-heavy" configuration, there just are not enough young people paying into the system to keep it solvent.

There must be an overhaul of the medical services that are now being dispensed in Japan. Japanese people have been conditioned to go to a doctor or a hospital at the drop of a hat for minor ailments like common colds and stomach aches.

Hospitals and doctors in Japan have a tendency to over prescribe medication and other expensive tests for relatively minor aches and pains. The current system makes it advantageous for them to do so because they receive money back from the government for every procedure performed.

Currently, for any surgery or invasive treatment, patients usually stay in the hospital for one month. In the United States, insurance companies want patients dismissed as soon as possible, sometimes on the same day as a surgery.

The system in place now must be reformed in Japan to make it more cost effective, efficient and solvent. Now that fewer and fewer elderly people are living with their children, placing the primary care of these people on the shoulders of the socialized health care system, excessive treatments must be stopped to save money for more serious ailments and diseases.

Many elderly people go to the doctor or hospital on a daily basis as a sort of "social" gathering to see friends and to chat. These people arrive in the early morning to get a place in line and to see their friends, which plugs up the system for those who are truly in need of medical care that is more urgent. This is a burden on a system that is already strained.

(3) A raise in the mandatory retirement age.

Since retirees are living longer, often their quality of life is much better which allows them to work past the 60 to 65 retirement age.

Luckily, many older people in Japan prefer to work and are quite happy to do so. With people living into their 90s, retiring at 60 means that many people have a three decade retirement.

The declining population in Japan has many colleges and universities wringing their hands. Attracting enough students to fill its slots is a challenge now and will only get more competitive in the coming years as educational institutions of higher learning try to rethink their programs, doing what they can to stay afloat…my university included.

Finally, Japan will be forced to open its doors to more immigrants willing to relocate here to work. When this does happen, the face of Japan will change considerably. Within the next generation or so, Japan most likely will take on the appearance of a "mosaic" rather than the homogeneous face it now has.

Actually, it is already happening.

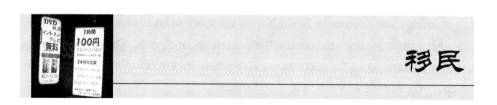

移民

直到最近,外国人真正去办理移民手续获得日本公民身份,从而成为真正意义上的日本人,还是十分罕见的。长久以来,绝大多数决定定居日本的外国人都是出于工作原因,并且十分乐意往返于日本和自己的祖国,他们只需一张工作签证或永久居住证便足够了。

在申请并获得永久居住证之前,我曾有一张有效期为三年的教授签证。拥有永久居住证,使我得以合法自由地出入日本,并且想在此工作多久就工作多久。但这并不等同于获得了日本公民身份,而是可让我自由地在这里工作和生活的长期签证,这类似于美国的绿卡,持有绿卡的外国人可以在美国长期居住。

众所周知，日本在20世纪80年代遭受了泡沫经济的冲击，日本因此不得不放宽对海外劳动力的入境限制，并赋予他们一个新的身份。当时劳动力的紧缺迫使日本打开国门让国外劳动者和非技术工人从事许多日本人不愿做的工作。

这和美国的情况很相似。美国需要来自墨西哥的季节工人分别于夏秋时节在东西部偏北地区、冬春两季在佛罗里达和加利福尼亚采摘农产品。在美国工作和居住好些年之后，这些工人中有很多人选择在美国安家。

我认为，日本政府的初衷是想让那些外来工人在日本工作一小段时间以解决日本的劳力紧缺问题，然后带着收入以及掌握的将来用得上的工作技能回到自己的国家。

日本政府没有料到的是，这些来自经济不发达、政局动荡或深陷战乱的国家的外来工人最后决定留在日本。

部分外来工人与日本人结婚生子并安家落户，还有一些则非法居住在日本，继续干别人不愿意干的活。政府对此基本上睁一只眼闭一只眼，因为这些人弥补了日本劳动力的不足。

30年转瞬即逝，目前日本的大城市有一些外国人聚居的社区，这些社区里全都是来自同一民族的外国人。政府没有出台具体计划帮助这些人融入日本社会，所以当外来工人没能很好地适应日本文化，没有被当地主流社会接受时，问题就出现了。

这样只会让情况恶化，因为有关方面不是尽力去帮助这些新来者与日本人一起生活和工作，而是建立外来移民聚居地，使得他们与外界隔离开来，他们的日本邻居因此质疑他们的生活方式，反倒加剧了日本主流社会对这些外来移民的偏见。

有关上述情况的一个恰当例子可以追溯到20世纪80年代末。当时日本爱知县南部小镇保见丘急需劳动力来填补严重的劳力短缺，镇上的官员想到了一个解决措施，就是雇佣日裔巴西人。他们的体貌特征与日本人无异，甚至有日本姓氏，但从民族和文化角度看，他们则是纯粹的巴西人。

他们的祖父母为了寻求更好的生活从日本迁徙到巴西，首次移民浪潮后的第一代日裔巴西人在巴西很可能基本保持着日本人的生活方式。

然而随后的每一代人都变得更像巴西人，一直到20世纪80年代，绝大部分的日裔巴西人怀着和他们祖父母一样寻求更好生活的愿望回到日本找工作。

日本政府设立了一种新型工作签证，使这些第二代和第三代日裔巴西人在日本工作变得更容易，同时取消了以往申请日本工作签证所需的繁琐手续。

但问题是，他们与曾经的日本文化根基相去甚远，他们更乐于认同巴西的文化和传统而不是日本民族的文化遗产。

他们几乎都没有真正地掌握日语，来日本前从没吃过日式食物，对日本的礼仪、传统和文化也一无所知。

小镇的官员认为，既然他们长得像日本人，他们的言行举止也一定像日本人。由于没有制定任何计划来帮助这些新来的移民适应新的环境和生活，问题很快就出现了，日本主流社会认为与他们在同一社区生活的是巴西人。

我记得当时的一篇报道历数了巴西人种种让当地日本人震惊不已的行为，其中最让当地日本人受不了的是，一些巴西人会穿着泳裤进入公共澡堂，把日本人用来泡澡的浴池当成了热水浴缸。

很少有日本人会否认廉价劳动力对日本汽车工业产生的经济影响，廉价劳动力使日本汽车产业在国际市场上颇具竞争力。这是那些雇佣大量外国劳工的公司在"实时生产系统"这一汽车生产体系下获得的短期收益。

这种体系可以降低企业运营成本，因为汽车公司不是把所有组件都交给一个工厂生产，像丰田这样的公司会将其大部分配件分包给一些更小的公司生产，而这些小公司则十分依赖日裔巴西移民所提供的廉价劳动力把每一个零部件"及时"运输到装配线，这样就可以缩小工厂的规模并减少储存大量配件所需的费用。

这种现象的负面影响是，虽然这些工人中很多已经取得永久居住权，可以无限期地待在日本，但他们被官方列为"临时工"（尽管他们每周至少工作40个小时，甚至更多），这就意味着公司不需要给他们全职员工的待遇，不必给他们买医疗保险或缴纳养老保险，致使许多工人无法享受正当的医保和真正的养老金待遇。

从长远来看，公司为了节省开支而不付给工人足够的工钱，不主张他们享有合理的社会医疗保险和退休福利，那么当这些人得了衰竭性的慢性疾病或当他们老了该怎么办呢？

日本政府并未全力解决这些问题，因为该国政府过分担心经济能否峰回路转，而事实上日本汽车工业目前发展迅猛，让欧美同行眼红不已。

目前，他们就像鸵鸟一样把自己的头埋到沙子里，假装一切都很好。在接下来的20年，日本的人口结构将会发生巨变。到那时，移民的子女开始结婚成家，彻底改变日本的人口面貌。而在此之前，一个更严重的问题将会困扰这些外来者的后代，那就是教育。

在日本没有法律规定这些移民的孩子必须接受义务教育，虽然大多数孩子确实会上学，但辍学率非常高，因为没有系统的项目教授这些移民子女第二语言日语（JSL），导致他们的日语写作能力及在以日本人为主的学校里的交际能力都很弱。很多社区意识到移民子女的需要，正在建立更多的JSL项目。

对于土生土长的日本儿童来说,每年必须掌握所学日本汉字以便能够正常阅读和写作,已经很不容易了;而对于那些被送到以日本人为主的学校学习的移民子女,在没有针对性的帮助和辅导的情况下,要想掌握日本汉字无疑难上加难。

这将在未来产生巨大的社会影响。一旦这些孩子长大成人却没有适当的教育和技能以获得一定社会流动能力,他们就将沦落到社会经济的更底层,因为除了干体力活,他们没有能力做任何有技术含量的工作。

目前日本正处于一个巨大的十字路口,日本人口数量之少已经岌岌可危,致使全国部分小学关闭,并使一些大学的办学前景堪忧,因为这个浪潮最终会导致很大一部分综合性大学、独立学院、大专和职业学校缩小办学规模,甚至关闭。

不管日本是否愿意承认,它的未来与大量的外国移民密切相关,这些以到日本短期工作、弥补日本不断扩大的劳动力缺口为目的的外来移民最终会永久居留在日本。他们会结婚生子,并与其他人一道,不断改变日本的面貌。

日本会通过提供正当的签证、保险、退休金以及教育来欢迎这些外来工人,让他们在日本社会更有作为吗?还是仅仅把他们当做劳力,不给这些工人平等的权利以及合适的生计,当不再需要这些人时就把他们驱逐出境?日本究竟会作何选择?让我们拭目以待。但如果日本过去的指令和态度是预兆的话,未来对于这些希望把日本称作家园的外来工人来说,是十分凄惨的。

美国在对待外来工人方面显然做得也很糟糕,这就是为什么在2016年的总统大选中,这个问题在某种程度上起了决定作用。日本必须开始接受这一严酷的现实:为了保持自身竞争优势和国际地位,日本必须接受这些移民并让他们融入日本社会,赋予他们平等和有尊严地同日本人一起工作生活的机会。否则在将来,日本同样会发生目前美国正在上演的令人轻蔑的争论。只有时间可以证明一切。

Immigration

Until recently, it was quite rare for foreigners to go through the actual immigration process where they take Japanese citizenship, making them, in essence, Japanese. Traditionally, the majority of expatriates that decided to call Japan home were people who chose to come here for professional reasons and were quite happy to glide back and forth between Japan and their home countries, being satisfied with a "work visa" or "permanent residency".

Previously, I used to have a three-year "professor's visa" until I applied and received "permanent residency". This allows me to come back and forth to Japan freely and to stay and work legally for as long as I wish. It is not Japanese citizenship but a long-term visa that allows me more freedom to live and work here, similar to an American "green card" that resident aliens are granted who reside in the US for an extended period of time.

The proverbial "bubble" economy that Japan enjoyed in the 1980s made it necessary to loosen the restrictions regarding "visiting workers", giving them a new status. A shortage of laborers during that time period required Japan to open its borders to allow laborers and unskilled workers to do the jobs that many Japanese people refused to do.

This is similar to the situation in the United States, where migrant workers from Mexico were needed to pick produce during the summer and autumn seasons in the upper Midwest and in Florida and California during the winter and spring seasons. Many of these workers, after years of working and residing in the United States, opted to make the US their home.

The original intention of the Japanese government, I believe, was that the migrant workers would come into Japan to shore up the labor shortage for a short-term stint, and then return to their home countries with money in their pockets and hopefully some new job skills that they could then use there.

What the government didn't count on was that many of these people who came from countries where the economies were not doing as well, had political strife or were at war decided to stay in Japan.

Some of these workers married Japanese nationals, had children and set up house. Others lived illegally, continuing to do the jobs that no one else wanted to do. The government officials largely turned a blind eye to such practices, because a need was being filled.

Fast-forward 30 years, and now we have communities in the larger cities where pockets of foreign nationals live together, creating entire neighborhoods of non-Japanese from the same ethnic background. No concrete programs were introduced to help these people assimilate, so there are instances where problems have arisen when the foreign workers haven't adapted well to Japanese culture and now were then shunned in Japanese mainstream communities by the locals.

This only exacerbates the situation, because instead of trying to assist these newcomers to Japan to live and work alongside their Japanese counterparts, little ghettos were created where these foreigners became isolated, making their Japanese neighbors suspicious of their ways of living, which in turn fueled the tendency of mainstream Japanese to become insular in their thinking toward these newcomers.

A good example of this dates back to the late 1980s, when a town in the southern prefecture of Aichi, Homigaoka, desperately needed workers to fill a severe labor shortage. The town officials thought a solution would be to employ ethnic Japanese-Brazilians. Physically they looked Japanese, even having Japanese surnames. Ethnically and culturally, however, they were 100 % Brazilian.

Their grandparents had emigrated from Japan to Brazil in search of a better life. Probably the first generation after the initial wave of immigrants lived a largely Japanese life in Brazil.

Each ensuing generation, however, became more Brazilian until the 1980s, when the large majority of the Japanese-Brazilians who, like their great-grandparents before them who were searching for a better life, came back to Japan to find work.

The Japanese government created a new type of working visa to allow these second and third generation Japanese-Brazilians to work in Japan more easily (cutting out much of the bureaucratic red tape normally required to work in Japan).

The problem was, though, they were so far removed from their Japanese roots that they readily identified with their Brazilian culture and traditions more so than their Japanese ethnic heritage.

Nearly all of them had no real Japanese language skills, had not eaten Japanese food prior to coming to Japan and had no idea about Japanese etiquette, traditions or culture.

The town officials assumed because they "looked" Japanese that they would "behave" like Japanese. With no programs in place to assist these newly arrived immigrants to fit into their new surroundings and life, problems soon arose with mainstream Japanese who found themselves sharing their community with the Brazilians.

I remember a newspaper article during this time that listed all the improper things the Brazilians were doing that horrified the local native Japanese population. One of the biggest offenses to the locals was that some of the Brazilians would go to the local public bath wearing swimming trunks—treating it more like a "hot tub" than the intended "bath tub".

Few people here can deny the economic impact that cheap labor has had on Japan's auto industry, making it quite competitive on the world market. This is the short-term gain companies enjoyed by employing so many foreign workers in the "just in time" auto-manufacturing system.

This system allows for a lower overhead because instead of having all the components made in one location, companies like Toyota subcontract much of the production to smaller companies that are very dependent upon the cheap labor that the Brazilian-Japanese immigrants offer. Each component is delivered "just in time" on the assembly line, which cuts down on the size of factories and the need to stock so many parts.

The down side to this is that these workers, many of whom now have permanent residency and can stay in Japan indefinitely, are categorized officially as being only "part-time" workers (even though they work a 40-hour or more week), which means companies do not have to pay wages as high as for full-time employees, or pay into the health-insurance or pension-fund schemes for these employees, leaving many without proper health care and with no real retirement plan in place.

In the long term, by saving money now by not paying the workers sufficient incomes and by not insisting they have proper socialized health insurance and retirement benefits, what will happen to these people when they have debilitating, chronic illnesses or when they are elderly?

These questions haven't been fully answered by the Japanese government, because it is too worried about the prospect of the economy maintains a turn-around and the fact that the Japanese auto industry is going gangbusters at the moment, placing Japan in a position of envy by the US and European automakers.

For the time being, they are like ostriches with their heads in the sand, pretending all is well. The next 20 years will see huge demographic changes in Japan when the children of the immigrants begin to marry and have families, and become a part of changing face of Japan. Before this occurs, however, a more serious problem is plaguing the offspring of these newcomers: education.

There is no law that requires compulsory education of the children of these immigrants in Japan. Although the majority does attend school, the dropout rate is high, because there are no systematic programs in place to teach Japanese as a second language (JSL) to these immigrant children, so their written Japanese and ability to function in mainstream Japanese schools are weak. Thankfully, many communities are realizing this need and are offering more JSL programs to these foreign families.

It is difficult enough for native Japanese children to keep up with all the *kanji* characters they must learn each year to be able to read and write properly. It is doubly difficult for children who are thrown into a mainstream classroom with no remedial assistance or special tutoring.

The future social implications of this are tremendous. Without proper education and know-how that would allow these children to have some semblance of social mobility once they become adults, they might be cast into an even lower socioeconomic bracket because they will not be able to perform any worthwhile jobs other than menial labor.

Japan is at a huge crossroads currently. The population of Japan is dangerously low which has caused elementary schools across the country to close, which is currently making universities jittery as this wave eventually will cause a good number of universities, colleges, junior colleges and trade schools to either scale back or close.

Japan's future, whether it wants to admit it or not, is going to be closely intertwined with a large migration of foreigners who will come to Japan for short-term work to fill the growing shortage of workers, but who will end up staying on permanently. These foreigners will then marry, have children and become a part of the changing face of Japan.

Will Japan embrace these people by offering them proper visas, insurance and pension schemes, as well as education, to make them more functional in society? Or will Japan use them for labor only, denying these workers equal rights and a proper livelihood by casting them away when no longer needed? It will be interesting to see which direction Japan takes. If past directives and attitudes are any indication, however, the future looks rather bleak for these immigrant workers who are hoping to call Japan home.

The United States certainly has handled the immigration of workers to the US horribly, which is why the 2016 election was decided in part on this issue. Japan might be having the same contemptuous debate the United States is having in the future if it doesn't start accepting the harsh reality that in order for it to maintain its competitive edge and world standing, it will have to accept and assimilate immigrants into its society, offering these workers a way to live and work alongside Japanese people that gives them equal footing and personal dignity. Only time will tell.

流浪汉

20世纪80年代后期，我第一次到日本居住。当时每一位第一次见到我的人都会不可避免地问我这样一个问题：为什么美国会有那么多流浪汉？

这个问题总让我很戒备，因为它的确曾经是，而且现在依然是美国的一个污点，即使美国是世界上最富有的国家之一，且以个人自由、追求幸福和机会平等为本并以此为傲。

我从来没能给出一个让人满意的详细回答，因为人们无家可归的原因有很多。

我在华盛顿特区以大学实习生的身份为印第安纳州州长工作期间，必须从住处步行前往国会山。每天我都会经过一个公园，那里聚集了很多流浪汉，当时的我处于易受影响的年纪，使我震惊的是，这些人竟都这么年轻。

他们为什么不工作，没有家？知晓问题的答案得益于我的经历，我很幸运能和一位来自英国的援助工作者住在一起，他设立了一个施舍处，给国会山周边的流浪汉提供食物。在周末我常常会主动帮忙分发食物。这对我来说是一次有趣的经历，我因此学会了感激，感激自己有房子、食物、家人、朋友和使我幸福快乐所需要的一切。我的英国室友无私奉献，帮助他人，是他使我学会了感恩，这是十分宝贵的。

他还向我解释了为什么有些人会流落街头。因为当时是20世纪80年代早期，他们中很多人都是近10年前回国的越战老兵，因无法再次融入美国主流生活才成为流浪汉。

几乎所有无家可归的男男女女都曾遭受过心理创伤，大部分人沉迷于酒精或毒品；有些人穷困潦倒同投资不当最终血本无归有关；还有的就是决定逃离主流社会的生活及其责任。在美国，导致人们无家可归的主要原因与日本形成鲜明的对比。

在日本，流浪汉问题是在20世纪90年代初著名的泡沫经济爆发之后才出现的。在那之前，日本几乎不存在有人无家可归的现象。然而，渐渐地，以前的美好时光不再，很多中年男性失去了工作，而且往往得不到家里的支持。

这些流浪汉，有些是出于羞愧，另外一些因为妻子忍受不了失业的丈夫，将他们赶出家门。他们涌入大城市，在公园或桥梁底下搭建的小帐篷里度日。

在日本，成为流浪汉主要是因为经济困难而陷入困境。有趣的是，他们不会像美国的那些同病相怜者一样遭受精神疾病、酒瘾和毒瘾的折磨。

日本流浪汉尽管接受救济金，但仍保持着个人尊严，他们通常会将用塑料防水布和箱子搭建的临时帐篷周围打扫得干净整齐。

在东京，我常常看见流浪汉帐篷外的晾衣绳上挂着新洗的衬衣，简陋的小屋前整齐地摆放着鞋子，因为在日本文化里，穿鞋进屋是不可接受的。

当然，日本流浪汉也有不讲究卫生的、患有精神疾病的以及沉迷于酒精和毒品的，但是相较于北美和欧洲，这类人在日本所占据的比例要低很多。

在日本，流浪汉似乎有着强烈的社区意识。他们中的大多数人会与他人正常交往，会为保持居住地的整洁出一份力。他们能自给自足，在便携式的电热板上做饭，利用大多数公园内还算干净的公共厕所来洗漱、洗碗和洗衣服。

最近几年，日本流浪汉的数量开始回落，这要归功于更加强劲的日本经济。东京政府试图通过向他们提供就业培训和两年政府津贴，帮助他们自食其力，从而重新安置大部分无家可归者。

在个人手机普及之前，我在东京各处乘坐火车和地铁时，注意到那些流浪汉为了换取废旧杂志和漫画书为别人擦洗汽车，随后他们会在街上折价转卖这些杂志和书籍赚钱。这些东西通常没怎么用过，再卖出去的可能性很大。同时，这也是自给自足的做法。然而，如今很少人买旧杂志和旧漫画，人们更愿意在手机上读文章和看漫画。

如果在20世纪90年代初经济泡沫破灭时有网吧的话，大部分流浪汉很可能会成为网吧难民。如今，经济拮据的年轻人会在网吧里转悠，表面上看他们不是流浪汉，但实际上他们确实是。

网吧难民和居住在大桥底下油布帐篷里的真正流浪汉的唯一不同，就是他们出没的地点。过去让流浪汉露宿街头和现今让年轻人陷于困顿的社会弊端几乎没有什么两样，他们在公共场所勉强度日，都没有一个可以真正称之为"家"的地方。

奇怪的是，自从日本流浪汉问题变得十分突出之后，就再也没人问我关于美国流浪汉的问题了。世道真是挺有意思的。

Homeless People

When I first arrived to live in Japan in the late 1980s, one question I inevitably was asked by people I first met was: Why are there so many "homeless" people in America?

This always put me on the defensive, because it certainly was, and still is, a stain on the fabled tapestry of one of the wealthiest nations in the world, which prides itself on being a country based on personal freedom, the pursuit of happiness and equal opportunity.

I could never give a boxed answer that was satisfactory; there are many reasons, circumstances and situations which caused people to find themselves homeless and with no place to go.

When I worked in Washington, D.C., for the governor of Indiana as a college intern, I had to walk to Capitol Hill from the place where I lived. Each day I passed through a park where homeless people gathered. What struck me at that impressionable age was how young all the homeless people looked to me.

Why couldn't they work? Why didn't they have homes? To help answer these questions, I fortunately shared a house with a British aid worker who ran a soup kitchen to help feed the homeless who lived around Capitol Hill. On many occasions I volunteered to help serve food there on the weekends. It was an interesting experience that has stayed with me, making me appreciate having a home, food, family, friends and everything I want or need to be happy. My British roommate was selfless in his devotion to helping others and taught me some very valuable lessons about gratitude.

He also explained to me how some of these people ended up on the streets. Since this was during the early 1980s, many of the men were Vietnam vets who could not readjust to mainstream life after arriving back from the war nearly a decade before.

Most all of the people—men and women—suffered from some sort of mental illness, and the majority were addicted to alcohol or drugs. For others, the reasons for the downward spiral had to do with bad financial investments where they lost everything, while others just decided to check out from dealing with the responsibilities of living in mainstream society. The majority of these reasons are in stark contrast to Japan's onslaught of homeless people.

The homeless problem in Japan did not begin until the proverbial economic bubble burst in the early 1990s. Up to that point, homeless people virtually did not exist in Japan. Slowly, however, once the good times stopped rolling, many middle-aged men found themselves jobless and, in many cases, without family support.

Men who found themselves homeless—sometimes out of shame, and in other instances, because wives were fed up with out-of-work husbands and kicked them out—gravitated to large cities where they set up little tent cities in parks and under bridges.

The majority of homeless people in Japan were largely due to financial reasons, falling upon hard times. Interestingly, Japanese homeless people were not plagued by the mental illness, drug addiction and alcohol dependency that their American counterparts are.

Japanese homeless people tend to maintain a sense of personal dignity while on the dole. Generally, they keep the area around their makeshift tents made out of plastic tarps and boxes quite orderly, clean and neat.

In Tokyo, I often observe freshly washed shirts hanging on clotheslines outside their tents, as well as their shoes neatly lined up outside their shanties because to wear shoes inside one's home is culturally unacceptable here.

Of course, there are also homeless people here who have no personal hygiene, are mentally ill and have alcohol and drug problems—the percentages of these types, though, are much lower in comparison to North America and Europe.

There does seem to be a strong sense of community among the homeless in Japan. Many can be seen socializing with one another, as well as pitching in to keep the area where they live tidy and neat. They are quite self-sufficient, cooking meals on portable hot plates and using the somewhat clean public restrooms located in most Japanese parks to wash themselves, their dishes and clothes.

In recent years, the number of homeless has been falling, thanks to a more robust economy. Tokyo has tried to relocate a large percentage of homeless men by offering them job training and two years of government-subsidized rent to help get them on their feet.

Before the onslaught of personal cellphones, while riding the trains and subways around Tokyo, I noticed homeless people scouring the cars for discarded magazines and comic books which they discounted and resold on the street to make money. Usually these items were only slightly used, making their resale quite possible. Again, this has to do with self-sufficiency. However, today, few people purchase such items as they prefer to read articles and comics on their cellphones.

The large majority of homeless people, mostly men, probably would have become net cafe refugees had such places existed when the economic bubble burst back in the early 1990s. Today, young people who find themselves in the financial doldrums can maneuver about the cafes, maintaining a semblance of not being homeless, when in fact that is what they are.

The only difference between the Net Cafe Refugee and the truly homeless person who lives under a bridge under tarps is circumstance. The social ills that caused the old-timers to live on the streets is nearly the same as those that now cause this younger generation to fall on hard times, living from hand to mouth in public spaces, not having any real place to call "home".

Curiously, after Japan's homeless problem became so prominent, I was never again asked that question about America's homeless problem ... funny how that works.

我刚到日本时，离婚现象在这里还很罕见，我只是偶尔遇到离过婚的人。如今，日本的离婚人数正快速赶上美国。离婚目前在日本还是不常见的，依然伴有随之而来的负面成见（尤其是针对女性），但是，社会正在慢慢接受这一现象——主要原因是其普遍性以及人们别无选择。

在日本完全没有"共同监护"的概念。最近，我在文化课上给学生看了一个视频，里面描述了共同监护的复杂性。视频中的父母对哪周该由谁照看孩子而推搡争吵，男孩在父母分配自己和他们在一起的时间时显得不知所措。

共同监护制度在美国很常见，孩子们对于和爸爸或妈妈轮流生活没有任何想法。这只是美国家庭生活的一个方面，再平常不过了。

日本没有共同监护制度，这可能是因为文化上的原因。日本法律规定，父母离婚后只有一方能够拥有孩子的完全监护权，这在很大程度上和父母之间已经没有婚姻关系有关。因此，在社会上他们被认为是毫无瓜葛的。

父母中没有监护权的一方有义务分担抚养孩子的经济费用，扮演这一角色的通常是父亲。在日本，孩子的监护权在绝大多数情况下会判给母亲。

没有监护权的一方可以探望孩子，但离婚协议并未对此做出明确规定。父母看望自己的孩子，和他们通电话或互通信件被认为是天经地义的权利。虽然法律条文没有对这些做出规定，但这些是允许的，因为有先例可循的，同时也是一种惯例。

但是，据我观察，没有法定监护权的父母就算会看望自己的孩子，也是偶尔为之。婚姻关系一旦在法律上终结，似乎除了在经济上补偿抚养费之外，其他所有的关系也都跟着终结了。

随着越来越多的日本人和外国人结婚，他们之中有一部分人以离婚收场一点也不奇怪。这促使法院审视与离婚相关的一些习俗，因为西方人，尤其是北美人要求进行"共同监护"。有时候，为了和平解决此类纠纷，法官们确实得动一番脑筋才行。

在日本，离婚很容易。从法律上说，离婚所要做的就是夫妻双方达成共识，在一份正式表格上加盖私人印章（判子）并在市政府登记。如果双方同意这么做，这婚就离成了。没有必要让家事法庭介入。离婚申请一旦提出，就会受理并通过。

其他绝大多数国家没有这样的制度，这可能是世界上最简便的离婚制度之一。我阅读相关资料得知，将近90%的日本离婚者都采取了这种方式。

近来一个让人吃惊的趋势是，日本退休人群的离婚率居高不下。孩子长大成人各自独立后，许多夫妻决定终止婚姻关系。孩子曾经是维系夫妻关系的纽带，大多数夫妻将孩子抚养成人后，他们却不知道如何彼此相处。

我曾在一档脱口秀节目上看到一位妇女谈论自己不久前的离婚，她看上去60岁左右。她说当孩子在家和读大学的时候，她为了孩子而维持着婚姻。但丈夫退休后，她决定宁愿独自生活也不愿每天忍受自己的丈夫。丈夫退休前，她觉得自己还能自由地做喜欢的事，但丈夫退休后总待在家里，她就无法忍受整天和他待在一块儿了。

有些年长的夫妻达成了某种事实离婚的约定，免去了从法律上结束婚姻关系的麻烦。这些夫妻通常同在一个屋檐下生活，但会分开居住，妻子可能住在楼下，而丈夫则住在楼上，从不相互问候，各过各的生活，就像已经离了婚一样。

这一做法使他们无需经受离婚带来的公开羞辱，从而保全了面子——当一对夫妻出于种种实际的原因，在法律上没有离婚，而实际上已经"离婚"，邻居们很可能还被蒙在鼓里，认为一切如常。

在日本，人们对父母离婚的孩子也抱有成见。父母常常会等所有孩子都成家后才申请离婚。没有哪个正直体面的家庭愿意自己的孩子和离异家庭的孩子结婚，好像离婚也会传染似的。因此，他们虽生活在痛苦之中，却佯装幸福，直到子女结婚成家，才会离婚。我的一位日本朋友曾被他母亲催婚，不是因为她想抱孙子，而是她急切地想和我朋友的父亲离婚。朋友结婚后没几个月，他父母就离婚了。

在我看来，日本女性在离婚时毫无疑问是吃亏的一方。有一些针对女性的贬义词，比如"出戻り"，指离婚后回娘家的女人。再比如"傷物"，指那些因为无法再次销售变现而降价的"破损商品"——换句话说就是次等货。这些词很刺耳，因此很多女性在跟丈夫离婚这个问题上犹豫便不难理解了，因为她们在离婚后会被社会打上耻辱的烙印。

一个更现代的针对离婚男女的词组是 X（指在婚姻状况一栏中打的一个 X），意为"离过一次婚"，就像英语词汇 one strike（一次挫折）。在美国，大部分离婚的人最终会再婚，但是在日本，情况就不一样了。年轻人更有可能再婚，而大部分中老年人在离婚后通常不会再婚。

Divorce

When I first came to Japan, divorce was still rather rare. Only occasionally did I meet someone who had divorced. Today, the numbers are catching up rather quickly with those in the United States. It's still not as common here, and there tends to be a negative stigma still associated with divorce in Japan (especially toward women), but slowly society is making allowances for divorcées—primarily because of its prevalence and because people have no choice.

The idea of "joint custody" is a totally foreign concept in Japan. Recently,

I showed a video clip in my culture class that showed just how complicated an arrangement can be. The parents were jostling and arguing about whose turn it was to have the child that week. The boy stood bewildered as his parents tried to divide his time between them.

This system is so common in the US that kids don't think anything about being ferried from parent to parent. It is but one aspect of American family life that has become ordinary.

In Japan, there is no system of "joint custody", and this could be due to cultural reasons. Legally, only one parent after the divorce has sole custody, and this largely has to do with the fact that the parents no longer are legally bound to one another, so they are viewed by society as being completely separate.

The parent who doesn't have custody is expected to participate in the financial cost of raising the child by sharing the expenses associated with the child. This is usually the father. An overwhelming majority of custody cases in Japan are awarded to the mother.

The parent who doesn't have custody is allowed visitation, but it isn't expressly stipulated in the divorce settlement. It is considered a natural right of a parent to be able to see his/her child, call by telephone or exchange letters. There is no "legal provision" for these types of contacts, but it is allowed as a matter of precedent and practice.

It is my observation, though, that often the parent who does not have legal custody generally does not see his or her children regularly, if ever. Once the marriage is severed legally, it seems that all association is then cut off, except for financial remuneration as a sort of "support" payment.

With more and more Japanese marrying foreigners, it is only logical that a certain percentage of these marriages end in divorce. This is causing the courts to have to rethink some of the customs associated with divorce because Westerners, especially North Americans, want and demand some sort of "joint custody" arrangement. At times, it does leave judges scratching their heads trying to figure out how to amicably solve these types of disputes.

Divorce is quite easy in Japan. All that has to be done legally is for both people to have mutual consent; they must affix their personal seal (hanko) on an official form and then have it registered at the city office. If both agree to it, then it is a done deal. There is no need to have a family court involved. It is accepted and settled upon filing.

This type of system is quite rare in most other countries and is probably one of the easiest in the world. I read where about 90% of couples in Japan who divorce do so in this manner.

A recent trend that is surprising is the high percentage of divorces between couples who are in their golden years; after the children are raised and on their own.The children were the bond that held the couple together, most likely, and when they finished raising the children, they were at a loss with one another.

I saw a talk show where a woman was talking about her recent divorce. She looked to be about 60-year-old. She said that when her children were at home, then in college, she had a purpose. But when her husband retired from his job, she decided that she preferred to be alone rather than to have to put up with him every day. When he worked, she felt she had some freedom to do as she pleased, but after he was home day in and day out, she couldn't stand to be around him.

Some older couple have worked out a sort of divorce without legally going to the trouble to dissolve the marriage. These couples often live in the same home but separately. The wife may live in the downstairs and the husband upstairs, never exchanging greetings and going about their lives as if they were divorced.

This system allows them to save face by not going through the actual public humiliation of a divorce—the neighbors are none the wiser, most likely, thinking that everything is normal, when in fact they are for all practical reasons, "divorced" without legal registeration.

There is also a stigma associated with the children of divorced parents in Japan. So parents will wait until all of their children are married before filing for a divorce. No upstanding family wants their child to marry someone from a divorced family, as if it were something contagious. So, they live in misery, putting on a happy facade until the children marry, then they divorce. A Japanese friend was being pressured to get married by his mother—not because she necessarily wanted to have grandchildren but because she was eager to divorce his father. As soon as he married, it was only a matter of months before his parents divorced.

Japanese women in Japan certainly get the short end of the stick in divorces, in my opinion. There are a number of derogatory terms used toward women, such as "demodori" which refers to a woman who goes back to her parents' home after the divorce. Another term, "kizumono", means "damaged goods" like those that are on a discount table because they likely cannot be sold again—"seconds", in other words. These are quite harsh and it is understandable why women are hesitant to divorce husbands, because of the stigma associated with them afterwards by society.

A more modern term used for both men and women is "batsu ichi" meaning "one failure", like the English term "one strike". In the US, a majority of divorced people eventually remarry, but in Japan, this is not the case. Younger people are more apt to remarry, but the majority of middle-aged to older Japanese who divorce often do not remarry.

收养

收养在日本极为罕见,即使有人收养了孩子,收养孩子的父母往往也会尽力不让邻居和朋友们知道。

我刚来日本永久居住时,我办公室里有一位司机,他和他太太年纪轻轻、精力旺盛且十分幽默,也就是说,他们有可能成为理想的父母。

一次,我们讨论婚姻和家庭问题时,他们坦诚地告诉我,他们无法生育,虽然为此伤心,但他们接受了一辈子无儿无女的现实。

我当时是个涉世未深的20来岁美国小伙。我马上提出建议,让他们从遍布日本的众多孤儿院里收养一个孩子。他们夫妻俩都看着我,好像我头上长角了似的。

做丈夫的很快说,这个办法行不通,他妻子也点头认同。我不明白为什么,要他们做进一步解释。似乎他们本身不反对收养别人家的孩子,而是他们的家族会反对他们收养孩子。

在日本,很多人看重血缘关系,对收养怀有根深蒂固的厌恶。当一个孩子不管由于什么原因成了孤儿,这个孩子的大家族通常会接管他,将其养大直到成年。

如果大家族没法养育孤儿,大部分家庭宁愿把这个孩子送到政府办的机构——孤儿院,也不愿让一个完全陌生的家庭收养他。

这对没有孩子的夫妻把这些都告诉了我,还说他们担心自己的家庭不会像对待他俩亲生孩子那样对待收养的孩子。另外,他们担心,如果孩子不是他们亲生的这一事实曝光,学校里的同学和老师不知会对孩子做出什么,邻居又不知会怎样对待他们。

当然，这是近 30 年前的事了，也许随着米娅·法罗、罗西·欧多内尔、麦当娜、安吉莉娜·朱莉等好莱坞明星收养孩子的国际新闻层出不穷，日本社会会因此进步一点。

于是，我决定最近在大四学生的"跨文化研究研讨"班提出这个问题。首先，我通过回顾近年来引人注目的收养案例及美国夫妇到亚洲或中美洲收养孩子这一现象提出话题。我还跟学生们提及我家族里有四个收养的表兄弟，在我成长阶段，他们在我生活中起着非常重要的作用。

对于很多美国人选择收养来自不同民族和种族的孩子，我的学生很是惊讶。我跟他们解释说，"孩子就是孩子"，很多美国人只想体验拥有孩子的快乐，因此，当决定从国外收养孩子时，孩子的民族背景常常就不是问题。

简单讲解后，我问学生对收养有何看法，有趣的是，几乎全部学生都认为人们收养孩子是一件好事，孩子在充满关爱的家庭里生活比在孤儿院里生活好多了。

然而奇怪的是，当我询问他们之中有谁会考虑收养一个孩子，没有一个人表示愿意收养。我换了一种问法问他们，要是因为某种原因无法拥有自己的孩子，他们是否愿意收养别人家的孩子。

同样，没人认为自己能那么做，给出的理由与前面提到的大体一样——大家庭对于完全接纳收养的孩子存在顾虑，社会对被收养孩子的态度，孩子在学校可能受到欺负，还有一个原因是担心收养的孩子与亲生子女性格不合。

很明显，30 年来日本在收养孩子这件事情上没有太多改变。因为我所做的研究虽然规模小且不太科学，但也反映了日本人对待收养的传统态度。

我的一个外国朋友和他的日本籍妻子生有两个儿子，大儿子跟一个一直生活在孤儿院的高中同学是好朋友，在这个同学年满 18 岁时，必须离开孤儿院，他基本上没地方可以去。

我朋友的儿子问他父母，他的同学在适应孤儿院之外的生活、接受一些工作培训并找到工作之前可否在他们家住一小段时间。当然，他父母同意了。

这个男孩最明显的特征是，他真的没有任何与家庭有关的体验，他一直待在孤儿院，从来没有体验过正常的家庭生活。

比如，他们说，不管他的餐盘里有什么，他都会吃个精光，这是孤儿院的一条规矩：不管你喜不喜欢，都得把给你的东西全部吃光。另外，他在吃饭时默不作声，这是孤儿院的另一条规矩。

他们给他买了些衣物，他开始在衣服的标签上写上自己的名字，这在孤儿院里是必须要做的。他觉得在我朋友家独自住一间房不舒服，因为他习惯和同伴们一起住。

那个男孩刚到我朋友家，他们就得知那天正好是他的生日，于是他们准备了生日蛋糕和蜡烛，要给他一个惊喜。男孩感动得哭了，因为他从来没见过生日蛋糕。

当许多家庭不想做晚饭时，他们通常会订披萨吃。男孩从未有过和一家人一起点外卖吃，吃什么、吃多少都随意的体验。

不用说，一想到男孩没体验过大部分家庭认为理所当然的事，我朋友及家人的心都碎了。最后，那个男孩前往东京，在一家寿司店当学徒学一门手艺，使自己成为一个对社会有贡献、自食其力的人。

日本孤儿在政府办的孤儿院里成长与美国孤儿在寄养家庭生活的原因相互映衬——都是父母去世、孩子被照看者抛弃、虐待和忽视等。

在日本，人们极少讨论孤儿，他们被关在社会的大门背后，几乎成了日本社会中的一个无形群体。人们对在孤儿院长大的孩子无疑持有偏见，这使他们进入主流社会时很难找到适当的工作、住房以及与人建立婚恋关系。

我相信，在人们注重自己的外表以及在别人眼中形象的日本社会，许多日本家庭不太喜欢让自己的孩子跟在孤儿院长大的孩子结婚，其中的原因是社会对孤儿的偏见。

这很可能是我个人的文化偏见在起作用，我来自一个这样的社会：人们认为孤儿由审查合格、愿意领养孩子的家庭抚养更有利。在我看来，孩子在毫无生气和人情味的孤儿院长大，比在一个家庭里生活要糟糕得多。

也许美国的寄养体制在日本根本行不通，因为日本人反感收养别人的孩子。如果收养孩子在日本被认为是这么不好的一件事，我深信，想要寄养一个孩子的家庭也会遇到同样的问题。

我这一生曾有很多机会去旅行和看世界。旅行中我常做的一件善事，就是去所到国家的孤儿院看看。我在波多黎各生活时，曾多次与几位来自尼加拉瓜的朋友造访我家附近的一所孤儿院。

当我问孤儿院院长，我能做点什么，她只是说："请尽可能多抱抱这些婴儿，他们需要人们的拥抱。"我拥抱了孩子们，虽然这看上去只是一个小小的善举，但我却受到了很大触动。

想到只是抱抱婴儿就能对婴儿的一生产生影响，我懂得了一些很有价值的东西：千万别低估一次小善举的力量。

重要的不是我付出了多少，而是我收到的回报：对一个人做了点有用的事的感觉，对方当时最需要的，只是一个充满关爱的拥抱。

据报道，日本政府办的孤儿院里生活着大约 3 万名弃儿。有时会有人考虑收养孩子，而孩子的法定监护人或亲人往往会拒绝收养申请，选择让孩子待在孤儿院。

这些人也许抱有这样一个期望：将来有一天，这些弃儿的父母或有经济能力的近亲会回来将孩子从孤儿院带走，抑或是那些虐待、忽视孩子的父母会改过自新，从而能再次照顾孩子。

很不幸的是，上述情况很少发生，孤儿的整个青少年时期最终都会在孤儿院里度过。人们几乎都认为，如果孩子没法与自己的父母生活在一起，与其被没有血缘关系的家庭收养，还不如待在孤儿院。

由此产生了一个有关"弃婴安全岛"合法性的问题，即一旦一名儿童被遗弃在那里，法院将裁定该名儿童是被正式遗弃了，因其父母有一天回来将其领走的可能性微乎其微，所以理论上一辈子都要待在孤儿院里。

日本户籍制度只在家庭登记表里依法记录诸如结婚、出生和死亡等人生大事，传统上还是认为收养、离婚是使家庭蒙羞的事。

20世纪80年代晚期，日本修改了相关法律，使被收养的孩子可以将出生时的姓氏改为收养家庭的姓氏。而在这之前，被收养的孩子的两个姓氏都要登记在册，这基本上成了被收养的醒目标志。

在法律修改之前，被收养的孩子在社会生活的许多方面都会受到歧视。此外，在孤儿院长大的孩子在接受高等教育、找工作以及心智足够成熟时建立男女关系等方面都很难得到公平对待。

孤儿院能保证里面的孩子有地方住、有东西吃、有衣服穿，可以读完高中。一旦他们成人了，原则上他们就独立了，如果他们要上大学，必须自己负担学费。不用说，这些孩子通常付不起学费，所以，大部分孩子不会继续上大学。

收养孩子的家庭有时会立即搬去一个没人认识他们的地方，以避免任何可能出现的问题或来自外人的歧视，以及其他家族成员的反对。

奇怪的是，日本的老年夫妻或年长的单身女性出于继承的目的而收养一个儿子却是常有的事。日本社会似乎接受这样的收养，但收养的"孩子"常常是成年人，而且这么做是因为法律上的原因，比如延续一个家庭的姓氏。

日本人讨厌收养也许源于佛教文化的影响。敬仰祖先的理念是佛教文化的重要组成部分，同时，它还可能有助于人们所笃信的家庭和群体内部血缘应当纯正的观念得到持久的延续。因此，被认可的血缘纽带从宗教角度显得十分重要。

我来自一个接受和欢迎收养的文化环境，有时很难理解日本人为何对收养孩子一事如此大惊小怪。为什么不让父母和孩子成为一家人？收养对于膝下无子而又十分想要孩子的父母，和从此能拥有一个真正的家庭并在家庭氛围中成长的孩子来说，是一件双赢的事情。

在过去的几十年里，日本确实经历了一些影响深远的社会变革：允许妇女成为职业女性，有些妇女有时候为了事业而放弃做母亲；年轻一代日益摒弃长辈所坚持的无聊习俗以争取更多的个人自由和独立,这令长辈们忧心忡忡;从由家庭成员照顾自家老人、疗养院之类机构数量寥寥,转变为此类机构为数众多而与孩子生活在一起的老人数量越来越少。

只有时间才能说明一切。也许在不久的将来,日本的年轻一代会接受收养的观念。就像过去的传统被现在的观念更替,年老的一代将最终面对现实。

Adoption

Adoption in Japan is something that is quite rare, and when it does happen, the parents often do all they can to keep this fact a secret from neighbors and friends.

When I first came to Japan to live permanently in the late 1980s, there was a staff member who worked in my office as a driver. He and his wife were young, energetic and a lot of fun. In other words, potentially ideal parents.

Once when we were discussing marriage and family, they admitted to me that they were not able to have children of their own, and although saddened by this, they had accepted that they would always be childless.

Being a naive twenty-something American, I immediately suggested that they adopt a child from one of the many orphanages that are located all over Japan. They both looked at me as if I had a horn growing out of my head.

Quickly, the husband said it was not an option, while his wife nodded in agreement. I was puzzled as to why, so I pressed them to explain their reasoning further. It seems that although they personally were not opposed to adopting a child from another family as their own, their families would be against it.

In Japan, many people have a rather deep-seated aversion to adoption, placing greater importance on blood relations. Often when a child is rendered parentless within a family, for whatever reasons, the extended family of the child will often take the child to raise through adulthood.

If this is not an option, then many families would prefer the child be placed in a government-run home—orphanage—rather than to allow complete strangers to adopt the child.

The childless couple who was telling me all of this also said that they worried their families wouldn't accept an adopted child the same way they would a biological child. Besides, they were afraid of what might happen to the child at school by classmates and teachers if it were ever found out the child was not their own, or how neighbors would treat them if the truth were ever discovered.

Of course, this example is nearly 30 years old, and perhaps Japanese society has evolved a bit with all of the internationally reported adoptions of Hollywood stars like Mia Farrow, Rosie O'Donnell, Madonna and Angelina Jolie.

So, I decided to present this question to my fourth-year "Cross-Cultural Studies Seminar" class recently. I first presented the topic by reviewing the high-profile adoptions in recent years; and the trend in the United States for couples to travel to Asia or to Central America to adopt orphaned children. I also related to them that in my family I have four adopted cousins who were a very important part of my life while growing up.

My students were surprised that many American couples opted to adopt children from different ethnic backgrounds or races. I explained that a "child is a child" and many American couples just want to experience the joy of having a child, so the child's ethnic background is often not an issue when deciding to adopt from a foreign country.

I asked the students how they felt about adoption after the short presentation. It was interesting that nearly all of my Japanese students felt that it was a good thing for people to adopt children, and it was better for a child to be in a loving home rather than to be in an orphanage.

Curiously, though, when I asked if any of them would consider adopting a child, not one said they would. I changed the dynamic of the question by asking that if for some reason they couldn't have a biological child of their own, would they then consider adopting a child from another family.

Again, no one felt that they would ever be able to do that, offering as reasons much of what I mentioned earlier—extended family concerns about accepting the child fully into the family, society's attitude toward the child, potential bullying at school and an additional reason, worrying that the personality of the child would not fit that of a child that was a biological son or daughter.

Obviously, not much has changed in 30 years, because the attitude in my small, unscientific study seems to mirror what has been traditionally the attitude in

Japan toward adoption.

A foreign friend of mine and his Japanese wife have two biological sons. The older son befriended a boy in high school who had lived in an orphanage his entire life. When the boy turned 18 years old, he had to leave the facility and basically had no place to go.

My friend's son asked his parents if he could come to their home for a bit until he could get used to living outside the orphanage, get some job-training and find employment. They, of course, agreed, and the boy came to live with them.

What was most noticeable about the boy was the fact that he hadn't really ever had any "family-based" experiences. He always had been in the facility and never did normal family things.

For instance, they said he ate absolutely everything on his plate, no matter what. This was an orphanage rule—to eat every bit of what is given to you whether you like it or not. Also, he was completely silent during meals, another rule at the facility.

They purchased some clothes, and he started to write his name on the label, which was necessary in the orphanage. He had his own room in their home, which made him uncomfortable because he was used to being in a room full of people at night.

Soon after he arrived to their home, my friends learned it was his birthday, so they prepared a birthday cake with candles as a surprise. The boy was so touched that he cried because he had never seen a birthday cake.

As is typical in most families, they would order pizza on some nights when they didn't want to cook. He had never experienced eating carry-out food as a family—eating what and how much he wanted.

Needless to say, it broke their hearts to think he had not experienced many of the ordinary things that most families take for granted. He eventually was able to relocate to Tokyo where he is training as an apprentice in a sushi shop, learning a trade that will make him a productive, self-sufficient member of Japanese society.

The reasons children end up in government run orphanages in Japan mirror why American children end up in foster care—the parents are deceased, the children were abandoned, abused, or neglected by their caretakers.

Seldom do people in Japan discuss orphaned children, making them almost invisible to society because they are kept behind closed doors. There is a stigma attached to a child who has grown up in an orphanage, making it difficult when they are placed into mainstream society to find proper work, housing, and to form lasting relationships with others.

Many Japanese families, I'm sure, would not be so keen to have a child marry a person who grew up in an orphanage due to the societal attitude toward such people, in a country where appearance is everything and image by others is taken very seriously.

This is probably where my personal cultural bias comes in, coming from a society and culture where it is believed that children are better off in "foster care" with families who are vetted and willing to accept the child into their home. The sterile and cold surroundings of a facility, in my logic, must be far worse than being placed in a family home.

Perhaps such a system of foster care would never work in Japan due to the aversion of caring for a stranger's child. If adoption is viewed so gloomily in Japan, I'm sure the same issues and problems surrounding a family who wanted to adopt would be the same for a family who wanted to foster a child.

I have had so many opportunities in my life to travel and see the world. One thing I often tried to do on these trips was to visit orphanages in the countries I visited. When I lived in Costa Rica, I visited a number of times an orphanage near my home with a couple of friends from Nicaragua.

When I asked the caretaker at the orphanage what I could do, she just said, "Please hold as many babies as you can...they need human contact." I did and although it was seemingly a small contribution, it was powerfully moving for me.

To think that by merely cradling a baby can make a difference in that child's life taught me something very valuable: Never underestimate the power of a simple act of kindness.

It wasn't the act of giving so much, but it was what I received in return—the feeling of having done something of use for a fellow being who, at that moment, most needed something as easy as a caring touch.

It is reported that there are some 30,000 Japanese children living in government orphanages. When a child is considered for adoption, it is not uncommon for the legal guardian or next of kin to reject the application, opting for the child to stay in the orphanage instead.

There is a longing, perhaps, by these people that someday the parents who abandoned the child will return, or an extended family member might be able to afford to take the child, or the abusive or neglectful parent will reform and be able to once again care for the child.

Unfortunately, these cases are quite rare, and the child ends up spending his/her entire adolescent life in the facility. It is almost an attitude that if children can't live with the parents, then it is somehow better for them to live in an institution rather than to be adopted out to an unrelated-by-blood family.

One issue that arose regarding the legality of the baby hatch is that once a baby is left there, it is up to the courts to rule the baby officially "abandoned" or the baby could theoretically be left in an orphanage its entire life because of the possibility the parents might come back someday to pick the child up.

The Japanese system of "koseki", which legally records such life events as marriages, births and deaths in a family registry, traditionally viewed adoption or divorce as being blemishes upon the family name.

In the late 1980s, the law changed and made it possible for adopted children to have their birth name changed officially to the adopted family name. Before, both names were registered, which basically served as a neon sign saying ADOPTED.

Prior to the change in the law, it was easy for adopted children to be discriminated against in many parts of society. Still, it is difficult for children who grew up in children's homes to get a fair shake when it comes to receiving higher education, securing employment and being emotionally stable enough to get involved in relationships.

Orphaned children are guaranteed a safe place to live, along with food, clothing and education, through high school. Once they become adults, they are basically on their own, and if they want to attend university, they must pay for it themselves. Needless to say, the kids normally do not have the resources to pay for college tuition, so a large percentage does not go on to university.

Families who do adopt sometimes will move immediately to a place where they are not known in order to avoid any potential problems or societal prejudices the couple might face by outsiders, and to deal with unsympathetic family members who might oppose the adoption because the child isn't related by blood.

Curiously, it is common in Japan for an elderly couple, or older single woman, to adopt a son for inheritance purposes. This seems to be acceptable by society, but usually the adopted "child" is an adult, and it is done for legal reasons to carry on a family name, for instance.

The aversion to adoption in Japan might have its roots in Buddhism culture.

The belief in ancestral worship is an important part of Buddhism, also, which perhaps helped to perpetuate the belief in the idea of "pure" and "impure" blood within families and groups of people. This makes a recognizable bloodline important for religious reasons.

Coming from a culture where adoption is accepted and embraced, it is sometimes difficult for me to understand what all the fuss is about in Japan regarding adoption. Why deny parents and children the opportunity to become a family? It's a win-win situation for the childless parents who desperately want a child, and for the child who would benefit from having a real family and home life to grow up in.

Japan has experienced some far-reaching social changes in the last few decades: allowing women to become professionals who sometimes choose to forgo motherhood for careers; or where young people increasingly have rejected the stodgy customs of their elders for more personal freedom and independence, causing the older generation to wring their hands with concern; and changing from a nation that had families caring for their old people, going from having few nursing home-like facilities to having many such facilities with fewer older people living with their children.

Only time will tell, but there might come a time in the not-so-distant future where adoption will be embraced by younger generations. Just like past traditions being cast aside for more modern ones, the older generation will just have to deal with it.

宠物

30年前，日本宠物大多仅仅被视作一种财产；而今，宠物被人们当作孩子一样宠爱着，并成为日本家庭里的一员。

一些主人宠溺它们，喂它们吃人吃的珍馐美味，这种做法确实过火了，宠物们因此患上了肥胖、糖尿病、心脏病等疾病。

我的一位日本朋友喜欢在吃饭时给她的三只小腊肠狗喂食，它们尤其喜欢奶酪。突然有一天，较小的那只变得无精打采，郁郁寡欢。

她急忙带小狗去看兽医，才发现小狗的肠胃不适合吃奶酪。在服下泻药后，小狗总算安然无恙了，但是医生责备我的朋友并建议她严格控制宠物的饮食。出于关爱，她把它们给宠坏了；但她也意识到这样做对它们是不利的。

流行时尚往往会对日本人购买服装、汽车甚至宠物时的决定产生极大影响。当电影《101只斑点狗》首映后，许多人也迫不及待地想去购买一只这样的狗。

但问题是，幼犬惹人怜爱，让人不禁想要拥它们入怀，但它们很快就会长大并需要更多空间和照顾。公寓适合养小型犬，而不是大型犬。而且，斑点狗对幼童也不是很友善，如果被激怒可能会张口咬人。其结果是许多因一时冲动购买斑点狗的人不得不放弃喂养，因为让它们和幼童一起待在狭小的空间里实在不适合。

另一个例子就是吉娃娃。几年前，电视上播放了一则贷款广告，其中主角是一只长毛吉娃娃，吉娃娃因此迅速走红。宠物店里的吉娃娃供不应求，致使其价格飙升。

该借贷公司看到吉娃娃突然爆红潜在的巨大商机后，决定让吉娃娃参与公司正在进行的广告活动。这是明智的决定，该公司通过在众多不同的广告中不断使用吉娃娃挖掘商机从而续写辉煌，其中一则广告是吉娃娃结婚的场景。人们对小吉娃娃爱不释手，都忍不住要买上一只。

这和美国塔可钟公司在广告中播放会说话的吉娃娃后出现的吉娃娃热并无太大不同。同样，该公司投顾客所好，向市场推出了众多以这种可爱的大眼睛小狗为特征的商品，创造了一个围绕这一形象的产业。

许多日本宠物主都渴望拥有一只品种独特、具有罕见特征的宠物狗，使得这样的狗身价倍增。举个例子，要是哪种宠物狗的皮毛颜色与众不同，或是异色瞳，又或者是个头小到可以放入手提包里，人们便会喊着非去宠物店买一只不可。

于是问题来了，犬只供不应求，诱使犬类繁育者们以更快的速度繁育更多的幼犬。缺德的育种者为了尽可能多地牟利，利用种犬与其兄弟姐妹或后代繁殖幼犬以满足市场对犬只的巨大需求。由此造成的悲惨后果是，越来越多的小狗出生时就患有严重的遗传病，这使它们痛苦不堪，也让对小狗宠溺有加的主人心碎不已。

有些遗传疾病在宠物狗出生时就表现得很明显，而其他疾病症状则是在多年以后才突然显现出来。这不仅让主人的情绪大起大落，还要花费巨额费用为宠物治病。

近来已转变了对待宠物的态度的日本宠物主，会像美国的宠物主一样不惜代价拯救如孩子和家人般的宠物。

最近，与我关系甚好的朋友一家得到了一个惨痛的教训。家里的小男孩很想要一只宠物狗，他们认为那种不掉毛的小型鬃毛狗是最佳选择，于是从狗舍购买了一只。这只狗在买回后的几月内状态很好，然而有一天它突然发病，最后死在去看兽医的路上。

尽管尸检还查不出具体的死因，但众所周知的是，过度繁育会导致小狗骨骼过于脆弱。这只狗因颅骨破裂造成了脑出血。

不用说，小男孩几乎崩溃了，伤心之余，他为小狗制作了一座佛教祭坛，并把小狗的照片及玩具堆放在它的骨灰盒周围。一家人都悲痛不已。

日本人有时会花费 8,000 至 10,000 美元不等的高价购买稀有或因具有不寻常特征而备受追捧的宠物狗。

这些人并没有清楚地认识到，为了得到一只白色的腊肠狗（十分稀少）或是蓝色皮毛的吉娃娃，这些携带某种隐性基因的宠物狗被人为地与其可能携带同种隐性基因的直系后代不断进行繁殖，以保持其特性。

在一窝具有理想特征的幼犬中可能只有一只是健康的，其余的则都严重畸形或残疾——要么没有眼睛，要么缺少一只爪子，要么智力低下。但是无良的繁育者们仍然会觉得 10,000 美元一只的售价值得他们那么做，就算一窝幼崽中的大部分要被抛弃也在所不惜。

不幸的是，这个问题不光出现在日本，美国也存在大量类似的情况。不同的是，美国制定了许多法律来保护动物和宠物主们的权益不受缺德繁育者的侵害。制定和颁布动物保护的相关法律不久也将在日本成为常态，因为当前的宠物热丝毫没有快速消退的迹象，宠物主们也会要求有关方面做出改变以保护他们自身和身处险境的动物们。

目前我没有养宠物，因为我工作忙碌，时常出差，这样对宠物不太公平。

但是，如果我真要养宠物，我可能会领养一条需要救助的狗。

我所了解的一些最出色的狗都有着随处可见的外型，经过多次杂交已经无法辨认是哪个品种。在被救助或收养后，它们往往精神抖擞、健康可爱，是心怀感激的伙伴。

如果你计划养一只宠物，请考虑到动物收容所收养一只，那里有许多值得收养、非常不错的动物正静候佳主。如果你已经养了宠物，别忘了给它们做绝育手术。

Pet

Thirty years ago, Japanese pets were, for the most part, just things that were considered to be mere possessions; today, pets are coddled and doted over like children, making them an extension of the family unit.

Indulgent pet owners can go overboard, trying to feed their pets food that is best reserved for human consumption. This has led to diseases like obesity, diabetes and heart ailments.

A Japanese friend loved to give her little trio of Dachshunds bites from the table; they especially were fond of cheese. Suddenly, one day the little one was lethargic and unusually low-key.

A quick trip to the veterinarian revealed that the dog's penchant for cheese didn't agree with its system. With the aid of a laxative, the dog was all right in the end, but the doctor scolded my friend and suggested she put all her pets on a strict diet. She spoiled them out of love, but realized it wasn't in their best interest to do so.

In general, Japanese people are influenced greatly by trends and fads which affect their decision-making when purchasing items related to clothing, cars, and even pets. When the movie *101 Dalmatians* first hit the silver screen, a number of people rushed out to buy one of these dogs.

The problem was that as puppies they were cute and cuddly, but they soon grew to be very large dogs requiring a lot of space and care. Apartment living is best suited for smaller canines, and not the larger ones. Also, Dalmatians aren't known for their sweetness toward small children, having a tendency to be nippers if provoked. The end result was that many of these impulsive owners were forced to unload these dogs because of the impracticality of keeping them in a small space with small children.

Another example, is Chihuahuas. A number of years ago, a loan commercial aired on TV featuring a long-haired Chihuahua; instantly there was a Chihuahua boom. Pet shops couldn't keep up with the great demand for these animals, so this caused the price of these dogs to skyrocket.

The loan company, after seeing the huge potential of this sudden fad, decided to make this Chihuahua a part of its ongoing advertising campaign. Cleverly, the company continued riding the boom it created by using this dog in a number of different scenarios, one of which featured it married with little Chihuahua puppies all around. People couldn't get enough of this cute little Chihuahua and had to have one.

This isn't too much unlike the US boom that occurred after the airing of the talking Chihuahua dog in the Taco Bell commercials. Similarly, Taco Bell used this interest to market a variety of goods featuring that big-eyed, adorable dog, creating a whole industry around this one character.

Many Japanese pet owners relish owning a unique or unusual type of dog with rare features, making it highly prized. For instance, if the animal has an alternative coat color to what is the norm, or has two different eye colors, or is so small it can fit into a handbag, people clamor to buy these from pet stores.

This is the problem. The demand is outstripping the supply, tempting breeders to produce more dogs more quickly. Unscrupulous dog breeders, trying to make as much money as they can, are breeding parent dogs with offspring and siblings in order to keep up with the high demand. The sad result is that more and more dogs are being born with severe genetic disorders, causing pain and suffering to the dogs and heartbreak to the doting owners.

Some of the genetic diseases are obvious from the time the dogs are born, but others stay hidden until years later when the symptoms suddenly appear, causing the owner to endure an emotional rollercoaster, not to mention spending huge amounts of money, trying to cure or care for the animal.

The newly reformed Japanese pet owner will spend any amount of money, like a devoted American pet owner, to save a pet that is like a child or family member.

Very good friends of mine recently learned this lesson the hard way. Their little boy so desperately wanted a pet dog. They agreed that a toy poodle, which is small and doesn't shed hair, would be the best choice. They purchased the dog from a breeder. The dog was perfectly fine for several months, and then one day it had a seizure and died on the way to the veterinarian's office.

Although an autopsy was inconclusive as to the exact cause, it is well-known that one symptom of over-breeding are brittle bones. The dog's skull was fractured and the brain hemorrhaged.

Needless to say, the little boy was crushed. He grieved by making a Buddhist altar for his little dog, arranging her photo and toys around the cremated remains. The entire family was completely heartbroken.

Japanese pet owners sometimes pay anywhere from $8,000 to $10,000 for some of these rare or highly sought after dogs with unusual features.

What isn't clearly understood by these people is that in order to get a Dachshund with white fur (very rare) or a Chihuahua with a bluish coat, the dog, which has a recessive gene, is bred over and over with direct offspring who also will likely have the same recessive gene in order to get that peculiarity.

One puppy with the desired characteristic in a litter may be healthy while all the others are grossly deformed or crippled—no eyes, one paw missing, mentally deficient. But, unethical breeders still feel that selling one for $10,000 is worth the effort, regardless if the majority of the litter has to be put down.

This problem unfortunately is not unique to Japan. Similar cases abound in the United States as well. One difference, however, is the amount of regulations in place to protect animals and pet owners in America from unethical breeders. This, in time, will also be the norm in Japan because the pet boom shows no signs of declining anytime soon, and pet owners will demand changes be made to protect not only them but also the animals at risk.

I currently do not own a pet because of my hectic work and travel schedule. It just wouldn't be fair to the animal. But, if and when I do get a pet, it likely will be a dog, and it will be one that comes to me through rescue or adoption.

Some of the best dogs I have ever known are the ones who are just run-of-the-mill dogs, so mixed that it is impossible to discern clearly which breed is dominant. They are often hearty, healthy, loving and, if rescued or adopted, very appreciative companions.

Please consider going to an animal shelter if you are planning to get a pet. There are so many deserving and wonderful animals waiting for just the right owner. If you are already a pet owner, please don't forget to spay or neuter your animals.

第四部分
日本生活

Part 4
Japanese Life

房屋

由于日本地理位置特殊，常年遭受各种极端天气的袭扰，因此人们在设计房屋时会将这些因素考虑在内。比如，除了最北部的岛屿北海道外，日本每年都会经历降雨量相当大的"梅雨"季节。这就是日本之所以如此植被茂盛、郁郁葱葱的原因所在。

如大家预期的一样，日本的夏季酷热难耐、湿度极大，因此房屋必须建得通风透气，这也是为什么自古以来日本建筑一直将关注的焦点放在如何防止房屋发霉上。

为了通风，传统的房屋一直都建造得轻巧柔韧。即使是在日本北方，房屋也不像美国北部地区那样密不透风。

另外，由于日本频繁遭受强地震袭击，结构柔韧的房屋更能抵抗震动。这就是为什么日本中世纪的城堡都用木头而非石头建成。地震时，木头能够弯曲摇晃，而砖石结构的建筑很可能会倒塌。

然而不幸的是，木结构的房屋不耐火，因此，千百年来，日本大部分城堡都因敌对势力蓄意纵火或遭怪异的雷击而被付之一炬。

火，以及对火的恐惧，一直萦绕在日本人心头，挥之不去。因为房屋都是用木头建的，一间挨着一间，加之许多是建在居民区的狭窄街道上，远离大道，一旦发生火灾，大型消防车难以进入现场，烈火会很快蔓延，烧掉某一区域内的不少房屋。

在古代，每晚都会有人手持两块木头在街道上边走边敲，进行巡逻，提醒大家在睡前熄灭炉火。有些地方至今依然保留着这样的做法。我记得几年前在日本南部的一个小村庄就听到过这样的敲击声。

在日本，除了房屋主要是木头建成的以外，人们通常还会将地板抬高以增加其与潮湿地面之间的间隔。如今，有些新的房屋建在水泥板上，有别于传统的建筑方式。这些房屋往往装有"地暖系统"以便过冬，并通过一定的设计防止房屋出现霉变现象，发霉是长久以来困扰日本房主的问题。

传统的日本房屋极少有固定墙面和铰链门，而是由可移动墙面建造而成，这些起到隔断房间作用的墙面称为"襖"（隔扇或拉门）。另外，拉门和外墙上的窗户都是用纸糊的，好让空气和光线穿透。这些看上去很结实又能保护隐私的门窗，是用障子纸糊的，而且确实非常轻薄。

就算不待在有固定墙面和铰链门的房间里，日本人也能找到属于自己的私人空间。尽管障子基本上都是纸糊的，人们还是觉得有属于自己的空间，哪怕家人就在另一边闲聊。尽管容易坏，而且有时对有孩子的家庭来说是件麻烦事，因为小孩觉得用手指在拉门的纸方格里戳洞很有趣，但这种门窗纸封不仅功能多样而且外观也优雅。

由于推拉门可以很方便地开关，日式住宅的房间有多种用途。白天，在房间中央摆上一张矮桌，并在矮桌周围放一些座布团，就可以用来招待客人喝下午茶。

到了晚上，把桌子推到一边，房间就成了卧室。置于半边墙壁的壁橱，白天用来放置床上用品，壁橱旁边的另半面墙通常会摆放一个叫做"神龛"的壁龛。神龛内一般会挂一幅传统书画卷轴，并在神龛底部配上一定式样的工艺品或插花。

房间地板是"榻榻米"（草垫），墙壁通常是用一种传统的绿色土质材料砌的。即便是按西式风格设计的日本房屋，通常也会保留至少一间传统的日式"榻榻米"房间。但因为不便于保养，有些新房子干脆舍弃"榻榻米"，转而选择安装更耐用、更便于清洁的地板。

当然，在像东京那样的大城市，拥有带庭院的房子，要花很多钱，因此许多家庭选择租公寓或者买高层大楼里的公寓。一般公寓通常是2LDK（两间卧室，附带一个集客厅、餐厅和厨房功能于一身的区域），虽然按美国的标准不算大，但供日本一个四口之家居住是没有问题的。

但如果可以选择的话，日本家庭还是想要拥有属于自己的房子。在日本，这个愿望和在其他国家一样强烈。最近越来越多的日本人已经能通过借款买地建造一个简朴的家实现这一愿望，这一潮流被称为"我的家"。

日本传统房屋

Homes

Since Japan is geographically positioned in such a way that it experiences every extreme in weather, houses are designed to take this into account. For instance, with the exception of the northernmost island of Hokkaido, Japan goes through a rather heavy rainy season called "tsuyu" every year. This is why Japan is so lush and green with thick vegetation.

As expected, the summer's sweltering heat and high humidity make it necessary for houses to be able to breathe. This is why, since ancient times, Japanese architecture has focused on how to protect homes from mold and mildew.

Traditionally, homes have always been made light and flexible to allow air to move through easily. Even in the snow country where houses aren't as tight and sealed as they would be in the northern areas of the United States.

In addition, since Japan suffers from frequent and powerful earthquakes, a flexible structure is more able to sustain a robust jolt. This is why Japan's beautiful medieval castles were all made of wood and not stone. The wood would bend and sway during an earthquake; whereas a brick or stone structure would most likely just topple over.

Unfortunately, though, the wood structures didn't hold up so well to fire, and the majority of Japanese castles throughout the centuries fell victim to blazes either intentionally set by an enemy faction or by freak lightning strikes.

Fire and the fear of fire always occupy Japanese people's minds. Because houses are built of wood and are so close together, coupled with the fact that many are built on narrow streets in neighborhoods off main thoroughfares, it's difficult for big fire engines to enter in an emergency. A raging fire can quickly become widespread, burning a number of homes in an area.

In the old days, each evening, a man would walk the streets with two pieces of wood that he clanged together to remind people to put out their stove fires before bedtime. In some places, this custom still exists. I remember hearing it in a small village in southern Japan a number of years ago.

In addition to homes being made primarily of wood in Japan, the floors are generally raised to add space between the structure and damp ground. Today, newer homes are sometimes being built on cement slabs, which are a departure from traditional methods. These often are equipped with "floor heating" for the winter and are somehow designed to resist potential mold issues that are always a concern for homeowners here.

A traditional Japanese home has few stationary walls with hinged doors. Instead, homes are built with movable walls that act as room dividers called "fusuma". Also, paper sliding doors ("shoji") between rooms and paper window coverings to outside windows allow air and light to pass through; these offer the appearance of being substantial and private but are made of rice paper and are actually very thin.

Japanese people can find privacy in their own personal space besides being shut up in a walled room with a hinged door. Even though "shoji" doors are primarily made of paper, people can still feel they have privacy, even with family members on the other side chatting away. Although fragile and sometimes a nuisance for families with small children for they find it amusing to poke holes in the paper squares with their little fingers, this type of covering is quite versatile and elegant in appearance.

Japanese homes, because of the moveable doors that can be opened or closed with ease, allow rooms to be used for a variety of purposes. By day, they can be used for entertaining guests for afternoon tea, using a low table in the center of the room surrounded by cushions called "zabuton".

At night, the table can be pushed to the side of the room, which is then transformed into a bedroom. A closet located on half of a wall (called an "o-shire") stores the bedding during the day; the other half of the wall next to the closet usually features an alcove called a "tokunoma". The "tokunoma" normally has a traditional scroll hanging in it with some type of art piece or flower arrangement displayed on the floor of the niche.

The flooring in this room is "tatami" (straw mats), and the walls are normally made of a traditional earthen material that is green in color. Japanese homes that are Western in design will usually have at least one traditional Japanese "tatami" room. Because of the upkeep, though, some new homes lay flooring which is longer-lasting and less trouble to clean, forgoing "tatami" altogether.

Of course, in the big cities such as Tokyo, owning a home with a yard is so expensive that many families rent apartments or purchase condominiums in high-rises. A typical-style apartment is usually a "2LDK" (two bedrooms with a combined living/dining/kitchen area). Although small by the US standards, this type of apartment can be occupied by a family of four in Japan with no problem.

Given a choice, however, Japanese families prefer to have their own homes. The dream of owning one's own home in Japan is as strong as it is in other countries. Recently, more and more Japanese have been able to realize this dream, a trend referred to as "My Home"—securing a bank loan, buying land and building a modest home for one's family.

泡浴

生活中鲜有像传统日式泡澡这样既惬意又奢华的事情。上千年来，日本国民真正地使洗澡这件事情臻于完美——将打理个人日常卫生这一普通的过程提升为一门充满仪式感的不折不扣的艺术。在我看来，这可以算是日本极其宝贵的文化财富。

对于日式泡澡，许多第一次到日本的游客都多少有两方面的顾虑：泡进别人泡过的水里，以及和陌生人一起在公共澡堂里沐浴。

说实话，我第一次来日本时，也不喜欢脱个精光和一群陌生人待在一起，或是泡在一些人用过的浴盆里。

然而，仅仅泡过一次之后，我便迷上了泡澡。现在的我一扫此前所有的顾虑，酷爱各种传统日式泡浴：家庭盆浴，公共澡堂浴，以及日语里称之为"温泉"的温泉浴。

需要注意的是，日式浴缸的使用方法和其他国家使用浴缸的方式不同。日式浴缸仅仅用以泡澡而非洗澡。水很干净而且热气腾腾——有时候热得好像要烫伤你的皮肤似的。

因此，实际上，人们并非按照西方人的做法，在满是肥皂泡的脏水中扑打拍腾着洗澡。日本的浴缸仅仅用来浸泡身体和放松身心，跟特定用途的热水浴盆类似，只是不穿泳裤，也没有按摩泡泡。

泡热水浴往往比日式泡澡更令我担忧，因为日式泡澡要求洗浴者在进入浴缸前，先仔细地往身上抹肥皂，擦洗并用水冲干净身体，之后再踏入热水中，这样才合乎日本礼仪。

　　大多数人都知道热水浴池和游泳池一样，其水中都含有大量的氯，泡完以后还需要冲澡，因此他们事先没有洗澡就直接进浴池了。

　　从幼童时代起，日本的儿童就开始接触传统日式泡澡，并早早地学习如何正确清洗他们的身体。在日本家庭中，儿童几乎总是和父亲一起沐浴。

　　从孩子们还是婴儿时起，通常就是父亲陪孩子们洗浴，好让母亲在晚餐后得到片刻的歇息。大多数日本成年人都能拿出一张和父亲一起在浴缸里的照片，照片里的他们通常还是小宝宝，照片一般由母亲来拍摄。这种孩子和父亲一起洗浴的做法会一直持续到孩子们长到能够独自洗浴为止。

　　作为一种家庭出游方式，许多日本家庭会在周末前往公共或天然温泉浴场泡澡。一些新开业的和更加现代化的公共浴池会提供"家庭浴室"，母亲、父亲以及孩子们——一家人可以在这私密之所一起泡浴。

　　古时候，有许多（允许男女一起泡浴的）公共混合浴池，这在今天已不那么普遍了。于19世纪末来到日本的基督教教士们极力反对这一习俗，最终，他们的努力基本上成功了，只有提供若干户外浴池、叫作"露天風呂"的传统"温泉"得以保留。而现今依旧有很多这样的露天浴池允许男女一起沐浴。

　　当朋友们从美国来访时，我喜欢带他们到我最喜爱的山间传统"温泉"，那里提供各式各样的浴池，其中就包括混合式共用露天浴池。

　　这个特别的浴场实际上是一家传统的日本旅馆，远离喧嚣，甚至连电都没有，手机收不到任何信号。对于想要完全摆脱一切烦恼的游客来说，这是个彻底放松身心、摆脱现代科技束缚的好地方。夜里，旅馆及周围的庭院会点满油灯，呈现出奇妙而梦幻的景象。

　　夏日里，客人们穿着棉质"浴衣"（夏季和服）穿梭于各个浴池之间，享受着各式各样的浴池，每一个浴池对人体都有不同的疗效。这些浴池里的矿泉水因其有助于缓解诸如关节炎等慢性疾病的药用价值而闻名全国。

　　泡浴者到旅馆周边体验各式浴池之前，首先会在室内用肥皂清洁体表皮肤。

　　冬日里，乘雪地车是前往该旅馆的方式之一。客人抵达后，旅馆会为其提供专用的冬季和服；冬季和服比较厚，能让辗转于各个浴池的客人感到温暖。

　　客人们学着在寒冷的天气里快速脱掉衣服，扑通一声跳入户外浴池温水中，身子马上就会暖和起来。静静地坐着，欣赏冬雪缓缓地飘落在头上，这可真是一派宁静祥和的景象。

　　日本民族十分保守，因此，他们会在进出浴池时用小毛巾遮挡身体的重要部位。浴室四周设有未用墙壁隔断的洗浴间，里面配有小壁镜供每位客人

日式泡浴

洗浴时使用。

洗浴者坐在离地面不高的低矮小凳上，用小水盆舀水冲洗身上的肥皂泡。即使旁边的人近在咫尺，洗浴者却有旁若无人之感。

实在难为情或介意身体外露的人，可能会觉得在日式公共浴池洗浴是一种难以忍受的折磨；但事实上，这是日本人生活中十分平常而自然的一部分，没有人会过多地注意其他洗浴者。或许坐在接近地面高度的低矮小板凳上，面前就是小壁镜，能给人一种心理上的隐私感。

对于那些害羞和没有经验的人而言，或许他们在去共用浴池沐浴前，最好先尝试保护隐私的家庭泡浴。家庭浴盆通常又宽又深，沐浴者脖子以下的部位都能没入水里。

日本浴室最为绝妙的一点是，洗浴者不必因为担心水花四溅而束手束脚，因为整个浴室都是防水的，水花溅到墙壁上、天花板上以及地板上，都没问题。

再者，淋浴喷头也不是固定在墙上，人们可以取下喷头，坐着或站着用喷头冲洗身体和头发。这样也让清洗浴池变得相当容易。人们擦洗浴室时，可以穿着从超市买来的塑料靴子。

实际上，人们还会购买许多和沐浴有关的物件，用以沐浴。洗浴者会用浴缸盖保持水温；冬日里人们泡浴时，盖上浴缸盖有助于保持浴缸内的热度，因为一般的日本浴室是没有供暖设施的。

人们用搅拌棒搅动非自动控温式浴缸内的水，以确保热水均匀地散开。桶、凳子，还有小斗勺，是在沐浴过程中清洗身体时要用到的。又长又窄的澡巾是用来擦洗身子的，澡巾粗糙的质地让我想到了砂纸，基本上起砂纸的作用。

一般来说，日本人都有宛若丝绸般光滑的细腻肌肤。我认为这和他们的日常沐浴习惯有莫大关系。日本人——哪怕是孩子——在公共浴室表现出来的细致常令我感到震惊。孩子们观察并模仿他们的父母,一遍又一遍专心致志地擦洗着自己的小身板。

这些粗糙的澡巾可以去角质,去除身上的死皮细胞。这能让皮肤保持细腻与光滑。因为很多美国人选择在早晨淋浴,不使用任何澡巾,所以他们只是洗掉身上大部分的污垢和灰尘,而无法去除所有的死皮细胞。

而我依旧坚持晨浴,因为这是美国文化的一部分。尽管如此,我也热衷于睡前来一次既奢华又放松身心的日式泡澡。这算得上是两全其美,各取所长。

Bath

There are few things in life are as satisfying and luxurious as a traditional Japanese bath. Over the millennia, Japanese have truly perfected bath-taking—elevating a mundane process of daily hygiene into a veritable art form, one that is steeped in ritual and, in my opinion, could be regarded as a precious and treasured cultural asset of Japan.

Many first-time visitors to Japan are a tad apprehensive about two aspects of taking a Japanese bath: entering bath water that has been used by someone else; and bathing with strangers in communal or public baths.

Admittedly, on my first visit to Japan. I, too, was not very keen about baring it all with a group of strangers, or getting in a tub after several people had already used it.

However, after just one time, I was hooked. All apprehensions were cast aside, and I am now a big fan of all types of traditional Japanese baths: the home bath, communal or public bath and the hot spring baths known as "onsen" in Japanese.

It is necessary to keep in mind that the Japanese bathtub is not used in the same way people use a bathtub in other countries. The Japanese bathtub is used only for soaking and not washing. The water is clean and steamy hot—so blistering sometimes that it seems like it's going to scald your skin.

So in reality, one is not really bathing in the true sense of the word, meaning splashing about in soapy, dirty water as is the custom in the West. The Japanese bathtub is used only for soaking and relaxing, similar to a hot tub's intended use, except without swimming trunks and massaging bubbles.

I tend to be much more apprehensive about getting into a hot tub than I am about entering a Japanese bath, because before entering the actual bathtub, proper Japanese etiquette obliges the bather to first thoroughly soap, scrub, and rinse off their bodies before setting foot into the hot water.

Most people enter a hot tub without bathing, knowing that so much chlorine is in the water that, like a pool, a shower afterward is needed.

From early childhood, Japanese children are exposed to traditional Japanese baths and learn early on how properly to wash their bodies. In Japanese families, children's bath time is nearly always done with Dad.

From the time the children are babies, Dad is the one who usually bathes with the children giving Mom a short break after dinner. Most every adult Japanese person can pull out a photo with Dad in the bathtub, usually as a small baby, taken by Mom. This custom of children bathing with Dad continues until they reach an age when they can bathe alone.

As a family outing, many Japanese families will visit a public or natural hot spring bath on the weekend. Some newer and more modern public bath facilities offer a "family bathroom" where an entire family can bathe together in privacy—mother, father and children.

Quite numerous in the old days, mixed public baths (that allowed both men and women to bathe together) are not so common today. The Christian missionaries who came to Japan in the late 1800s tried very hard to nix this custom and eventually were largely successful except for traditional "onsen" that often feature several outdoor baths called "rotenburo". A number of these allow both men and women to bathe together still today.

When friends visit from home, I like to take them to my favorite traditional-style "onsen" in the mountains that offers a variety of baths, including a communal outdoor bath that is mixed.

This particular bathhouse is actually a traditional Japanese inn. It is located so far away from civilization that it has no electricity. Cell phones are unable to pick up any signal. For travelers wanting to truly get away from it all, this is the place to go for total relaxation, away from the clutches of modern technology. At night, oil lanterns are lit all around the inn and the surrounding grounds, giving it a magical and surreal appearance.

In the summer, guests scurry from bath to bath in their cotton "yukattas" (summer kimonos) enjoying all the various baths, each boasting different health benefits. The mineral water in these baths is well-known around the country for its medicinal value that helps relieve chronic conditions such as arthritis.

The bathers first bathe inside with soap to clean their skin before going outside to try out all of the different baths located around the inn.

In the winter, one way to access this inn is by snowmobile. Upon arrival, special winter kimonos are offered to guests; these are thicker, giving people a semblance of warmth as they go from bath to bath.

Guests learn to disrobe quickly in the cold weather, plopping themselves down in the immediate warmth of the outside baths. It is indeed serene to sit quietly, enjoying the winter snow falling gently upon your head.

Japanese, as a people, are very modest, so a small towel is used to cover the important parts as one enters and exits the bath. There are wall-less stations all around the periphery of the bathroom equipped with a small wall mirror that each person uses while bathing.

Bathers sit on small stools, low to the ground, utilizing a small washpan for rinsing the soap off their bodies. Even though the next person is only inches away, one has a feeling of being alone.

Really self- or body-conscious people may find a Japanese public bathing experience to be much too torturous to bear; but in fact, it is such a common and natural part of Japanese people's lives that no one pays to other bathers much attention. Perhaps by sitting low to the ground and in front of this small mirror, psychologically it gives one a sense of privacy.

For the shy and uninitiated, perhaps the privacy of a home bath would be best to try first before bathing in a communal bath. Home baths are typically wide and deep, allowing bathers to submerge up to their necks.

The most wonderful part about a Japanese bathroom is that bathers don't have to be careful about splashing water about, because the entire room is water-resistant. The walls, ceiling and floor can be sprayed with water without worry.

Also, the shower nozzle is not attached to the wall—it can be detached to rinse your body and hair while sitting or standing. This also makes cleaning the bath quite easy. Little, plastic boots are sold at supermarkets that can be worn while scrubbing down the bathroom.

In fact, there are a number of interesting bath-related accessories that people buy for the bath. A cover is used between bathers to keep the water hot; and in the winter, it helps to hold the heat in the bathtub while the person is bathing, because the typical bathroom is unheated.

A stir-stick is used for non-temperature controlled baths to make sure the hot water is evenly distributed. A bucket and stool, as well as a smaller ladle-like container are used for the actual body-washing portion of the bath. A long and narrow washcloth is used for scrubbing the skin. Its rough texture reminds me of sandpaper, and it basically has the same effect.

Generally, Japanese people have beautiful skin, often resembling silk. I believe this has a lot to do with the bath ritual they perform daily. I am always amazed at how thorough people are, even children, when bathing at a public bath. Children scrub and scrub their little bodies with such determination, learning by observing and mimicking their parents.

These rough washcloths exfoliate, sloughing off dead skin cells from the body. This keeps the skin smooth and silky. Since many Americans opt for a morning shower, forgoing the use of any type of washcloth, they are only washing off the dirt and grime for the most part and not all of the dead skin cells.

I still insist upon a morning shower, because this is a part of my culture. In addition, though, I relish taking a luxurious and relaxing Japanese bath before bed. The best of both worlds.

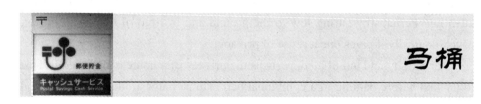

马桶

日本人不光在马桶的基础设计上精益求精，还让如厕这样普普通通的日常需要实现了华丽转身，使之成为一种让外国游客痴迷不已的绝妙体验。

曾有这么一件事：2005年，麦当娜时隔近12年再次来到日本举办演唱会。在一场新闻发布会上，当着娱乐记者的面，她对满屋子的人表示自己对日本加热马桶座圈甚是想念，在场的人深谙其意，忍不住咯咯窃笑。

如果你居住在寒冷地区，一个电动加热马桶座圈就成了必需品，这不仅是为了享受。而在那些对中央供暖系习以为常的人看来，安装加热马桶座圈似乎奢侈过头了。

但对我们这些无法享受中央供暖系统的人来说，在睡了一夜之后醒来，使用这样的坐便器确实是一大早第一件受人欢迎的事。臀部接触温暖的马桶座圈要比忍受冰冷的塑料座圈带来的一阵刺激好受很多。相信我。

西式马桶在日本被广泛使用是二战结束之后很久的事，当时的日本正逐步成为工业化、现代化的发达国家。当流行使用西式马桶后，日本的马桶制造商立刻开始改进其原有设计，使其功能更加多样化和实用化，从而促进其在日本家庭中的普及。

比如，日本马桶的一个普遍特征是将洗手池嵌入其水箱的顶盖之中。绝大多数日本马桶都装有一个小水盆和水龙头供人们上完厕所后洗手，而不是安装独立的洗手池。水龙头里流出清水供如厕者洗手，同时流入水箱，供下一位使用者冲洗马桶。

这种别出心裁的设计，既节水，又使马桶具备了多种功能。毛巾架通常安于马桶一侧，方便使用者在洗手后拿毛巾将手擦干，其洗手用水则会流入水箱。

最近，一位印第安纳州的朋友来日本看望我，她对马桶的这一特征以及加热座圈印象尤为深刻。她特地给我家的马桶拍了张照给她的先生看，并称赞这样的设计很节水。不得不说，我赞同她的看法。这样更加环保，因为冲洗的水使用了两次，这一点很有意义。

绝大多数日本居民家中的马桶安装在单独的房间里，和浴缸以及用于刷牙洗脸水槽是分开的。用来洗手以及刷牙洗脸的小房间叫做"洗面所"（通常里面放有洗衣机，同时做洗衣房使用）"風呂"或浴室则紧邻洗脸盆间。

当我第一次到访日本时，常在厕所门上见到"W.C."的字样，这个缩写词借用自英式英语，是"抽水马桶"的简称，标明是厕所。

日本人认为在同一处所如厕和梳洗太过污浊，因此厕所几乎总是独立设置。一个例外情况是，很多小型公寓使用"整体浴室"——整个盥洗室安装了马桶、洗手池、浴盆等设施。西式酒店房间通常也有这样的一体式盥洗室。

然而，在日本生活30多年后，不得不说，我喜欢将马桶与浴室及洗脸盆完全独立开来，从卫生角度来看，将这两种功能区独立开来是十分有必要的。

研究显示，无论什么时候，冲洗马桶的水中所含的微小秽物颗粒总是不可避免地会被冲到空气中。如果牙刷、毛巾、肥皂以及浴盆和马桶同处一室，污浊不堪的水汽就会沾到这些物件上。

我注意到，现在美国的一些新房已经开始将马桶置于独立的小房间，与洗浴间隔开，这一房屋设计上的变化肯定会大受欢迎。

日本人对于来自厕所的交叉污染十分在意，他们甚至给客人提供了专门在厕所内使用的拖鞋。这些拖鞋通常是塑料的，便于清洗，并且只在厕所里穿。

有时候，这些拖鞋上会有"W.C."的字样，因此，如果有人在上完厕所后忘记把厕所专用拖鞋脱下来，所有人都会知道。这确实很尴尬，尤其是在宴会上，主人不得不向某位客人指出，他/她在上完厕所后忘了换回普通毛绒拖鞋。

目前日本流行"卫洗丽"马桶，或称坐浴盆式马桶，这些马桶盖科技含量极高，现在已经安装在全日本的百货商店、写字楼和饭店的公共厕所内。大多数在过去15至20年间建造的民宅使用的马桶普遍都有这样的功能。

这种马桶并不是什么新奇玩意儿，它们由一家美国公司于1964年首次引入日本。但在进入日本市场仅仅两年后，这种"气压冲洗坐便器"就实现了国产化，接下来的事大家就都知道了。这种马桶在今天的美国鲜为人知，如今在日本却是很普遍的设备。它们在过去的50年里不断发展。

一位在泰国居住了40多年的美国朋友曾来日本探望我。我们去了东京游览，住在一家价位十分经济的酒店。即便是这样普通的酒店也在每一个房间安装了比较讲究的坐浴盆式马桶。

我的朋友对酒店房间里马桶的特殊功能印象深刻——加热座圈、用以清洁臀部的水可以调节温度和压力，还有专供女性使用的清洗模式。他开玩笑说，为了在房间享受智能马桶，他都可以不出门去游览东京。他决定也要在他曼谷的家中安装这种"卫洗丽"坐便器。

不了解情况的人都会是这种反应。日本的坐浴盆式马桶确实把人惯坏了，一旦你体验过这种最新潮的奇妙装置，再用普通的马桶，就会觉得平淡无奇了。

然而，这样的奢侈享受需要付出高昂的代价。但这并不会使那些想要在家安装这种马桶的日本人望而却步。正如美国人认为厨房里没有门上安有饮水机和制冰机的冰箱、自动洗碗机和垃圾处理机，日子就没法过一样，日本人觉得没有"卫洗丽"坐便器也是难以想象的。日本的厨房很少有刚才提到的在美国厨房里常见的便利设施，但绝大多数日本人都使用智能马桶。

房屋建造商们也理所当然地在新建的卫生间内为这种坐便器安装额外的供水设备，所有马桶后部都装有用以连接加热座圈的电源插座。一些更新潮的型号带有遥控器，用户就无需扭过身来笨手笨脚地触摸所有装在马桶座圈一侧的按钮了。

我知道，如果售价能够降低的话，这一科技发明会迅速风靡美国。很少有美国人愿意花1,000美元购买一个马桶座圈。有趣的是，大多数美国人在购买汽车时倒是毫不手软,极尽奢侈,他们看中的是汽车的舒适和时尚而非单纯的功用。

为什么不将这样的态度拓展到人们每天都要花不少时间使用的东西上呢?这种马桶的高价物有所值,一旦你用了这样的高科技马桶,普通的马桶就再也无法满足你了。

日式马桶

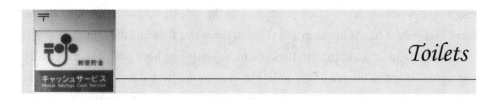

Toilets

The Japanese have not only perfected the basic design of the hardware used in Japanese toilets—they have magnificently transformed the mundane need for daily elimination into a surreal experience that makes visitors to this country swoon with contentment.

A case in point: In 2005, Madonna returned to Japan for a concert after a nearly 12-year absence. When she met with entertainment reporters at a press conference, she commented to the packed room that she had missed terribly Japan's warm toilet seats. This remark caused the attendees to chuckle, knowing exactly what she meant.

Living in a cold climate makes having an electric toilet seat that stays warm a necessity and not a mere indulgence. For people who take for granted central heating, it might seem like a superfluous extravagance to have a heated toilet seat.

However, to those of us without the luxury of central heating, it is indeed a first welcome thing in the morning upon waking up from a night's sleep. Being greeted with a toasty-warm toilet seat rather than a burst of icy-cold plastic on one's derriere is much appreciated—trust me.

Western-style toilets were not generally used in Japan until well after World War II had finished and Japan was forging ahead in becoming a first-world, industrialized and modern nation. Once it became trendy to have and use Western-style toilets, Japanese commode makers immediately started to improve upon the original design, making them more versatile and practical for widespread use in Japanese homes.

For instance, a standard feature on Japanese toilets is a sink that is built into the design of the lid on the toilet tank. Instead of having a separate sink to wash one's hands after using the facilities, a small basin and faucet can be found on most Japanese toilets. When it is flushed, the clean water washes the person's hands, filling the tank, which will then be used by the next person to flush the waste away.

This is an ingenious design, saving water and making the toilet multi-functional. A towel rack is often positioned to the side of the toilet, in order for the users to dry their hands after rinsing them in the water that fills the tank.

Recently, a friend from Indiana came to visit me here and was especially impressed with this feature of the toilet...as well as the heated toilet seat. She made a point to photograph the toilet in my home to show her husband, commenting that it was such an efficient use of water. I have to agree with her. It is more environmentally sound, and makes perfect sense to have a double-use for the water that will eventually be flushed away.

Most toilets in Japanese homes are in separate rooms, away from the bathtub and sink used for bathing and washing one's face and brushing one's teeth. A small room called a "senmenjo" (which usually doubles as a laundry room with a washing machine) is where people wash their face, hands, and brush their teeth. Next to this washbasin room is the "ofuro" or bathroom.

When I first visited Japan, it was common to see the letters "W.C." on all lavatory doors to toilets. This acronym was borrowed from Great Britain, short for "water closet", which labeled the toilet room.

The W.C. is considered by Japanese to be much too dirty to be combined with washing and grooming oneself, so it is nearly always separate. The one exception is in many efficiency apartments which utilize a "unit bath"—an entire bathroom including toilet, sink and tub in premolded pieces. Also, Western-style hotel rooms often have all-in-one bathrooms.

Having lived in Japan for over 30 years, though, I have to say that I like having the commode completely separate from the bath and sink-basin. It just makes hygienic sense to keep the two functions isolated from one another.

Studies have shown that anytime a toilet is flushed, it sends small particles of waste from the flushed water out into the air. If toothbrushes, towels, soap, and a bathtub are in the same room, these items get covered in this sullied mist.

I noticed that some new homes in the United States are beginning to separate the two areas of the bathroom by isolating the toilet in its own little room. A welcome change in house design, for sure.

Japanese are so finicky about cross-contamination from the toilet that special slippers are even provided for guests to use while in the toilet. These are usually plastic, making them easy to clean, and are worn only in the toilet room.

These slippers will sometimes have the letters "W.C." on them, so if someone forgets to take off the "toilet" slippers after using the facilities, everyone will know. An embarrassing situation indeed, especially at a dinner party, when the host has to point out to a guest that he/she forgot to change back into the regular house-slippers after using the toilet.

The current rage in Japan is the "washlet" or bidet-style toilet. These are very high-tech and are now being placed in public restrooms all over Japan in department stores, office buildings and restaurants. Most homes built in the last 15~20 years have as a standard feature this function on the family toilet.

These are nothing new, first introduced to Japan in 1964 by an American company. However, after just two years on the Japanese market, the "Wash Air Seat" went into domestic production, and the rest is history. Virtually unheard of in the United States today, these types of toilets are now standard features here.

And they have evolved over the past 50 years.

An American friend who has lived in Thailand over 40 years came to visit me. We were touring Tokyo and staying at a very reasonably priced hotel. Even this modest hotel had installed in each room one of the fancier models of these bidet-style toilets.

My friend was so impressed with all the bells and whistles included on his hotel room toilet—heated seat, temperature and pressure-controlled water for the derriere and a separate mode for women to use—he jokingly said he could forgo seeing Tokyo in order to stay in his room to enjoy the toilet. He was determined to get these washlet toilets installed in his home in Bangkok.

His reaction is typical for the uninitiated. Japanese bidet-toilets are certainly spoiling, and once a person has experienced one of these new-fangled contraptions, ordinary toilets just seem, well, humdrum.

However, this type of luxury comes at a hefty price. This is no deterrent to Japanese people who gladly fork out the money to have these installed in their homes. Just like Americans who think they can't live without a refrigerator with a water dispenser and icemaker on the door, automatic dishwasher or garbage disposal in the kitchen, Japanese people feel the same way about their washlet toilets. Rarely do Japanese kitchens have any of the amenities just mentioned that are typically found in American kitchens, but the majority of toilets in Japan are "washlets".

Home builders regularly, as a matter of course, include an additional hookup for water for these in new bathrooms, and an electrical socket can be found behind all toilets to plug in the heated seat. Some of the swankier models come with a remote so the user doesn't have to twist around to fumble with all the buttons found on the side of the toilet seat.

I know that Americans would embrace this technology in a New York minute—if the price would come down. Few Americans want to pay up to $1,000 for a toilet seat. Interestingly, luxury options when purchasing a car is something that most Americans don't flinch at, choosing comfort and style over pure function.

Why not let this attitude extend to the one place where people do spend a goodly amount of time on a daily basis? It is well worth the high price, and once you try one of these high-tech toilets, you'll never be satisfied with the common, run-of-the-mill toilet ever again.

垃圾回收

总的来说，在日本全境，人们都必须将垃圾分成四大类：可燃物、塑料、金属和玻璃。我们城市的分类则更加具体，在主要的类别中又细分出更多的类别。我们需要将垃圾细分为12个不同的类别，这对于只有一两个房间的公寓住户来说，确实是个大问题。

这一制度生效之初，市政府向所有"町内会"（邻里协会）分发录像带。这是日本的邻里街坊组成小型联合会，也就是住在特定区域的居民组成协会，协会成员每个月缴纳一小笔费用。

作为协会成员，每个家庭每周都会收到张贴在纸夹板上有关临近的节日及城市法令等内容的通知，这些纸夹板会挨家挨户传递。居民一看完纸夹板上的消息，就会将纸夹板传递给隔壁邻居。

有一个月，街坊四邻之间传阅的纸质通知换成了一段给每个家庭成员观看的视频。这是一段半专业人士拍摄的视频，视频里一位中年家庭主妇按照海报上垃圾分类的规定，欢快地把她家的垃圾分门别类装入不同的垃圾箱。

她甚至把罐子、瓶子以及速食食品的塑料包装袋都清洗干净。她还在洗碗槽上方装上晾衣绳用来晾干塑料袋，之后才把它们丢入恰当的容器。

我认识的大部分美国人不愿意关注这些小细节；但在日本，绝大部分人会对垃圾进行分类，并尽心尽力地做好。对于按规定分类垃圾这件事，我当然不会敷衍了事，因为我害怕被好事的邻居或自愿充当"垃圾警察"的巡逻队成员发现，后者偶尔会出其不意地出现在垃圾收集点，以确保大家正确投放垃圾。

朋友和家人从印第安纳州来日本探望我时，每当他们将废弃物丢进垃圾筐时，我都得密切注意，生怕他们出错。

我所在城市执行全日本最为严格的垃圾回收制度。而我家乡的人们早已习惯将所有垃圾一股脑丢进同一个垃圾箱，要他们摒弃想都不想就把废弃物直接丢进垃圾筐这一习惯，着实不易。

我得承认，就连从日本其他地区来本市的日本朋友，我都需要特别留意，因为他们很难弄清什么垃圾该往哪儿丢。和他们所在的城市比起来，本市垃圾回收规定之严格常常令他们吃惊不已。

市政府曾分发（用日语和英语撰写的）详细介绍垃圾分类的海报，帮助居民对垃圾进行正确分类。海报底部写有"让我们减少垃圾"的宣传语。在这句话的旁边还有一句不吉利的警示语："千万不要违规丢弃垃圾，这是法律严格禁止的。"我可不想因为没有正确分类垃圾而进监狱！

垃圾基本上分为"可回收"和"不可回收"两大类。一月之中，我们有两次机会可以将罐子和瓶子拿出屋外丢弃。其中，各种罐子必须按铝制、铁制和常规金属制加以分类。

喷雾罐必须戳穿以释放其中的气体。海报上一位男士用锤子和钉子戳穿罐子的画面着实把我吓得不轻。因此，我通常会跳过这一步。

瓶子必须按颜色分类：无色、棕色以及"其他"颜色。这些仅限于装食物和饮料的瓶子（其他类型的瓶子属于完全不同的种类，需要在其他日子丢弃），而瓶盖则被归于"混杂塑料"之列。

硬纸盒和纸板箱则是每个月回收一次。牛奶盒和果汁盒必须清洗、晾干、切开以便摊平；纸板盒必须弄平整，并用纸芯绳绑好。

一个月里，我们有两次机会处理"杂纸"（纸袋、礼品盒或纸巾盒——但纸巾盒顶端的塑料条必须扯掉并归入混杂塑料类）。另外，透明的可回收塑料瓶一个月回收两次，包括装水、饮料、果汁或茶的可回收容器。

由于日本人会对几乎所有食品进行过度包装，因此混杂塑料一周收集一次。在日本，一个普通的四口之家所产生的垃圾之多，令人吃惊。

混杂塑料包括除可回收的瓶子之外的任何东西，如方便面杯、薯片袋、洗发水瓶、蛋盒，甚至包括为防儿童误食而设计的玻璃纸背衬打孔装药的药袋。但这类塑料不包括必须按"不可燃烧垃圾"处理的牙膏管。

诸如水壶、平底锅、塑料玩具、灯泡、鞋子、电池、陶瓷和水桶等废弃物，每月收集两次；真正的大件物品，如木质家具、小型加热器、自行车、旧地毯、弹簧床垫以及钢制的书架、床、书桌等，则每月收集一次。

所幸，市政府每月会对可燃废弃物进行两次收集，包括厨房湿垃圾，还有旧衣物、填充玩具、小树枝、园艺剪枝以及一切可以燃烧殆尽和不属于其他任何类别垃圾的东西。

我已经养成了一整套把垃圾分门别类装进小袋子再丢进屋外稍大垃圾袋的习惯。周二到周五，有人会来我所在的街区收垃圾，人们投放垃圾的时间不得早于当天早上6点，也不能晚于早上9点。

清晨时分，天刚蒙蒙亮，我就提着垃圾袋，跌跌撞撞地走向垃圾收集点完成日常的垃圾处理工作，但这是我和同样上那儿倒垃圾的邻居们互相问候的好时机。有时我们几个人会凑在一起开即兴"井户端会议"（字面意思是井边聚会），基本上就是"闲话会"。

这样的闲聊能让我了解街坊邻里发生的事，也可确保他们没有在议论我。

最近，大家在纷纷议论"某某人"没有用"透明"垃圾袋装可回收垃圾，也没有用"绿色"垃圾袋装易燃垃圾。当然，我在听到这一议论后装出一副很吃惊的样子（意识到大家知道我在忙乱时会混用不同颜色的垃圾袋）。这还真管用，看到我假装对自己的糟糕行为感到很吃惊，大家很满意。

因此，当你下次毫不在意地把果汁盒丢进厨房的垃圾箱时，想想我在世界的另一端，为了把果汁盒装进透明的垃圾袋便于回收而清洗、晾干并用剪刀将它剪开的情景吧，我可是在为保持世界清洁尽一份绵薄之力呢。

Recycling Garbage

Generally, all over Japan, people are required to sort their garbage into four basic categories: burnable, plastics, metals, and glass. My city has taken this one step further by subdividing these into even more groupings, within the main categories. We are expected to divide our garbage into twelve different categories, which is quite a problem for people who live in a one or two room apartment.

When this system first went into effect, the city distributed videos among all of the neighborhood associations (chonaikai). Neighborhoods in Japan are grouped together into small alliances; residents living in a particular area form an association and pay a nominal monthly stipend to be a part of this organization.

In return, each household receives weekly announcements on a clipboard that is passed from neighbor to neighbor with bulletins about upcoming festivals, city ordinances, etc. Once the resident sees the information on the clipboard, it is passed to the next neighbor.

One month, instead of the usual papers being circulated around the neighborhood, a video was included to be watched by everyone in each household. The video was semi-professionally made, featuring a middle-aged housewife cheerfully separating her garbage into various containers while consulting a prescribed poster that outlines exactly how it is to be done.

She even went as far as to wash out cans, bottles and the plastic food pouches found in instant-types of meals. She had rigged a small clothesline above her sink that she used to dry the plastic bags before disposing of them into the proper receptacle.

Most people I know back home couldn't be bothered with such detail, but the vast majority of people here separate their garbage and are quite dedicated to doing it properly. I certainly don't fudge on the prescribed manner of separating garbage for fear of being caught by a nosey neighbor or by one of the roving patrols of volunteer "garbage police" who occasionally make surprise visits at the collection points to make sure people aren't improperly disposing their trash on the wrong day.

When friends and family from Indiana come to visit me here in Japan, I have to watch them like a hawk when it comes to the disposing of unwanted items in the wastebasket.

My city, has one of the most stringent recycling programs in the country. People from home are so used to tossing everything into one container that it is hard for them to break the habit of disposing unwanted items directly into the wastebasket without thought.

Admittedly, I have to even pay special attention to Japanese friends visiting from other areas because they have a difficult time in knowing "what trash goes where". They are often surprised at how strict my city's recycling regulations are in comparison to where they live.

The city issued (in Japanese and English) a detailed poster to assist residents in the correct way to sort their trash. Towards the bottom of this poster is the phrase "Let's reduce our garbage"; next to it, however, is an ominous warning: Never illegally dispose of your garbage. This is STRICTLY PROHIBITED by law. I for one certainly don't want to go to prison for not separating my trash!

Basically, garbage is divided into "recyclable" and "non-recyclable" categories. Twice a month, we are allowed to put out cans and bottles. The cans must be divided between aluminum, steel and regular metal cans.

Spray cans must be pierced with something to release the gas. The picture shows a man using a hammer and nail to puncture the can, which scares the dickens out of me, so I usually forego this little step.

The bottles must be separated by colors: colorless, brown and "other" colors. These should only be food and drink bottles (other types are disposed on another day in a totally different category). The caps on the bottles are placed in the category called "miscellaneous" plastics.

Once a month, cartons and cardboard boxes are picked up. Milk and juice cartons must be washed, dried and cut so that they lay flat. Cardboard boxes must be flattened and bundled using "paper-based" cord.

Twice a month, we are allowed to dispose of "miscellaneous paper" (paper bags, gift and/or tissue boxes—the plastic strip must be removed from the top of the tissue box, however, and placed in "miscellaneous plastics"). Also, "clear recyclable plastic bottles" are picked up twice a month and these include water, soft drink, juice and tea containers that can be recycled.

Because Japanese over-packages most everything that is food-related, "miscellaneous plastics" are picked up once a week. It is amazing how much trash is generated by a typical family of four in Japan.

These plastics include anything other than the recyclable bottles, like instant noodle cups, potato chip bags, shampoo bottles, egg cartons, and even the childproof medication packages where the medicine is punched through the cellophane backing. However, toothpaste tubes which must be disposed with "non-burnable refuse".

Twice a month, items such as pots, pans, plastic toys, light bulbs, shoes, batteries, ceramics, and buckets are picked up. Once a month, really big items are picked up, including wooden furniture, small heaters, bicycles, old carpets, spring mattresses, and steel items like bookshelves, beds and desks.

Thankfully, twice a week the city picks up burnable refuse which is the "wet" garbage from cooking; also, old clothes, stuffed toys, twigs and garden clippings, and anything that can be burned cleanly and that which is not included in any of the other categories.

I have developed quite a system of sorting all of these items into small bags that are placed in larger trashcans outside. In my neighborhood, trash days occur from Tuesday through Friday, and the garbage must be put out on the day, not before 6:00 a.m. and not after 9:00 a.m.

In the early morning, I must tumble down to the trash collection site at the crack of dawn, bags in hand, to do my nearly daily trash ritual. It is a good time to greet neighbors, though, who are doing the same. Sometimes several of us have an impromptu "idoatakaigi" (literally "meeting around the well") which is basically a "gossip session".

This catches me upon what's going on in the neighborhood, and ensures that they aren't talking about me. A recent topic was how "someone" wasn't using the required "clear" trash bags for the recyclable and the "green" trash bags for the burnable trash. Of course, I feigned shock at this revelation (knowing that I have been known to mix bag colors from time to time when in a pinch). It worked. Everyone was satisfied with my seemingly surprise at such atrocious behavior.

So, the next time you carelessly dispose of a juice carton in your kitchen trashcan, think of me on the other side of the world first rinsing it out, drying it, and then cutting it with scissors in order to place it in a clear trash bag to be taken away, making my small contribution to keeping the world clean.

发廊

　　日本拥有为数众多的发廊和理发店，其数量之巨，和人口完全不成比例。来日本的外国人鲜有注意不到这一现象的。几乎在每个角落、每条街道，都会有一家美容店、发廊或是理发店。

　　我倒真不觉得日本人的头发比其他地方的人长得快，或是他们的头发更浓密。但说来奇怪，此地到处都是发廊。我的头发从前很浓密，不好打理；但这么多年过去，如今头顶已然相当稀疏——但无论怎样，我每月依然会至少花上一个下午的时间去理发店打理头发——管他有没有头发。

　　日本发廊和美国发廊之间最大的差别大概在于，前者为确保顾客能有愉悦而惬意的体验，对细节的关注到了极致。

　　毕竟，行业竞争十分激烈，将数量有限的潜在顾客揽进门，确实是"适者生存"的体现。正如每周都有新的发廊开张，也有一些老的发廊关门。

　　为顾客提供额外的服务，并加倍努力，只为让顾客满意，是日本美发行业的真实写照。

　　顾客在日本发廊可以享受到无微不至的服务。从门口的迎宾员到洗头工，从理发师到接待员，为使顾客尽可能感到舒适，发廊全体员工都格外努力。比如，在日本理发时，洗头工会在顾客的脸上敷一块薄纱，以防飞溅的泡沫不经意间进入顾客的眼睛。

　　关于为何使用这样的面纱，至少日本人一直以来都是这样跟我解释的。但我倾向于认为，这样做多半是出于为顾客营造更多私密空间的谦逊谨慎的服务态度，因为顾客与洗头工如此近距离地面对面，可能会让顾客感到不舒服。

一个简单的解决办法就是将顾客的脸遮住，从而避免任何尴尬和目光接触。或许这是将顾客面部遮住的另一个理由——如此一来，顾客和洗头工都不会觉得有必要相互攀谈。除了洗头工问顾客几个常规的问题外，如"水温是否合适？""头部哪里痒？"整个洗头过程中没有过多的闲聊。当然，这些问题的回复一般都是"水温正合适""不，我的头不痒"。

很多年前，一档电视栏目在一家生意兴隆的发廊的洗发池里安装了一个隐藏式摄像头。摄像头拍到了这样的情形：尽管所有的顾客都说自己的头不痒，但每个洗头工帮顾客洗完头后，顾客总要抬手挠一下自己的头部。尽管洗头工愿意帮挠一下头，但或许顾客觉得叫洗头工帮自己挠头的做法太颐指气使。谦逊至关重要，麻烦别人，就算是麻烦服务行业的从业人员，都是不谦逊的表现。

然而，正是在洗头工用洗发剂为顾客洗头这一环节，顾客最为放松。这份迫不得已的宁静令人神清气爽，让顾客得以神游异地。洗头工用上各式芳香的洗发产品给顾客做5~10分钟的头部按摩，的确是排除一切杂念、彻底放松精神的好时机。

美国人往往喜欢用漫无目的或毫无意义的老生常谈打发时间，这是我们在文化上的一个特点。因为长时间的沉默让我们感到不自在。在日本，沉默除了有时候是独自思考的宁静之外，并不一定是出于无聊、愤怒或其他任何潜藏的原因。沉默不语并没什么不妥。

我已学会享受这一层面的日本文化，享受驾车在山间长途穿行，其间无需借助毫无意义的交谈消磨时间。

我光顾的那家理发店在冬天会为顾客提供热茶或咖啡，在夏天则会提供冰爽的大麦茶或冰镇咖啡。当然，店里的杯子优雅精致，精心挑选的饮料和最新的杂志一道，整齐地摆放在做发型的台面上。

为了避免顾客的衣服沾上剪下的碎头发和化学制品（如染发剂和烫发溶剂），部分理发店会将轻便的和服套在顾客出门所穿的便服之上，以使顾客的衣服干净如初。

美发服务完成后，所有员工常常会将顾客送到门口，鞠躬感谢他们的惠顾。这样细致的服务，价格自然不菲，但也不至于高得离谱。

这里的理发店同样有红白蓝三色相间的条形图案的转筒这一理发店的标志。在日本发廊，我最喜欢做的事情之一就是刮胡子，而这是我在美国的理发店从未做过的事。

准备剃须前，理发师先把热气腾腾的毛巾敷在客人的整个面部，为的是打开毛孔；尔后在整个面部涂上大量的剃须热泡沫，接着就用直剃刀刮脸。

在日本，额头、鼻子，甚至耳朵顶端，只要是脸上的毛发都会被剃掉。不瞒你说，在理发店刮胡子时最能让人放松身心的就是清理耳朵。

理发师用一个像小勺子般的工具，轻轻地刮掉所有长在耳垂周围及耳道中的细毛。不得不承认，第一次让人清理耳朵时，一个陌生人拿着细长的金属工具探进我的耳道深处让我觉得有些许紧张。这和我小时候学到的传统观念——不要用小东西掏耳朵——完全不符。幸运的是，这些人都训练有素，而且他们将工具探进耳朵时都极为小心。

作为一种向丈夫表达爱意的方式，日本妻子很乐意帮丈夫清理耳朵。丈夫将头枕在妻子大腿上，一副服服帖帖的样子，以显示对妻子的绝对信任。同样，日本的孩子也会将头枕在妈妈的大腿上让妈妈帮忙给自己清理耳朵。

一旦你放松下来，原先的恐惧消散之后，掏耳朵就变成了一种很愉快的体验，乐于接受且十分欣赏的体验。

时下一种新式的发廊和理发店十分流行——没有其他服务的单剪，价格便宜。在这类的理发店，顾客从自动贩售机购买一张票，然后按到店顺序排队理发。

发型师用喷雾瓶将顾客的头发打湿，尔后单纯修剪头发，没有洗头、按摩、饮料或日本理发店通常提供的其他服务。在这种新式流水线服务的理发店，通常要花上60到90分钟的全套美发服务被压缩到仅仅15分钟左右。

最初，这种"即进即出"的理发店，主要面向的是手头吃紧的学生群体和没有多少时间享受全套服务的工薪族。如今，无论男女，都会光顾这样的理发店，因为人们比以往更有"円"（金钱）意识，在消费上尽量寻求折扣或廉价商品。

我在此地有一位很要好的朋友，她想让我母亲体验一回日本美发服务，因此，为了表示对我母亲的心意，她请客让我母亲体验全套美发服务——头部和背部按摩、洗头、护发，以及做一个时髦的日式发型。

我母亲很喜欢这次体验，并对有机会享受这一皇室般礼遇的美发服务十分感激。我的继父第一眼看到她剪的小平头时，着实吓了一跳，因为他习惯了母亲之前的美式发型，不过他很快就习惯了这样的新发型。

如果你以后来日本旅游，在动身前可不要着急精心打理头发，你可以在到达日本后好好体验一番那非同寻常的美发服务。我敢保证，你绝对不会后悔。

Hair Salons

Japan has a disproportionately high number, per capita, of hair salons and barbershops. This fact rarely goes unnoticed by foreigners who visit Japan. Just about every corner, and certainly on nearly every street, there is a beauty shop, hair salon or barbershop.

I don't really think people's hair grows faster here than in other places, or that they have more of it, necessarily, but for some quirky reason, we are inundated with hair salons. Over the years, my hair has gone from being so bushy and unmanageable, to being quite thin on top…but no matter, I still treat myself at least once a month to an afternoon at the hair salon—hair or no hair.

Perhaps the biggest difference that sets Japanese hair salons apart from their American counterparts is the attention to the minutest of details to ensure that the customer has a pleasurable and enjoyable experience.

After all, competition is keen, and getting the finite number of potential customers through the door is certainly a case of "survival of the fittest". Just as new salons open on a weekly basis, a number of established salons close their doors.

Offering extra services, and going the extra mile to make sure the customer is satisfied, is a reality of the hair-design industry in Japan.

Being pampered is a part of the Japanese hair salon experience. Members of the salon staff—from the door greeter, to the shampooer, to the cutter, to the receptionist—all go out of their way to make you as comfortable as possible. For instance, when one gets a haircut in Japan, the shampoo-person places a sheer cloth over the client's face to protect the eyes from any wayward soap suds that might inadvertently fly around.

At least this is the reason I am always given by Japanese people regarding the face veil, but I tend to think it has more to do with modesty and discreetness to offer the customer more privacy. Being in such close proximity with the shampooer, face to face, could make the client uncomfortable.

The simple solution is to cover the person's face in order to avoid any awkwardness and eye contact. Perhaps this is another reason why the face is covered—so the client and shampooer do not feel obligated to engage one another in conversation. There is not a lot of chit-chat during this process except for a couple of predetermined questions the shampooer asks the client: "Is the water temperature all right?" and "Does your head itch anywhere?" Of course, the standard responses are "Yes, the water is fine" and "No, my head doesn't itch anywhere".

Many years ago a television program placed a hidden camera at the shampoo sink of a busy salon. Even though all the clients said their heads didn't itch anywhere, as soon as the shampooer finished, each person reached up to scratch a part of their head. Perhaps it would be too assertive to instruct the shampooer to scratch the head, even though she or he offered to do so. Humility is the key, and being a bother to another, even a service-related worker—is not being humble.

However, it is during the shampooing part of the process that the client is the most relaxed; the forced quietness is refreshing, allowing the customer to be transported to another place. It is meditative to have the head massaged for 5~10 minutes by the shampooer, using a variety of aromatic hair products in the process.

It is a cultural trait of Americans to pass time with banalities that often times have no purpose or real meaning. We are uncomfortable with prolonged silence. In Japan, silence is not necessarily an indication of boredom or anger or any other underlying reason other than it is sometimes peaceful to be alone with your thoughts. It's all right to have nothing to say.

I have learned to relish this aspect of Japanese culture, enjoying a long car ride through the mountains without feeling the necessity to fill the entire time up with inane conversation.

The shop I patronize offers customers hot tea or coffee in the winter, and a cold barley tea or ice coffee in the summer. Of course, the cups are dainty and elegant, with the latest magazines neatly laid out at the station where the hairstyling is done, along with the selected drink.

To protect the client's clothes from hair clippings and chemicals (like hair dye or perming solution), some shops offer customers a light kimono-wrap to wear over their street clothes to keep everything pristine.

Once finished the entire staff often walks customers to the door, bowing and thanking them for their business. Of course, such individual attention is not exactly cheap, but not outrageous either.

The same thing is true for barbershops featuring the tell-tale red, white and blue swirling striped poles. One of my most favorite things to do here, and something I've never had done in the United States, is to get a shave.

In preparation for the shave, the barber places steaming hot towels all around the face area to open the pores. Then, hot lather is generously put all over the face. A straight razor is then used to shave the face.

In Japan, everything on the face gets shaved—forehead, nose and even the tops of the ears. In fact, one of the most relaxing things to have done at a barbershop while getting a shave is to have your ears cleaned.

The barber uses a small scoop-like instrument to scrape gently away all the little hairs that grow around the earlobe and in the ear canal. Admittedly, the first time I had this done, it was a bit nerve-racking to have a stranger put a long metal instrument deep into my ear canal. It goes against all conventional wisdom given to me as a child that nothing smaller than your elbow should ever go into your ear. Luckily, these people are highly trained and are very careful when probing in the ear.

Japanese wives, as a way to show love for their husbands, will gladly do this little chore. The husband lies with his head in her lap, submitting completely as a way to show his absolute trust in his wife. Also, Japanese children lay with their heads in their mothers' laps to have their ears cleaned.

It is a pleasurable experience that you welcome and appriciate, once you relax and the initial fear dissipates.

A newer type of hair salon and barbershop is now quite trendy—the discount cut with no frills. In these shops, the customer buys a ticket out of a vending machine and waits in the order he/she arrived.

The stylist wets the hair with a squirt bottle and does a very standard haircut with no shampooing, massaging, beverage, or other perks normally associated with hair salons in Japan. The normal 60~90 minutes hair session of full-service salons is whittled away to a mere 15 minutes or so in these new types of conveyor belt establishments.

These "in-and-out" shops, at first, catered largely to students on a budget and salary men who had no time for the lengthy full-service treatment. Today, men and women both patronize these establishments because people are more *"yen"* conscious than in years past when it comes to seeking out discounts and bargains.

A dear friend of mine here wanted my mother to experience a Japanese hair salon, so as a gift, she treated my mother to a full-service treatment—head and back massage, shampoo and conditioning treatment, and a stylish Japanese-style haircut.

My mother loved the experience and was very appreciative to have had the opportunity to be pampered with the royal hair salon treatment. The close-cropped haircut, at first sight, did surprise my stepfather, who was accustomed to her American-style hairdo, but he soon got used to the new look.

If ever you find yourself traveling to Japan, forego getting coiffed before your trip and wait until you are here to have a unique hair experience. You won't regret it. I promise.

包裹服务

日本国土面积比美国要小，因此建立一套效率极高的邮政和投递系统要容易得多。然而，近年来，已经十分出色的日本邮政株式会社为了能与那些收费更低服务更优的私人快递公司竞争，不得不积极采取行动。

但是，总的来说，日本邮政服务能够十分出色地将邮件完好无损地准时送达目的地。

邮局在日本随处可见，这使得邮寄包裹以及购买邮票、明信片等十分便利。从我家出发步行2分钟，就有一家街区邮局，我每周都会光顾几次。从这家邮局出发，再走20分钟就到了另一家邮政分局。这些邮政分局规模虽小，但数量众多，提供人性化服务。在日本，邮箱到处都有，甚至在便利店里也不乏其身影，大大方便了信件的寄送。

日本的邮局还设立了邮政储蓄所。我本人除了有普通银行账户外，还办了邮政储蓄账户。日本的邮政银行自助柜员机提供英文操作指南（文字版和语音版都有），我十分赞赏这种做法。

每当有朋友从美国到访日本，他们也可以通过这些柜员机提取他们美国银行账户里的钱，很是方便。有时候，普通日本银行对顾客持外国银行卡办理业务十分挑剔，只受理某些特定的银行卡业务。

现如今，邮政行业正努力提供多样化的服务，以期让客户体验便利和更加愉快的邮寄服务。但在过去，情况往往不是如此。当我初到日本居住时，只能通过邮政总局向国外邮寄包裹。而现在，全日本数千家邮政分局都可以对寄往世界各地的各类包裹进行称重和收寄，极大地方便了涉外邮递服务。

几家私人快递公司可在日本全境实现"次日达"服务。比如说，某天在东京购买的冷冻或冷藏食品通过冷链货车在第二天即可送达目的地。

日本人常常挑选当地的美食作为礼物馈赠给在外地的亲朋好友。对于食品而言，新鲜至关重要。因此，快递公司会尽一切可能将货物快速送达并使食物与寄出时的状态无异。

在日本境内寄送包裹的费用之所以如此低廉，可能是因为每天庞大的包裹数量。与此同时，由于快递行业利润丰厚，日本各快递公司之间的竞争也十分激烈。领先竞争对手的最好方式就是效率更高、价格更低并且更细心地处理所托运的货物。

我尤其赞赏日本私人快递公司对于细节的关注，他们对每一件包裹都格外仔细。我使用快递服务这么多年来，从未发生货品破损、丢失或错投的情况。我不敢说美国邮政可以做到这一点。

在日本，人们创造了一个几乎零失误的系统以追踪每一个包裹。包裹在邮寄时会贴上一个地区编码和一个更详细的编码，以便将货物送往目的地所在的街道。这些快递服务公司通常也会在不同地方揽收包裹，比如便利店、百货大楼、超市、酒水商店、干洗店甚至私人住宅。

在日本快递公司提供的各项服务中，我特别喜欢行李托运服务。在动身出国之前，我可以花10到15美元将我的行李箱从家里邮寄到我即将乘机飞离的机场。这确实让出行变得省心又省力，因为乘坐公共交通把行李箱带到东京可能是行程中最麻烦也最扫兴的一件事。把行李箱事先邮寄到机场，那么我只需在机场领取，然后办理登机手续即可。

返回日本时也是一样。在所有国际机场里的海关外面，都会有一些柜台可供旅客办理邮寄行李箱回家的业务。几乎所有住在东京市区之外的人都会使用该项服务。试图携带沉甸甸的行李箱上下楼梯，穿过拥挤的火车站并扛上公共汽车，对于哪怕最健壮的旅客来说也是吃不消的。日本往返机场的行李邮寄系统使这一切变得轻松了许多。

这些年来，这一包裹寄送系统可把我给惯坏了。有一次，当我试图通过一家美国快递公司将我的一个小行李箱从明尼苏达州寄往印第安纳州时，我着实被高得离谱的邮费吓了一跳。在日本很少有便宜的东西，但在日本境内邮寄包裹恰恰是其中之一。

Parcel Service

Since Japan is geographically smaller in comparison to the United States or China, it is much simpler to have an incredibly efficient and effective postal service and delivery system. In recent years, the already superb Japanese postal service has had to step up to the plate, however, in order to keep up with the private companies that can offer better services for less money.

In general, though, the Japanese postal service does a very good job in getting mail delivered in a timely fashion and without any damage.

Post offices are found everywhere in Japan, making it easy to mail packages and to purchase stamps, postcards and so on. Within a two-minute walk from my home is a neighborhood post office which I use several times a week. Within another 20-minute walk is yet another postal substation. These are small in size but are plentiful, making the postal service quite user-friendly. Mailboxes are located in many places—even in convenience stores—making mailing letters easy and convenient.

Post offices in Japan also have a banking section for savings accounts. In addition to regular banking, I maintain a postal account as well. I appreciate the postal cash machine dispensers, because they offer English instructions (both written and aurally).

Also, when friends visit from home, it is easy for them to get money from their US bank accounts using these cash machines. Sometimes regular Japanese banks can be fussy about foreign cash cards, recognizing some systems and not others.

Today, the postal service strives to offer a variety of services geared toward making the postal experience easy and more enjoyable for its customers. This wasn't always the case. When I first came to Japan to live, parcels addressed to foreign destinations could be mailed only from the main post office. Today, all of the postal substations (numbering in the thousands nationwide) can weigh and stamp any parcel going anywhere in the world, making it much more convenient to mail overseas packages.

There are several private companies deliver packages anywhere in Japan, usually overnight. For instance, frozen or refrigerated goods purchased in Tokyo one day are delivered the next day in a refrigerated truck.

Often Japanese will give food as gifts, choosing local delicacies to send to friends and family in other parts of Japan. Since freshness is all important with these types of items, the parcel services do everything in their power to ensure that the items are delivered quickly and in the same condition they were sent.

The reason why it is so inexpensive to mail boxes around Japan probably has to do with the sheer volume of parcels that are sent each and every day. Also, competition between companies is very keen, as it is a very lucrative industry. The best way to stay ahead of a rival company is to be more efficient, inexpensive and careful with the entrusted cargo.

I especially appreciate the private delivery companies' attention to detail. They handle each package with extreme care. Never in all the years of utilizing such services have I ever had anything broken, lost or misdirected. I can't say this about the US Postal Service.

In Japan, they have created a nearly foolproof system that tracks each package individually. When mailed, the package is given a regional code, then a more specific code that takes it to the street where it will be delivered. Also these delivery services regularly pick up packages from a variety of places—convenience stores, department stores, supermarkets, liquor stores, dry cleaners and even from one's home.

One service they provide that I particularly like is a suitcase delivery system. Before leaving on an international trip, I can mail my suitcases from my home to the airport I am leaving from for about $10 to $15 each. This really makes traveling hassle-free, because getting the luggage to Tokyo using public transportation can be the most difficult part of a trip and the most frustrating. By having the suitcases arrive before, all that needs to be done is pick them up and check in.

Returning to Japan is the same. Located outside of customs at all international airports are several counters for people to send their luggage back to their homes. Nearly all people who live outside of the Tokyo metropolitan area utilize this service. Trying to lug heavy suitcases up and down stairs, through busy train stations and onto buses is too much for even the heartiest of travelers. The Japanese system of mailing luggage to and from the airport makes it all that much easier.

This system of parcel delivery has spoiled me over the years. I had a severe case of sticker shock when I tried to mail a small suitcase from Minnesota to Indiana once using an American parcel service. There are few bargains in Japan, but mailing boxes and parcels around the country happens to be one of them.

宠物

记得30多年前我刚来日本定居时,在大街小巷都看不到流浪狗的身影,对此我十分诧异。我偶尔会见到流浪猫,却极少见到流浪狗。当我真的见到一只落单的狗时,我敢肯定它只是不小心走失了,而非真正的流浪狗。

过去,许多日本人会养狗,几乎只养在屋外,用短绳或链子将狗拴在小狗舍里或其他临时遮蔽物下面,有时候这些狗根本没有可以遮风挡雨的东西。

狗因此没有机会逃跑、跑动、玩耍或嬉戏,比如探寻、刨挖和追踪,当然还有到处嗅闻。看到这些宠物常年被拴在屋外经受风吹雨淋、严寒酷暑,我心里真不是滋味。由于大部分房屋并没有真正意义上的庭院,狗常被安置在房屋旁的狭窄过道里。

过去人们不遛狗,人和狗之间也没有任何真正有意义的交流。我刚搬来日本时住的是居民区的一间公寓,一户邻居也养了这么一条拴在屋外的狗。由于无聊和沮丧,这可怜的家伙只能日夜嚎叫。在过去,宠物,尤其是狗,往往被当成财产,而不是家庭的一员。

20世纪90年代初,我认识的一位美国朋友到一户日本人家里做客时,说主人家的狗在下雪天睡在门口的台阶上,好像怪冷的。主人却说那狗"喜欢"在雪地里睡觉。

然而,那家孩子却大声反驳说,她记得有一年冬天把狗放在屋里时,它似乎也很享受睡在温暖舒服的家里。哎,要是狗真的可以选择的话,我相信它会选择在哪儿睡觉。

时至现今,30年一晃而过,情况完全不一样了,宠物狗受到了主人前所未有的宠爱。日本过去几年的"宠物热",使日本人变得像美国人那样认真对待豢养宠物,十分溺爱自己的宠物。

多数日本家庭有将榻榻米铺在地板上的传统,但这种草席很脆弱,也不易维护。如果让宠物进屋,它会把尘土带进来,并且抓挠草席,伤害这些既昂贵又极易损坏的垫子。

如今,许多新房子都会铺上更耐用的硬木地板和油毡,这些对于在屋内养宠物更实用,宠物也被当作真正的家人看待。

我曾看到一个非常有趣的统计数据,也许可以解释在日本养宠物的人数暴增的原因。这一趋势促使宠物主们毫无顾忌地拥抱自己的宠物,把它们当成自己的孩子来对待。目前,日本家庭饲养了成千上万只猫狗作为宠物,这一数字已经超过该国 15 岁以下儿童的数量。由于日本人口多年来持续下降,我认为那些无儿无女的夫妇和单身居民正把本该给予孩子的关爱转移到宠物身上。养宠物不仅时尚,还能满足那些十分想要和另一个生命体建立身体互动的人的需求。照顾宠物让他们在无条件地爱护宠物的同时,也得到了来自宠物的爱。

我的一位好友和他太太最近来我家,当他从车里出来时,我发现他坐在后排座位。我问他为什么坐后排,他回答说:"哦,库吉(他宠物狗的名字)坐前面,所以我只好坐后面啦。"他们俩没有孩子,可以说他们那只腊肠犬就像他们的孩子,因为他太太把它当孩子一样宠着。

那天晚些时候,我们开车前往一家咖啡店,店外有露台,允许客人携带宠物。当然,在去咖啡店的路上,我和朋友坐在后排,他太太开车,库吉坐在副驾驶位置上。

朋友的太太有个背包,里面装有零食、水、便携式碟子、食物、玩具以及库吉的小外套。她准备了所有这些东西,出门时小狗可能用得着。

也许他太太就是日本时髦宠物主的典型代表。他们中大部分人在宠物身上会花很多时间和金钱,使得日本宠物行业利润可观且前景大好。据报道,日本喜爱动物的人一年就花了近 90 亿美元购买与宠物相关的商品,尽管每年的这一开销只有美国的 1/4,但比起 20 世纪 90 年代中期已经增长了近 50%。那时候宠物基本上都放在屋外,不加理会。

在日本养宠物的另外一个群体是年长或退休的人,这些老年夫妇的孩子已经长大成人,不和他们同住,因此他们觉得有宠物的陪伴很好,赋予他们的生活新的意义。

另外,由于年轻夫妇生育的孩子越来越少,意味着年老的夫妇没有那么多孙辈。况且,在过去通常是家中最年长的子女跟父母住在一起,陪伴父母,让父母的生活更有意义。如今,越来越多的老年夫妇跟孩子们分开居住,独自生活。养一只宠物可以填补一些老年夫妇的情感空缺,让他们觉得自己是被需要的,或者对他人是有用的——这也使他们得以将爱的能量和关怀转移到另一个生命上。

Pampered Pooches

When I first came to Japan to live over 30 years ago, I remember being amazed at the lack of stray dogs wandering the streets. I did see the occasional stray cat, but rarely did I ever see a dog—and when I did, I am sure it had gotten loose from its owner accidentally and was not a stray.

In those days, a goodly number of Japanese people did keep dogs, almost exclusively as "outside" pets, which meant they were tied on a short rope or chain to a tiny doghouse or other makeshift cover...and sometimes with no protection at all from the elements.

There was no chance for the dog to escape, run, play or do "dog" things, like exploring, digging, tracking and of course, sniffing anything and everything. This saddened me to see these pets relegated to a life of being tied up and left outside in all sorts of weather. Since most homes have no real yard to speak of, dogs were often kept in narrow passageways next to the house.

In those days, people didn't really walk their dogs nor have any real, meaningful interaction with them. The apartment I lived in when I first relocated to Japan was in a residential area. A neighbor had one of these "tied-up" dogs; the poor thing howled night and day from boredom and depression. Pets in those days, especially dogs, were basically regarded as possessions and not considered to be an extension of the family unit.

An American friend I know visited a family back in the early 90's and commented that the family dog seemed cold as it slept on the snow outside the front stoop. The owner replied that the dog "liked" sleeping on the snow-covered ground.

The owner's child, however, piped up and said that she remembered one winter when they let the dog inside the house and it seemed to like sleeping inside the warm, cozy home as well. Uh-huh. I am sure if given a real choice, we can guess which place the dog would choose to sleep.

Fast-forward 30 years today, and I am happy to report that the situation has changed completely, with pet dogs being indulged by pet owners in an unprecedented manner. The "pet boom" of the past few years in Japan has turned owners here into doting masters resembling that of the United States, where pet ownership is taken very seriously.

Traditionally, many homes in Japan used "tatami" straw mats as floor coverings which were quite fragile and very high-maintenance. It was virtually unthinkable to allow pets inside where they could soil, scratch, claw and potentially destroy these very expensive and delicate coverings.

Today, many new homes tend to use more durable coverings like hardwood floors and linoleum. This has made it more practical to have inside pets that do become like family members.

I once read a very interesting statistic which also might explain the recent surge in pet ownership in Japan, which has encouraged masters to embrace their pets completely, treating them like small children. Japanese families now own over tens of millions of pet dogs and cats, a figure which now exceeds the number of Japanese children who are under the age of 15. Since Japan has been suffering from a yearly decrease in population for many years, I think that childless couples and singles here are substituting the love and care they would normally give to a child to their pets. Animal companions are not only trendy, but fulfill an apparent emotional need for people who want to have some type of physical interaction with another living thing. Caring for a pet allows them to love the pet unconditionally, while receiving the same in return.

A good friend of mine stopped by with his wife recently; when he exited the car, I noticed he was sitting in the back seat. When I asked why he said, "Oh, Cookie gets the front seat, so I have to sit in the back." They have no children, so their dachshund is a surrogate child, of sorts, because his wife fawns over this dog as if it were a child.

Later that same day, we drove to a coffee shop that has an outside patio that allows pet owners the opportunity to bring their pets with them. Of course, my friend and I sat in the back seat, while Cookie sat shotgun in the front with his wife.

My friend's wife had a backpack filled with treats, water, a portable dish, food, toys and a little coat for Cookie. She prepared all of these things in anticipation of any need the little dog might have while on this little outing.

Perhaps she represents the modern or stereotypical pet owner in Japan. The majority of animal owners currently spend a lot of time and money on their pets, making the pet industry in Japan a very lucrative and ever-expanding business. It was reported that nearly 9 billion US dollars was spent in a year by Japanese animal lovers on pet-related items. Although it is a fourth of what Americans spend on pets every year, it represents nearly a 50 percent increase since the mid-1990s, when pets were basically left outside and ignored.

Another group of people who have embraced pet ownership in Japan are older or retired people. Couples who have grown children that live away find having animal companions to be good company, giving them a new purpose in life.

Also, since young couples are having fewer children, this means that older couples do not have as many grandchildren. In addition, in the past, the oldest child usually would live with the parents, giving them companionship and a purpose. Today, more and more elderly couples are finding that their children are living separately, leaving them to live on their own. Owning a pet fills an emotional void that some older couples have—to feel needed or useful, while also allowing them to channel their energies of love and caring toward another living thing.

第五部分
日本风俗

Part 5
Japanese Custom

茶道

无论是在上午还是在下午，无论是在招待客人还是在休息时，绿茶都是日本人首选的饮品。绿茶是在日本种植的传统茶品，日本人喝绿茶时不添加牛奶或糖。对于第一次喝绿茶的人来说，可能会觉得苦，但就像喝咖啡一样，慢慢地你就喜欢喝了。

我的表兄妹们来日本看我时，很想尝尝绿茶，于是他们在飞来日本的航班上指名要喝绿茶。当女空乘为他们送上绿茶时，他们要求在茶里面加糖和牛奶。我想，女空乘当时肯定一脸惊恐地看着他们，觉得不可思议并告诉他们："这是绿茶，不是英国茶。"

表兄妹们回答说他们知道那是绿茶，但还是想往里面加糖和牛奶。女空乘虽然有些不情愿，但还是满足了他们的要求。我敢肯定，她当时震惊不已，因为在她看来，往绿茶里加糖和牛奶是对绿茶的亵渎。

绿茶不仅是一种饮品，还是一种国民消遣，一种文化习俗，融合了自然之美、艺术创造以及宗教仪式，并在茶师与客人之间庄严的社交仪式，即"茶道"（在日语中意为茶艺品鉴之道）中达到登峰造极的境界。

奈良时代（710~794）的佛教僧侣将茶种从中国带到日本，初次引入了绿茶。然而，日本的茶叶种植产业直到公元1191年才真正开始形成。据说一位名叫"荣西"的禅师首次种植了从中国带回的茶种，使得茶叶种植慢慢流行开来。

今天，几乎有一半的日本茶，都产自东京南部的静冈县。当年，我在东京做高中交换生时，我的寄宿家庭带着我登上了一辆高速列车，前往位于静冈县东部的热海市度过了一个短暂的假期。

旅途中，我们穿越了"茶的国度"。透过飞驰中的列车车窗，映入眼帘的是经过精心修整的梯田式茶园，这般景象令人不由赞叹，一排排茶树随着整个乡村的丘陵绵延起伏。头戴宽边草帽的妇女们正低着头忙于采茶。

对于来到日本的游客而言，能参加一次正式的茶道仪式确实是大饱眼福。当我母亲初来日本的时候，我们受邀参加了一次茶道仪式。所有出席的妇女都穿着漂亮的丝制和服。这次的茶道仪式非常正式，也很有仪式感。茶道用的碗和餐具的搭配、就着茶一起品尝的上乘干甜品、陈放在茶室里的"床の間"和壁龛内的装饰，都是主人精挑细选的。

前来体验茶道仪式的客人,对仪式本身和主人都心怀敬意,因为主人辛苦地为仪式做准备,并从美感上考虑,让茶叶的色彩、质地及口感与不同季节相映成趣,从而让茶道仪式成为终生难忘的盛事。

事实上,每次茶道仪式都被认为是独一无二的,因为在相同的季节,和相同的客人在相同的氛围中品尝相同甜品的茶道仪式不可能分毫不差地再次发生。在时间的长河中,那个瞬间只会出现一次,永远不可能被完全复制。

茶道仪式要求客人"正坐",双膝并拢跪地,臀部坐压于足跟之上。对于日本人来说,跪坐不成问题,因为他们能以这种姿势坐很久。但对于不习惯长时间跪坐的人来说,这就成了一件难事。跪坐20分钟后,母亲就受不了了,最后欠起身子,告诉我说她的腿麻了。一位机敏的客人发现我母亲感觉不适,便为她找来一张凳子,母亲坐在凳子上既可以保持跪坐的姿势,又可以把腿部所受的重力转移到凳上。这样一来母亲很开心,正是因为这张凳子,她才得以尽情地享受这次茶道。

实际上,在茶道礼节方面,人们对外国游客的要求很宽松。我们对所体验的茶道一无所知,因此,大部分日本主人都会原谅第一次体验茶道的外国游客很多有违茶道正常程序或仪式的轻率言行,并给予他们一定的照顾。

参加茶道仪式的客人们一来,就被带到等候区,在这里他们可以喝用于茶道仪式的热水。通常,客人们会从他们当中选出一位"主客"作为领队。主客通常是一位德高望重的人,要么是老师,要么是一位长者。

主人对客人们的到来表示欢迎和感谢之后,客人们就由领队带往茶园,在这里他们可以坐在长凳上稍事休息,欣赏精心修整的茶园里的自然美景。

如果院里有"蹲踞"或石盆的话,客人会按照茶道仪式在里面洗手。洗手基本上是象征性的,表示客人在进入茶室之前,已经清除掉自己身上的任何尘世杂念,客人洗手的顺序就是主人在茶道仪式中为他们上茶的顺序。

客人们要进入真正的茶室,需要爬过一扇叫作"躙口"的小型推拉门,这要求客人们双膝跪地,蹲着身子进入茶室。别人告诉我,这样做象征着在茶室内没有高低贵贱之分,人人平等。

每位客人一进入茶室,就会毕恭毕敬地欣赏根据场合与季节挑选的悬挂在壁龛内的画卷,然后他们就根据之前在茶园里洗手的顺序,围坐在茶室四周。

之后,主人会用有数百年传统的方式,有条不紊、娴熟有度地备茶。碾磨好的茶与用木勺从铁质茶壶中舀出的热水混合在一起。随后,主人用一把传统的茶筅搅打茶碗里的茶。第一碗茶给主客喝,主客会先向主人鞠躬,然后双手接过,在抿第一口茶之前需要转动茶碗三次。

许多茶师用数十年学习、磨炼自己的茶艺。我就职的大学有一个茶道俱乐部，俱乐部中的许多学生在念小学或初中时就已经开始学习茶艺了。

茶道无疑是日本文化中极具代表性的组成部分，如果有机会的话，任何到日本的游客都应该去体验这种传统的艺术形式。

只是别往茶里加糖和牛奶。

茶道

The Way of Tea

Green tea is the Japanese beverage of choice in the mornings and afternoons, when entertaining guests and when taking a break. It is the only type of traditional tea grown in Japan, and it is served plain without any milk or sugar. For the first-time drinker, it may seem bitter; but just like coffee, it grows on you.

When my cousins came to visit, they were so excited to try green tea that on the airplane ride they asked for it. When the flight attendant served them, they asked her for milk and sugar. I guess she shot them a look of complete horror, announcing incredulously, "It's green tea, not English tea."

They responded that they knew what it was, but still wanted the milk and sugar. Begrudgingly, she gave them what they wanted. I am sure she was surprised that they would defile green tea with something as crass and vulgar as sugar and milk.

Green tea is much more than a beverage; it is a national pastime, a cultural institution of sorts, which incorporates the aesthetic beauty of nature, the creativeness of art, the ritual of religion, and culminates in a solemn rite of social interaction between the tea master and his/her guests in the "tea ceremony" ("sado", meaning "the way of tea" in Japanese).

Green tea originally came to Japan via China during the Nara Period (710~794) by Buddhist monks who brought tea seeds back to Japan with them. However, it wasn't until 1191 that an industry surrounding the cultivation of tea in Japan truly began. It is believed that a monk named "Eisai" planted seeds he brought from China and hence encouraged the widespread cultivation of tea.

Today half of all the tea grown in Japan comes from Shizuoka Prefecture, south of Tokyo. When I was a high school exchange student in Tokyo, my host family took me on the bullet train for a short vacation to Atami in eastern Shizuoka.

On our trip, we went through "the tea country". The perfectly manicured terraced tea fields were a wondrous sight to see from the window of the speeding train. Rows upon rows of tea plants covered the rolling hills of the mountains throughout the countryside. Women bent over in broad-rimmed straw hats busily picking the tea leaves.

For visitors to Japan, attending a formal tea ceremony is indeed a treat. When my mother first visited Japan, we were invited to partake in a tea ceremony. All of the women in attendance wore beautiful silk kimono. The tea ceremony is very formal and highly ritualized. Much care is taken by the host to select just the right combination of bowls and utensils to use, the perfect dry sweet that is eaten with the tea, and what decorations to use in the "tokonoma", or alcove, located in the tea room.

Guests approach experiencing the tea ceremony with a sense of reverence and respect for the ritual itself, but also toward the host who has made painstaking preparations, taking into account the season to match aesthetically colors, textures and flavors to make the ceremony a once-in-a-lifetime event.

In fact, each time the tea ceremony is performed, it is regarded as a singular occurrence or event that cannot be repeated exactly—the same season, the same guests, the same sweets, the same atmosphere. That moment in time can only happen once, and can never be exactly replicated.

The tea ceremony requires that guests sit "seiza" (sitting on one's knees). For Japanese, this is not a problem, as they are able to sit for endless periods in this position. Not so for people who aren't used to sitting like this for long periods of time. My mother, after about 20 minutes, finally leaned over and told me she couldn't feel her legs. An astute guest sensed my mother's discomfort and retrieved for her a small stool that allowed her to sit in the proper position, but shifted the weight from her legs to the stool. This made my mother very happy, and allowed her to enjoy the tea ceremony more fully.

Actually, foreign visitors are given much leeway in the etiquette department when it comes to the tea ceremony. It is such a foreign concept to anything that we experience, that most Japanese hosts forgive most indiscretions regarding the proper procedure and ritual associated with the tea ceremony and accommodate first-time visitors accordingly.

Upon arrival, guests for the tea ceremony are ushered into a waiting area where they are able to sample the hot water used in the ceremony. Often times, the guests will select from among them the "main guest" who will act as leader of the group. This is usually an esteemed person who is a teacher or the elder.

Once the host acknowledges them, they are led by the main guest to the tea garden where they may sit for a few moments on benches to enjoy the natural beauty of the meticulously kept garden.

If available, the guests will ceremoniously wash their hands in a "tsukubai", or stone basin. This is largely symbolic, representing that the guests cleanse themselves of any worldly concerns before entering the actual tea house. The order that the guests rinse their hands is the order that they will be served throughout the entire tea ceremony.

A true tea house requires that the guests crawl through a small sliding door called a "nijiriguchi". This requires that the guests crouch low on their knees to enter the room. I was told this symbolizes the idea that all are considered equal and no one person has status or prestige over another while in the confines of the tea room.

Each guest upon entering the tea room reverently admires the scroll hanging in the alcove (selected for the occasion and the season). They then seat themselves around the edge of the room in the order they decided earlier during the cleansing in the garden.

The host then prepares the tea in a very systematic and practiced manner that represents centuries of tradition. The tea is powdered and mixed with hot water from an iron teapot using a wooden ladle. The host then whips the tea with a traditional whisk made from bamboo. The main guest is served the first bowl of tea by bowing to the host before picking the bowl up and cupping it in both hands. The bowl is turned three times before taking the first sip.

Many tea masters have studied and honed their ability for decades. My university has a tea ceremony club, and many of the students who belong have studied it since they were in elementary or junior high school.

It is certainly a very representative part of Japanese culture, and any visitor to Japan, if given the opportunity, should experience this traditional art form.

Just don't ask for milk and sugar for your tea.

相扑

到访日本的游客只要看上几个小时的相扑比赛，就会迷上这项极具魅力的日本国技。

前不久，一位朋友从家乡到日本看望我，恰逢一项定期举行的相扑大奖赛赛事。她每天都坐在电视机前，满心期待地观看比赛，并猜测选手的胜负，看得十分入迷。短短几天时间，她就弄懂了比赛规则并为她最喜欢的选手们加油助威。

每个新赛季都会举行大奖赛。比赛场馆座无虚席，办公室职员则聚在办公室的电视机旁收看高段位选手比赛的赛况。尽管比赛通常只持续几秒钟，却依然让人看得心潮澎湃。

相扑运动之所以有如此的吸引力，其中一个原因是其近2000年的悠久历史。相扑运动的高度仪式化，是古代日本一项传承千年的优美艺术形式，至今保留了许多和过去相同的特征和传统。

毫无疑问，日本人热爱相扑并将其视为活着的民族瑰宝。晋升到横纲级别的顶尖相扑运动员就像超级明星一样受人欢迎，在杂志和电视广告中经常可以看到他们的身影。和其他运动一样，相扑运动员的肖像经常印在毛巾、卡片、海报、T恤以及其他任何想得到的纪念品上。

但是，不同于绝大多数运动，伴随相扑运动的崇高地位而来的，是从一开始就渗透于传统和礼仪之中的重大社会和文化责任。对于相扑运动员和观众而言，最重要的是尊重这项运动及其内涵。

不管一位相扑选手有多么强大，如果没有最高级别的冠军选手应有的尊贵气质，就不可能晋升为"横纲"。

这就是相扑和世界上其他多数体育运动的不同之处。相扑运动员的成功不仅取决于他的竞技水平，还在于他的言行举止是否足够尊重相扑这项运动及其历史悠久的程式化礼节，这一切都是对相扑选手场上娴熟技能以外的要求。

因其礼仪和传统，相扑运动被认为是一座过去时代的"活的博物馆"。在某种程度上说，它不仅是一项运动，更是一种表演。每一场相扑比赛都会把粉丝的思绪带回到日本的江户时代(1603~1868)。

在15世纪，常利用相扑运动员对武士进行训练。在对决中倒下意味着立刻死亡，因此，在倒下后凝聚力量和尊严重新站起来，是相扑职业精神的一种体现，这样的精神同样适用于武士。克服身体的极度疲劳，无论怎样始终都要保持站立姿势，倒下后再站起来，现今依旧是要教给年轻相扑手的经验教训。

相扑训练很艰苦，相扑运动员的全部日常生活都以相扑为中心。在整个训练和比赛期间，他们秉承相扑界前辈们数百年来的做法，全身心投入其中。

最年轻或段位最低的相扑运动员在早上四五点钟就要开始忙活了。他们必须准备好一天训练用的相扑台，还要运动放松自己，以便抗击很可能来自更高段位选手的击打。

年轻的相扑运动员必须学会保持身体的平衡、柔韧以及敏捷，这是在相扑台上取胜的三个关键要素，其目标是练就强有力的大腿并保持极低的身体重心。

说起相扑运动，绝大多数人想到的是运动员身躯庞大，梳着整齐的顶髻，轮番高高地抬脚顿足，这种顿足练习叫作"四股"（踏脚），年轻的相扑手每天至少要顿足500次。他们还要坐在地上，充分打开双腿，并向前屈身，直至肚子和脸都贴到地面上。大腹便便的相扑运动员要做到这一点绝非易事。但别担心，年长的相扑手会站在年轻相扑手的背上，帮助他们获得必要的柔韧性，这是一种痛苦但管用的办法。

传说在远古时代，领土争端有时候会通过相扑比赛来解决。"神的意志"决定比赛结果，因此人们会接受最后的成败。这种解决争端的方式更加和平，不那么血腥，远比现代战争中使用的"威慑与恐吓"手段好很多。

相扑运动员精心修剪的顶髻有两个作用：一是有助于防止运动员的头部

受伤；二是象征相扑运动的神圣感以及相扑手在相扑界的地位。

事实上，负责为相扑手梳理头发的人需要接受十年的训练才有资格打理顶级相扑运动员的头发。包括相扑在内，日本传统技艺师徒相传的传统历史悠久，一个家庭中的几代人往往都从事着祖传的营生。

相扑手别具一格的顶髻意义重大，因为发型师必须在相扑手的头发上涂抹大量的油，将其塑成银杏叶状。只有顶级相扑选手在赛前才可以留这种发式。如果一位级别较低的相扑手出场比赛、面对观众，他应该身着和服、脚踩木屐，并把头发扎成叫作"顶髻"的髻子（如果头发够长），这是江户时代日本男性的典型装束。

如前文所说，在比赛期间，只有顶级相扑运动员才有资格让人在头发上抹油并将其梳成银杏叶状。一旦顶级相扑手退役，他们会在"土俵"（相扑台）上举行一次特别的"理发"仪式。

身着正式和服的相扑手坐在相扑台中央，他的家人、朋友、其他相扑手以及名人相扑迷们则依次剪下他的少许头发。这是非常令人动容的仪式，在失去这一象征相扑手身份的显著标志时，他们往往无法控制自己的情绪波动。

在每届相扑大赛开赛前，40名专业人士会花费4天时间徒手搭建一座新的相扑台。相扑台被认为是神圣的场所——诸神聚会之地，因此在赛前搭建相扑台的人必须精挑细选。光是学会选用搭建相扑台的合适泥土就得花上10年工夫进行训练。

像2000年前一样，40位能手齐心协力，靠人力使用传统工具填充夯实泥土才能建起一个称心如意的土俵。

这些建造者被称为"呼び出し"，或是招呼员、迎宾员，他们除了建造相扑台之外还负责引导相扑手进入体育场并招呼他们上场比赛。此外，他们还担任比赛的裁判。

"招呼员"们从15岁起接受训练，终其一生都在锤炼技艺以建造完美的相扑台，并成为其中翘楚。他们参与协助相扑比赛的方方面面，包括浇水使相扑台保持湿润以免开裂、清扫相扑台中心松散的泥土以及在赛前和赛后给运动员递擦汗用的毛巾，等等。他们还负责在赛前举着赞助商的大型广告牌绕场展示。

相扑正在迅速成为一项国际性的运动。每年会举行数次表演赛，这些表演赛有时会在国外进行。目前，顶尖相扑手大多是外国人，他们已经主宰了这项运动，其中两位是蒙古选手，一位是正在向相扑更高级别发起冲击的保加利亚选手。

第一位升级到相扑大关级别（仅次于最高级别横纲）的外国人是一位名叫小锦的美国夏威夷人，他曾在20世纪90年代统治这项运动，他身材魁梧，过去能、现在依然能毫不费力地把个子小些的相扑手挤出场地。由于相扑联合会认为他缺少某种被称为"冠军的尊贵气质"的隐形品质,所以一直没能晋升为顶级相扑手。

随后另一位名叫查德·罗文的美国夏威夷人(日本人管他叫曙太郎)因被晋升为"横纲"而在相扑界傲视群雄。

日本当然希望相扑运动能够得到国际社会的认可,并且正在为此积极努力。但让日本人感到些许窘迫的是,外国选手正在逐渐主导这项运动,致使体型更小、力量更弱的日本相扑手被边缘化,在那些将相扑运动视为日本本土文化遗产组成部分的纯粹主义者看来,这是一道文化难题。

相扑表演

Sumo Wrestling

When a friend from home recently visited me, it happened to be during one of the regularly scheduled Sumo Grand Tournaments. Each day she sat mesmerized in front of the television, watching with great anticipation who would win the bout and who would ultimately lose. After only a few days, she had figured out the rules and was rooting for her favorite players.

This reaction to sumo wrestling is typical of visitors to Japan. There is something very absorbing about the national sport of Japan that hooks people after just a couple of hours of watching it.

Each new season brings a grand tournament, which packs the stadium where the bouts are held and has office workers huddled around their office televisions to watch the outcomes of the bouts of the higher ranked wrestlers. Although the bouts usually last a matter of a few seconds, it is very exciting to watch.

Part of the attraction is the history of the sport, dating back some 2,000 years. It is highly ritualized, reflecting an aesthetic art form of ancient Japan that has been passed down over the millennia, retaining many of the same aspects and traditions today as it did then.

Japanese people absolutely love sumo and consider it to be a living national treasure. The top wrestlers who reach the rank of "yokozuna" are treated like superstars. Magazine and television advertisements feature the popular wrestlers. Memorabilia, similar to other sports, feature wrestlers' likenesses on towels, cards, posters, T-shirts and any other imaginable type of souvenir.

Unlike most sports, however, sumo-stardom brings with it a huge social and cultural responsibility that is steeped in tradition and proper etiquette that dates back to its beginning. Having dignity and respect for the sport, and what it stands for, is of utmost importance to the wrestlers... and to the spectators.

No matter how strong or powerful a wrestler is, without a certain air of dignity that is associated with champion wrestlers of the highest rank, a wrestler will not be promoted to the rank of "yokozuna".

This is what sets sumo apart from other major sports around the world. A wrestler's success is not solely dependent upon his ability, but on the whole package of how he is able to conduct himself with respect to sumo and its long history of codified rituals; all of this is in addition to his adroitness in the ring.

Sumo is considered to be a "living museum" of a bygone era because of its rituals and traditions. In some ways, it is more of a performance than a sport. A fan is transported during each bout to a time that is reminiscent of Edo Period Japan (1603~1868).

In the 15th century, sumo wrestlers were used to help train samurai. To fall in battle meant instant death, so to muster the strength and dignity to get up after falling was an embodiment of the sumo ethic, one that served samurai warriors well. Conquering physical exhaustion, staying on your feet no matter what, and getting up after falling are lessons that are still taught to young sumo wrestlers today.

Sumo practice is hard. Wrestlers' entire lives and daily routines are centered on sumo. They eat, breathe and sleep sumo during the entire time they are training and wrestling, just as their predecessors have done for hundreds of years.

A wrestler's day begins at 4 or 5 a.m. for the youngest or lowest ranked wrestlers. They must ready the ring for the day's practice and exercise to get loosened up for the pummeling they will most certainly endure from the higher ranked wrestlers.

Physically, the young wrestlers must learn balance, flexibility, and agility— the three essentials for success in the sumo ring. The goal is to have extremely powerful thighs and a very low center of gravity.

When most people think of sumo, the image is of gargantuan men with neatly combed topknots, stomping their feet one at a time from a high position. This exercise is called "shiko", and young wrestlers do this at least 500 times a day. They also sit with their legs spread far apart, leaning down until their stomach and face touch the ring... not an easy feat to achieve with a huge belly of fat in the way. Not to fear, older wrestlers help the younger ones by standing on their backs to help get the needed flexibility. This is a painful, but effective technique.

In time immemorial, legend has it that territorial disputes were sometimes settled through sumo bouts. The "will" of the gods decided the outcome, so people would accept success or defeat. This is a much more peaceful and less bloody way to settle disputes, much better than the "shock and awe" methods of modern warfare today.

The topknot of sumo wrestlers which is so manicured serves two purposes: first, it is to help protect the wrestler's head from injury; and second, it symbolizes the sanctity of the sport and his position within the world of sumo.

In fact, the people in charge of coiffing the hair of a sumo wrestler have to train for 10 years before being allowed to touch the hair of a top-ranked wrestler. Apprenticeship of the traditional arts of Japan, including sumo, is a time-honored tradition with generations of family members often performing the same function as their ancestors.

The unique style of a sumo wrestler's topknot is significant because the hairdresser must mold and shape the hair, applying copious amounts of oil, into the shape of a ginkgo leaf. This style is reserved for only the top-ranked wrestlers to don before matches. If a lower-ranked wrestler goes out of his stable building into the public, he is always expected to wear a kimono with geta (wooden clogs) and have his hair tied in a topknot called "chommage" (if it is long enough) which was typical of men in the Edo Period.

As mentioned before, only the top-ranked wrestlers are allowed to have their hair oiled and combed in the "oichomage" (gingko leaf) style during tournaments. Once a top-ranked wrestler retires, there is a special "haircutting" ceremony that takes place in the ring.

The wrestler, dressed in formal kimono, sits in the center of the ring as family, friends, fellow wrestlers and celebrities who are fans take turns in snipping bits of his hair. This is a very emotional ceremony, and often the wrestlers aren't able to hold back the wave of emotion that engulfs them at having such a visible part of their sumo identity taken away from them.

Before every Grand Sumo Tournament, a new dohyo (ring) is made by hand by a legion of 40 specialists for 4 days. The dohyo is considered to be a sacred place—meeting ground for the gods —and only a select group of men are allowed to construct the ring before a tournament. It takes 10 years of training just to be able to choose the proper clay to use in the making of a sumo ring.

By hand, using only traditional tools—just as it was done 2,000 years ago— packed earth and the hard work of 40 specialists combine to make a good dohyo.

These men are called "yobidashi", or beckoners/ushers, who, besides making the dohyo, also beckon the wrestlers for their bouts and usher them into the stadium. They serve as referees, as well, for the bouts.

Yobidashi begin their training at the age of 15 and spend their whole lives honing their ability to create a perfect ring, and in becoming a "master yobidashi". These men assist in all aspects of the sumo matches, from keeping the ring moist with water to prevent it from cracking to sweeping the loosened earth from the center to handing sweat towels to the wrestlers before and after their matches. They also are responsible for carrying the huge advertising banners of sponsors around the ring before the matches.

Sumo is rapidly becoming an international sport. Several times a year, exhibition matches are performed, and sometimes these are done overseas. Currently, the top-ranked wrestlers are largely foreigners who have come to dominate the sport. Two Mongolian wrestlers are now the top-ranked wrestlers, with a Bulgarian wrestler working his way up the sumo ladder.

The first foreigner to be promoted to the rank of "ozeki", a step down from the top-ranking "yokozuna", was a Hawaiian by the name of Konishiki. He dominated the sport in the 1990s. He was, and still is, huge in size and could thrust a smaller wrestler out of the ring with little effort. He was never promoted to the top rank because of that intangible "certain something" that is referred to as a "champion's dignity" that the Sumo Federation didn't feel he possessed.

Later, however, another Hawaiian by the name of Chad Rowen (known as Akebono in Japan) did attain the ultimate pinnacle of the sumo world by being promoted to "yokozuna".

Japan certainly wants sumo to be accepted internationally and is working hard to get it recognized as such, but it is causing a bit of a quandary, as it is becoming too dominated by foreign wrestlers. By pushing smaller, less powerful Japanese wrestlers to the sidelines, it is creating a sort of cultural conundrum amongst the purists who see sumo as a part of its indigenous heritage.

邻里协会

日本各地的社区都建有一套独特的"邻里协会"制度，日语管这种协会叫"町内会"。这些准政府组织负责协助执行当地的行政职能，传递重要信息，协调社会活动以及筹划社区的节日活动。

"町内会"的历史可追溯到日本江户时代（1603~1868）。日本现行的邻里协会体系直接源自那个时代的体制原型，在当时，其形成的最初目的是为了让当地居民共同负责维持本地的法律和秩序，维护道德规范，以及收税。

1868年开始的明治维新揭开了推动日本现代化的序幕（汤姆·克鲁斯主演了以此为主题的电影《最后的武士》）。从此以后，这些地方协会就不再受政府官员的青睐，并最终丧失了曾经享有的权力。

然而，这一体制于20世纪20年代在城市中心区重新出现，并慢慢地扩展到全国各地。在20世纪40年代，统治日本的军国主义者认为，该体制是维持秩序十分有利且有效的办法，于是下令在全国所有城市推行"町内会"制度。

当时，邻里协会被赋予各种职权，其权力包括分配政府提供的口粮、培训当地民兵，甚至负责平息任何针对政府的抗议活动。

二战结束后，美国占领军废除了邻里协会制度，理由是美军认为邻里协会权力过大，甚至是反民主的组织。然而，在20世纪50年代，简化版的社区组织体系再次推广开来。这些邻里协会基本上是自发形成的团体，协助当地政府分发材料，包括社区通知、市政相关信息（如各种政府报告）以及有关社区节日和社会活动的通知。

如今，和20世纪50年代一样，这些协会在遍布日本社区的社会生活中起着非常重要的作用。在这种体制下，邻里以及社区之间可以正常往来，以达到交往的目的。拿我来说，我就期待收到住在我家右边的邻居挂在我家门上的告示板（回览板）。

我读完所有的通知后，就会把告示板拿到左边邻居家门口；邻居看完后又会把告示板传递给下一位邻居。这样一直传递下去，直到所有人都知晓通知。邻居们在传递告示板时，常常会站着闲聊一会。

实行这种体制能省很多钱，因为大家共享一份通知以及登载通知的纸张，就没有必要印刷大量纸质版通知，也能省下请人挨家挨户派送通知的费用或邮寄通知到各家各户可能产生的更多费用。地方政府充分利用了这一体制，节约了人力和开支。

加入协会的每户家庭轮流负责收取年费、分发简报及监督协会在特定街道的总体运作。

每位地方协会的领导要向监管大区域的领导汇报工作，大区协会由若干个小协会组成。之后，大区协会领导将与其他大区领导以及地方政府官员会面。

几年前，我所在街区邻里协会所属的大片区总协会新建了一座漂亮的社区中心，可供相关协会的居民使用。

老年人常在社区中心（配有厨房）吃便餐、做手工、进行社交聚会。当然，各种邻里协会也会在此举行会议。

除了挨家挨户传递的告示板外，大型社区公告牌摆放在整个社区最显眼的地方，上面张贴着各类相关信息供行人阅读，如当地的通知、政府竞选活动及居民应当知晓的即将来临的活动、节日等一般消息。

地方邻里协会行使的职能包括监督家庭垃圾的正确回收。我常常在天刚亮时就跌跌撞撞地走向指定的垃圾收集点，在那儿一个戴着官方样式袖章的人跟我打招呼，他要确保居民在正确的日期按规定投放垃圾。

邻里协会公告牌

Neighborhood Association

Communities all over Japan have a unique system of "neighborhood associations", known as "chonaikai" in Japanese. These quasi-governmental organizations are responsible for assisting in local administrative functions, distributing important information, coordinating social activities, and planning neighborhood festivals.

The history of chonaikai dates back to the Edo Period(1603~1868); the current system is directly descended from the original prototype which was initially formed to hold local residents communally responsible for maintaining law and order in their neighborhoods, preserving moral propriety, and even to collect taxes.

Once the Meiji Restoration (1868) started and a push to modernize Japan began (this was the subject featured in Tom Cruise's film The Last Samurai), these local associations lost favor with governmental officials, and eventually forfeited the legal authority they once enjoyed.

However, in the 1920s, the system gradually reappeared in neighborhoods in the urban centers and slowly spread over the country. In the 1940s, the militarists who were running Japan saw a very lucrative and efficient way to maintain order and made chonaikai mandatory in all cities across the country.

At this time, the neighborhood associations were given a variety of responsibilities which expanded their authority including the distribution of government rations, training residents in the civil defense of the community, and even being in charge of silencing any protests against the government.

After World War II, the US Occupation Forces abolished the system because it was viewed as being too authoritarian and even anti-democratic. Gradually, however, the 1950s reintroduced a pared-down system of community organizations, making these neighborhood associations largely volunteer bodies that assisted the local governments in the distribution of materials including community announcements, city-related information (like various governmental reports) and local notices regarding neighborhood festivals and social activities.

Today, just as it was in the 1950s, these associations maintain a significant role in the social lifeline for communities all across Japan. The system allows for regular contact between neighbors and neighborhoods, giving them a social purpose. In my case, I look forward to receiving the telltale clipboard (kairanban) propped up against my door, placed thereby the neighbor to the right of my home.

Once I have perused all of the announcements and notices, I walk it over to my neighbor on the other side. After they read through all of the information, they take it to the next neighbor until everyone has had a chance to see it. Often is the case where neighbors will stand and chat for a bit when exchanging the "kairanban".

This system saves quite a bit of money. Since announcements (and the paper they come on) are shared, there is no need for mass-producing reams of notices. Also, this system reduces the cost of having to pay someone to walk them door-to-door, or potentially more costly, mailing them to each individual household. The local government makes great use of this system, saving it manpower and money.

Each household in the association takes a turn being in charge of collecting the yearly dues, passing out the newsletter, and overseeing the general running of the association for that particular street.

Each of these leaders from the local associations reports to a general leader who oversees a larger area that encompasses a number of the smaller associations. This person then meets with the other larger associations and the local government.

A few years ago, the general association in the expanded area that my neighborhood group is attached to built a beautiful new community center that can be reserved by residents living in one of the connected associations.

Often, elderly people will use the facility for informal luncheons (it has a kitchen), making handicrafts, and to have social gatherings and get-togethers. Of course, the various neighborhood associations hold meetings there as well.

In addition to the clipboard that is passed from house to house, large community bulletin boards are placed in prominent places throughout the neighborhoods that post pertinent information for passersby to read. These include local notices, governmental campaigns, and general information that residents may need to know regarding upcoming events and festivals.

One function that the local neighborhood associations have been involved with is overseeing the proper recycling of household garbage. Every so often, as I stumble at the crack of dawn to the designated place where garbage is picked up, I am greeted by a person wearing an officious looking armband who is there to make sure that residents aren't improperly disposing of garbage on the wrong day.

小费文化

在日本，顾客给餐厅、酒店等场所的服务员小费这一行为，就算有，也并不常见。事实上，要是有人试图给服务人员小费，对方很可能觉得自己受到了侮辱。

有这样一个事例，曾有一个朋友从美国来日本看望我。我带她到餐厅吃饭，那是我最喜欢的餐厅之一，我也是那儿的常客。我的朋友对为我们服务的男服务员印象深刻，他在我们用餐过程中非常尽心和友好。

当我们准备离开时，我起身去收银台结账。朋友在收拾东西的时候，发现我没在餐桌上留小费。出于好意，也是为我请吃这餐饭尽点心意，离开前她在餐桌中央放了一张面值1000的日钞。

离开餐厅后，我们匆匆赶往另一地点赴约。几分钟后，一位服务员追着我们跑过来，气喘吁吁地喊着我的名字。我压根儿不知道他为什么追着我们跑，因为在离开餐厅前我已经反复检查，确认没有落下包和衣物。

追上我们后，服务员把那张日钞递给我，说道："您把这个忘在餐桌上了。"我完全被弄糊涂了，因为我很清楚自己并没有在餐桌上留下钱。由于我跟服务员说的是日语，朋友也不知道为什么钱会被退还给我，还以为是我在收银台多付钱了。

我转身对她说："真奇怪，他在我们吃饭的餐桌上发现了这张钞票，我不知道这是打哪来的。"她立即解释道，她以为我忘了付小费，钱是她留下作为小费的。然后我对服务员解释说，因为他在我们用餐期间服务周到友好，钱是我朋友留下给他的。

服务员的第一反应是困惑，接着很快露出不知所措的神色，继而又变得尴尬不已。对他来说，周到友好地为我们服务是他的职责，餐厅也因此付了他工资，他认为接受顾客的钱是不道德的，因为这本身就是他工作的一部分。

我的朋友试图把钱硬塞给他，但他只是恭敬地鞠躬道歉，直到我朋友从他手上接过钱。我感谢他特地把钱送回来，并解释说，在美国，饭后在桌上额外留些钱给上菜的服务员当小费是一种习俗。

他说他听说过付小费这种习俗，但仍然觉得接受一个常客（比如我），特别是造访日本的客人（比如我朋友）的钱很不自在。他很可能觉得让我这位来旅游的朋友对日本有个好印象是他的责任，因此他很乐意提供周到的就餐服务。

在日本，餐馆老板经常会给常客提供多加一道菜的服务（免费的）。近30年来，我经常光顾一家很特别的餐厅，这家餐厅有一群忠实的顾客，这些人喜欢坐在柜台边，而不是在餐桌就坐，这样就可以在老板做菜和上菜时和他闲谈。通常他会在晚上打烊时做一道特别的菜供大家享用，以感谢我们一直以来光顾他的生意。

每次回美国，我总是拿不定主意该给多少小费。说实话，我得在餐费之外再留下一些钱作为服务小费让我有些不快，因为享受服务本来就是用餐体验的一部分。

我想说的是，我明白小费作为这些员工的一种补充收入背后的经济意义。然而，日本没有付小费的习俗，我在此生活这么长时间后，也喜欢不用付小费的做法。

如果服务确实很差，是不是可以不付小费呢？我想，大多数美国人都觉得，不管服务好坏，留下小费是一种义务，在本质上把它看作用餐总花费的一部分，而不仅仅作为优质服务的一种奖励。

我想到一个给小费和收小费的双方都乐意的实例。在名叫"旅館"的传

服务生为我的朋友泰德和安德莉亚倒酒

统日式旅馆，客人通常会送给旅店服务员一点钱或一件礼物以表达谢意。

这种习俗叫"心付"，客人们通常在刚入住的时候就会给小费。在这类旅馆，老板娘通常会在门口迎接客人，帮助他们登记入住，然后带他们去房间。一到房间，老板娘就给他们奉上茶点，她还会负责客人住店期间的膳食，为他们准备睡觉用的蒲团，并在早上帮忙折叠卧具。

虽然现今的一些日本旅馆会把这种特别服务的费用自动加入账单，但一些更古老、更传统的旅馆则不会这么做。在这种情况下，向老板娘赠送某样东西就是一种很不错的举动。我记得当我还是一个高中生时，我寄宿家庭的太太为了感谢在日式旅馆帮助过我们的老板娘，送了对方一盒昂贵的巧克力而不是给现金。

要是给现金的话，就应该给新钞，且要用纸包好或装在信封里。在日本，如果不事先用不透明的纸把钱包好就直接把钱给别人是非常无礼的。同样，用旧钞送人在某种程度上说是不敬的行为，因为这说明送钱的人没有花该花的时间精心备好小费。

为了避免直接将零钱递给顾客而冒犯对方，商店服务员甚至会把零钱放在托盘里。在没有托盘时，我见过商店服务员小心翼翼地用一只手拿钱，另一只手平坦地放在拿钱的那只手的下面，宛如一个托盘。

传统上，如果一对夫妻入住旅店，应由妻子送上钱或礼物作为小费以表示感谢。男人管钱有失身份这一传统观念可以追溯到日本的武士时代。直到今天，许多丈夫仍把全部薪水交给妻子，妻子则掌管家庭的一切日常开支，支付账单，购买食物，甚至会将一小部分钱还给丈夫作为他们每月的零用钱。表面上，日本丈夫似乎在婚姻中处于完全主导的地位，但不要被这种假象迷惑了，真正的权利掌握在妻子手里，因为在幕后当家做主的是她们。毕竟，日本妻子不仅完全管理家庭日常生活，关心教育孩子，还掌管着钱财。在日本，妻子才是家中真正掌管财政大权的角色。

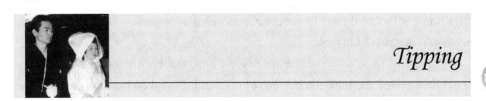

Tipping

The custom of patrons tipping service related workers in restaurants, hotels, etc. is not normally practiced in Japan—if at all. In fact, service related workers would most likely be insulted if someone tried to tip them.

An example of this was when a friend came to visit me here from back home. I took her to one of my favorite restaurants where I had become a regular. She was very impressed with our waiter, who was especially attentive and friendly throughout our meal.

When we prepared to leave, I got up first to pay the bill at the register. As she gathered her things, she noticed I didn't leave a tip on the table. So to be helpful and to contribute to the meal, she laid down a bill equivalent to about $10 in the center of the table before leaving.

We left the restaurant and began walking hurriedly to another place where we had a scheduled appointment. Several minutes later, a very out-of-breath waiter came running after us calling my name. I had no idea why in the world he would be chasing us down, because I had double-checked before we left to make sure we had all our bags and coats with us.

When he reached us, he extended the 1,000 yen bill to me and said, "You forgot this on the table." I was thoroughly confused because I knew I hadn't left any money on the table. Since I was speaking in Japanese, my friend had no idea why the money was being returned to me, figuring I had overpaid at the cash register.

I turned to her and said, "How strange ... he found this money on our table. I wonder where it came from." She immediately explained that she had left it as a tip, thinking I had forgotten to do so. I then relayed to our waiter that the money was left on the table by my friend, intended for him, because he was so attentive and friendly during our meal.

His first reaction was one of puzzlement, which then quickly turned to a look of bewilderment, then embarrassment. To him, it is his job to be friendly and attentive, because he is serving us in the capacity as a waiter, and the restaurant pays him a salary to do so. To accept money from a customer would be unethical, because it is a part of his job.

My friend tried to force the money on him, but he just bowed graciously apologizing until she took the bill out of his hand. I thanked him for going to the trouble to return the money and explained that in the United States, it is a custom to leave extra money on the table after a meal as a tip to the person who served the food.

He admitted he had heard of the custom of tipping, but was still uncomfortable accepting cash from a regular customer (such as myself), and especially from a guest (such as my friend) who is a visitor to his country. He most likely felt like it was his responsibility to make sure my tourist-friend received a good impression of Japan, hence his willingness to be so attentive and friendly during our meal.

In Japan, it is often customary for a restaurant owner to offer an added dish as service (meaning free of charge) to regular customers. One particular restaurant I have regularly gone to for nearly 30 years has a core group of diehard customers who prefer to sit at the counter instead of tables in order to chat with the owner as he cooks and serves the food. Often, as a token of appreciation for our continued business, he will make a special dish at the end of the night for all of us to share.

On trips home, I am always perplexed about how much a tip should be, and honestly, I am a bit resentful that I am expected to leave money over and beyond the cost of the meal for service that should be a part of the total dining experience.

I will say that I understand the economy behind tipping as a supplement to the workers' income. However, after living in Japan for so long where tipping is not a custom, I like not having to do it.

If the service is indeed poor, is it all right not to leave a tip? I think most Americans feel obligated to leave a tip regardless and, in essence, view it as a part of the total cost of the meal and not solely as an award for good service.

I can think of one instance in Japan when a type of tip is given and accepted willingly. In traditional-style Japanese inns called "ryokan", it is customary to offer money or a gift as an expression of gratitude to the hotel staff.

This custom is called "kokorozuke" and is usually offered at the beginning of the stay. In these types of hotels, the lady of the inn will usually greet the guests at the door, assist them in checking in, and then will accompany them to their room. Once there, she will serve them tea with some sort of snack. She will see to the meals during their stay at the inn, prepare the futons for sleeping and assist in folding the bedding in the morning.

Although in some Japanese inns today a service charge for this type of individual attention is added automatically to the bill, some of the older, more traditional inns do not. In these instances it is a nice gesture to offer some type of gratuity to the woman. As a high school student, I remember my host mother giving the woman who helped us at our ryokan an expensive box of chocolates in lieu of actual cash.

If cash is given, it should be in new bills wrapped in paper or placed in an envelope. It is rude to hand money directly to someone in Japan without first covering it with something opaque. Also, older bills can convey a certain degree of disrespect because it can mean that the person did not take the necessary time to prepare properly the "kokorozuke".

Even shops will place change on a tray as not to offend the customer by handing the money directly. If no tray is available, I have seen shop clerks gingerly hold out the money with one hand, while holding their other hand flat under the other hand like a tray.

Traditionally, if a couple is staying at the inn, it is the woman who gives the money or token of appreciation in the form of a gift as a tip. Historically, dating back to the days of the samurai, it was considered beneath a man's dignity to handle money. Still today, many husbands turn over their entire paychecks to their wives, who then handle all household related finances and expenses, pay bills, buy food, and even to give back a bit to the husband as his monthly allowance. Outwardly, it may appear that Japanese husbands are in complete control in the marriage, but do not be fooled by this illusion. The real power lies with the wives, because behind the scenes they rule the roosts. After all, Japanese wives have complete charge of not only running the household, the care and education of the children, but also the money. Japanese wives truly do hold the purse strings in Japan.

送礼文化

我喜爱日本的原因之一是该国的送礼习俗。我相信，所有国家都有类似历史悠久的习俗，但日本人在礼品授受方式上的固定做法，已成为他们丰富且充满活力的文化中根深蒂固和不可或缺的组成部分。

在日本，送礼是一门艺术。一年到头，人们都能在正式或非正式场合收到礼物。日本有个风俗，我特别喜欢，就是去别人家做客时送件小礼物，如一束鲜花、什锦水果、各式各样的小蛋糕等； 如果是参加晚宴，则常会带上一瓶酒供大家饮用。日本人不管去哪里做客，鲜有不带礼物的。礼物不必很昂贵，因为与礼物比起来，主人更看重的是那份心意，人们用这份象征性的礼物来表达对于主人邀请自己前往家中做客或吃饭的感激之情。

日本人在一年之中有两个全国性的送礼时节——仲夏时分的中元和年底的"歲暮"。每当此时，商店都会精心陈列商品，试图吸引顾客进店购买包装精美的礼盒。

每年12月13日至28日，大家常常互送礼物，尤其是有业务关系或社会关系的人，这一习俗叫送岁暮礼。这些礼物常用精美的盒子包装，有时可能是毛巾、咖啡、水果罐头、啤酒、洗涤剂等。每年，购买礼物的季节还未到，商家就早早地打广告宣传当年更受追捧的送礼商品。商品一旦卖出，商家就把它们装进盒子里，包装好，然后派送给收礼者。

岁暮礼不是出于纯粹的好意，而是一种"義理"（义务）。礼物的价格和质量，与送礼者的具体经济条件及其在当地的社会地位有关。为了避免事后因收礼者认为礼物太廉价或太昂贵（如果别人送你的礼物比你送出的礼物贵很多，那会十分尴尬）而造成误会，人们会因买什么价位和什么样的礼物而烦恼。

年轻一代圣诞时互送礼物，这一从西方传入的习俗，已经取代了岁暮礼。当然，这个时间节点最好不过了（都在12月底），况且互送圣诞礼物比送传统的岁暮礼灵活得多。

如果有人送我岁暮礼，我会很紧张，觉得必须马上出门买一件价值相当的礼物回赠送礼者。也许这看起来很可笑，但如果我不马上回礼的话，送礼者将来可能会请我帮更大的忙，因此，我要还清人情，这样就不会牵扯到什么义务了。

我从亲身经历中知道了这一点,也很快明白日本人是迅速还人情的,之所以这么做是为了避免因收到贵重礼物没有马上回礼而产生的压力。这在外国人看来十分麻烦,但送礼风俗可追溯到几个世纪以前,是日本保持社会礼仪机制运转的润滑剂。

几乎所有百货大楼、商店、精品店都会为顾客装箱和包装好所购买的商品。这一习俗棒极了,我去美国时就很怀念这样的服务。当我在印第安纳州购物,买好一件准备送人的礼物之后,我得考虑买包装纸、绸带及透明胶等用来包装礼物,以便送人时体面些。在日本,为感谢客人惠顾,商家会无偿提供该项服务。

日本商店之所以为客人提供这样的服务,是因为这是日本文化中根深蒂固的一部分,对于包装礼物这门传统艺术,每位营业员都训练有素。营业员把装有礼物的盒子放到纸张中央,然后用纸张将礼物裹上几圈,将礼物卷得紧紧的,最后就成了精心包装的包裹,备妥待发。

一年中另一个正式的送礼时间是七月中旬的中元节。同样,此时的送礼也是出于责任感而非好意。大家送的礼物很相似,连包装都和岁暮礼的一样。

但送礼物常常是有原因的。有时,出于策略上的考虑,人们会给某个特定对象送有一定价值的礼品;或许是送礼者在送礼季之前受过对方的帮助,因此觉得有必要送礼表达谢意,又或许是送礼者估计以后免不了还得麻烦人家,因此,一份贵重的夏季或年末礼品就可以缓解请对方帮忙所产生的歉意。不管是哪种情况,礼物都可能成为在与对方交际过程中的筹码。

这并不是说这些礼物一定有其他用意,因为在大多数情况下,人们在送礼时不会别有用心或是期望将来能获得什么好处。总的来说,日本人民是非常慷慨的民族,送礼是日本文化的天然组成部分。

在日本,礼物有时也可以用来还人情。比方说,如果你帮了我的忙,我会马上送你一份礼物表示感谢,这实际上就抵消了我可能欠你的人情。

有一次,一群学生来我家吃烧烤,当时我们想拍张合照。每个人都入镜,所以需要找人拍。当时我的邻居正在院子里干活,他理所当然成了帮我们解决难题的人选。

他很乐意地过来为我们拍照,当然,我对他的帮忙表示了感谢。正当他要走出我家后院时,一个女学生不假思索,很自然地俯身拿起桌上一盒未开封的饼干,轻松优雅地在他离开时递给他。

当时我想"天啊,她处事真老练"。整件事就让她随手办得妥妥帖帖,使我们不必因为邻居的帮忙而欠他什么人情。女学生此举,完全是一种基于文化的自然而然的反应。

要是在美国，一句简单的"谢谢"足矣，没人觉得拍张照这种小忙需要额外送什么东西表达谢意。

还有一次，离我一街之遥的一位邻居着实把我吓了一跳。他和女儿带着一篮色泽诱人的苹果来到我家门口，是那种自家种植的原生态苹果。我对他们并不太熟悉，他不得不告诉我他家的准确地址。他还向我坦言，事实上我们从未见正式见过面，只是时不时在街上互相打招呼罢了。

作为一个外国人，生活在日本农村地区的一个不利之处是我太过与众不同，以至于所有人都知道我是谁，可我却往往不知道其他人是谁。但是，就拿上面的例子来说，我至少对我的邻居还算有些许了解，但他这突如其来的慷慨之举倒让我有些不自在，并对他的动机多少有些怀疑。我一直在纳闷，他为什么突然间特地来拜访我，带着女儿一起前来又意欲何为？

仅仅过了两天，我就知道了问题的答案，并因此了解了他先前令人意外（并十分唐突）的慷慨之举的初衷。原来他是希望我能辅导他女儿英语。她那会儿正在准备高中的升学考试，需要课外辅导好让她达到入学标准。谜底终于揭晓了。

所幸的是，在她需要辅导的那段时间，我正好要出国去，免去了我为她辅导的义务。但这对女孩来说却不是什么好消息。尽管如此，我还是因为之前收了人家的苹果而对邻居怀有一丝歉意。

我突然想起，一两天前，一个学生送了我一包柿子。为求心安，我立刻取了一部分柿子给他们。这样一来，实际上就消除了我对这对父女可能的亏欠。

将收到的礼品再次赠与他人的做法在日本很是普遍，只要礼品完好未拆封，如是水果蔬菜的话，那一定得新鲜、品相极佳。我不太喜欢吃柿子，因此很高兴既能还了之前的人情又避免了可能的浪费。这真是双赢。

在日本，应邀到某人家做客时，人们习惯带上一份礼物，可以是一小束花，一份当作甜点的什锦水果或蛋糕，还可以是一瓶酒，随便什么都行。同样，这样的礼物可以帮你消除因为麻烦了主人而产生的歉意。

这一独特的送礼习俗现在已经牢牢地成为我个人文化的一部分，不管是在日本还是美国，每次应邀到谁家吃饭或是喝咖啡，我都觉得有必要带上一份礼物聊表谢意。

这是个很好的习俗。美国人显然不会指望客人送什么礼物，可如果真送了，他们还是会对此表示感激的。经过在日本这么多年的文化熏陶，两手空空不带任何谢礼就贸然上谁家吃饭，会让我觉得像没穿衣服一样不自在。

我对送礼这一风俗已经习以为常，甚至觉得应该从日本给身在美国的亲朋好友带些纪念品。回到印第安纳州却不带点什么给我要见的人，总觉得怪怪的。问题是，我已经没有什么可选的了，几乎所有想象得到的日本装饰品和小玩意儿都送遍了。

日本人已经将送礼的艺术升华成了一种民族美德。小到家庭作坊，大到连锁商店，几乎所有商家都认为替顾客（免费）包装礼品是理所当然的。

随便在什么地方都可以买到礼物，因为所有火车站、机场、旅游景点以及许多其他公共场所，都有销售"お土産"（土特产或纪念品）的柜台。

必须出差在外的商务人士回到办公室时，一定会带所去地方的特色食品让全体同事品尝，同事们对此满怀期待，这是在日本企业文化中根深蒂固的一个习俗。这些礼品数量不一（依办公室里的人数而异），并且，为了便于分发，每一块蛋糕或饼干都是独立包装的。

我在日本生活期间学到的一条宝贵经验，千万不要挑剔收到的礼物。我会心存感激地收下每一份礼物——即便是一些我不需要甚至不想要的东西。毕竟，我总是可以用来回礼的。

从历史上说，这些风俗很可能起源于中国，人们借此机会将礼物送给逝去祖先的灵魂。然而，在历经几个世纪之后，这些风俗变得越来越商业化，并演变成为一个完全现代的传统，不是核心家庭成员，而是不同的家庭和公司互送礼品。

我通常会在饭店为学生们举办一场圣诞派对。每年放寒假前，我们会一起好好吃上一顿，然后摸圣诞彩袋。这一美国习俗特别受学生欢迎，因为每个人都能得到一份礼物，他们不必担心自己会得到什么样的礼物。一件礼物最多值10美元，随机抽取，因此，大家不必担心礼物是否合适，是否好看。

礼品店

Gift Giving

One thing I love about Japan is the custom of "gift giving". I'm sure all cultures perform a similar time-honored gift-giving ritual, but there is something institutional about the way Japanese give and accept gifts, making it an ingrained and essential component of their rich and vibrant culture.

Gift giving in Japan is an art form. All throughout the year, people are given gifts for both, formal and informal occasions. One Japanese custom that I especially like is the giving of a small gift when visiting someone's home, such as a small bouquet of flowers, assorted fruits, or a variety of small cakes. If it is a dinner party, often people will come equipped with a bottle of wine to offer. Very rarely does a Japanese person go anywhere without some type of gift-offering in hand. This gift doesn't have to be expensive because it is the thought that is appreciated more so than the gift itself. It is a symbolic token of the visitor's appreciation for being allowed to visit or have dinner in the host's home.

Officially, there are two times a year that Japanese give gifts—"chugen", in midsummer, and "seibo", at the end of the year. Stores put up elaborate displays during these two seasons in an effort to lure customers into buying the exquisitely wrapped packages.

Between December 13 and 28 people often exchange gifts with one another, especially if they are associates in business or are involved socially. This is called seibo. These are elaborately boxed items which sometimes include towels, coffee, cans of fruit, beer, and even detergents. Every year stores advertise the more trendy items for that year well in advance of the gift-buying season. They are arranged nicely in boxes, wrapped, and then delivered to the recipient by the store where it was purchased.

This is not a spontaneous gesture of good will but usually a "giri" (obligatory) act. The cost of the gift and quality of the gift usually is related to one's specific economic and social status within the community. People fret over how much to spend and what to buy in these instances in order to avoid any misunderstandings later on because a gift was considered to be too chintzy...or perhaps too expensive (which would be embarrassing if someone gave you a gift considerably more expensive than the one you gave to them).

The custom of seibo has been replaced with the idea of exchanging Christmas gifts with the younger generation, an imported custom from the West. Of course, the timing couldn't be better (both occurring at the end of December), and the flexibility offered in exchanging a Christmas gift is much greater than that in a traditional seibo gift.

I tend to panic if someone gives me a traditional seibo gift. I feel obliged to go right out and have a seibo gift delivered to them of equal value. It seems silly, perhaps, but if I don't return the favor immediately, I may be asked a bigger favor in the future by these people and I want to clear the slate so there is no "obligation" involved.

I have learned this from experience, and realized quickly that Japanese people are very quick to clear the slate. This is in order not to have the pressure of having received an expensive gift without reciprocating it immediately. It seems like a lot of hassle to someone on the outside viewing in, but gift giving is a custom that goes back for centuries and it is the oil that keeps the social etiquette machine running in this country.

Just about any department store, shop, or boutique will offer to box and wrap anything you buy. This is a wonderful custom that I miss when visiting the United States. When I shop in Indiana and purchase an item to be given as a gift, I then have to think about wrapping paper, ribbon, and tape in order to make it presentable. In Japan, all of this is done free of charge in appreciation for shopping at the store.

Japanese stores perform this service for the customer because it is an engrained part of Japanese culture, and every salesperson is trained in the traditional art of gift wrapping. The clerks place the object off center on the paper, and then roll the box over and over, with the paper being tucked around it as it is rolled. The end result is an exquisitely wrapped package ready for delivery.

The other formal gift-giving time of the year is chugen which occurs in mid-July. Again, this is done more out of a sense of obligation rather than from a feeling of goodwill. The gifts are similar, with all of the same trappings as the end of the year gift tradition.

Often, however, these gifts are not given without some strings attached, meaning there is sometimes a strategic reason for giving a gift of a certain value to a particular person. Perhaps the giver had been assisted prior to the gift-giving season and hence feels an obligation to repay that assistance with a gift; or perhaps the gift-giver is anticipating the need to ask a future favor of the receiver, and an expensive summer or year-end gift will help ease the burden of asking for that assistance. In either case, the gift can be a sort of bargaining chip with the other person.

This is not to say these types of gifts aren't ever given just for the sake of giving, because in most instances, they are offered without any future expectation or ulterior motive. Japanese people, in general, are a wonderfully generous group of people, making gift-giving a natural part of their cultural being.

Gifts here are sometimes used to cancel out obligations to others as well. For instance, if you do me a favor and I reward you immediately with a "thank you" gift, then I have effectively neutralized the obligation I might have to you for the favor you did for me.

Once, when I had a group of students to my home for a barbecue, we wanted to take a group picture. Since everyone wanted to be in the photo, we needed someone to take it. Since my neighbor was working in the yard, he was the logical solution to our dilemma.

Happily, he came over to take our picture, and I, of course, thanked him for doing this. As he was exiting the backyard, one of my female students very naturally, and without consciously thinking about it, reached down to the table and picked up an unopened package of cookies that she then elegantly, and quite effortlessly, offered to him as he departed.

I thought at the time, "Boy, she's smooth." The whole transaction occurred in one well-ordered glide of her hand, thus canceling out any obligation we might have had to him for doing us this favor. It was a natural, cultural reaction for her to do this.

In the United States, a simple "thank you" would have sufficed, and no one would have felt the need to give anything further to the person for doing something as mundane as snapping a photo.

On another occasion, I was surprised by a neighbor who lived one street over. He and his daughter showed up at my door bearing a gift basket of beautiful homegrown apples in pristine condition. I was not so familiar with this neighbor and, in fact, he had to explain to me where exactly his house was located. Also, he admitted to me that we had never actually met in person, but we had greeted one another on the street from time to time.

One disadvantage of being a foreigner in rural Japan is that we stand out so much that everyone knows who we are, but often we have no idea who everyone else is. In this case, however, I was at least marginally familiar with him, but his sudden generosity made me a bit uncomfortable and somewhat suspicious of his motives. Why, I kept wondering, did he go to all the trouble to visit me—out of the blue—and why did he make a point of bringing his daughter along?

It took only two days to learn the answers to these questions and, in turn, his motives for the rather unexpected (and certainly abrupt) act of previous generosity: He was hoping that I would agree to tutor his daughter in English. She was preparing to take the entrance exam into high school and needed supplementary lessons to get her up to snuff. Mystery solved.

Fortunately for me, and unfortunately for her, I was going abroad during the time she needed the lessons, thus relieving me of any obligation. Be that as it may, I still felt a hint of indebtedness to this neighbor for the gift of apples I had received before.

Quick thinking on my part, I remembered I had a bag of kaki (Japanese persimmons) which had been given to me a day or so before by a student. Excusing myself momentarily, I gathered an assortment of these fruits and offered them to my neighbor, thus effectively canceling out any obligation I had—in kind—to him and his daughter.

The "recycling" of gifts is commonly practiced in Japan—as long as they are in their original, unopened packages or in the case of fruits and vegetables, fresh and in impeccable condition. Not being a huge fan of persimmons, however, I was happy to not only cancel out my prior obligation but to also unload something that likely would have gone to waste. A win-win situation.

When invited to someone's home in Japan, it is customary to arrive with some sort of gift-offering. It can be a small bunch of cut flowers, an assortment of fruits or cakes for dessert or a bottle of wine—just about anything. Again, this offering helps to cancel out any obligation that might have been incurred by "imposing" upon the host.

This particular gift-giving custom is now so firmly a part of my cultural-being that whenever I am invited to someone's home for a meal or coffee, whether in Japan or the US, I feel it necessary to contribute some sort of offering as a "thank you" gift to the host.

It is such a nice custom. Americans certainly don't expect gifts from guests, but appreciate the gesture all the same. After so many years of cultural conditioning in Japan, I feel naked arriving to someone's home for dinner without some type of appreciation gift in hand.

I have acculturated so much to this custom that I even feel the need to bring some sort of souvenir or gift from Japan to family and friends back home. I feel odd arriving back to Indiana without something to give the people I meet. The problem is, I've exhausted all of the possible options, having given just about every type of Japanese trinket and bauble imaginable.

The Japanese have perfected the art of gift-giving into a national virtue. From small mom-and-pop shops to huge department stores, nearly all of these enterprises offer "gift-wrapping" as a matter of course (and free of charge) to all their customers.

One can't swing a samurai sword here and not hit a place that has ready-made gifts for the picking. Every train station, airport, and tourist attraction—as well as a myriad of other public places—have counters where "omiyage" (souvenir gifts) can be purchased.

Business people who must travel away from their office on an official trip nearly always return with some sort of omiyage in the form of food for the entire office to enjoy. It is expected by the person's colleagues and is a firmly rooted custom in Japanese business culture. These gifts come in a variety of sizes (depending on how many people are in the office), and each cake or cookie is individually wrapped for easy distribution.

One valuable lesson I have learned while residing in Japan is never to look a gift horse in the mouth. I graciously accept whatever is offered—even if it is something I don't need or even want. After all, I can always recycle it.

Historically, these customs most likely originated in China and were occasions to offer gifts to the souls of one's dead ancestors. Over the centuries, however, these have become more and more commercialized and have become a full-blown modern tradition between people of different families or companies rather than an exchange of gifts within one's nuclear family.

Usually I host a Christmas party for my students at a restaurant. Every year, before the winter holidays, we have a nice dinner together and have a Christmas grab-bag. This American custom is especially enjoyed by the students because everyone gets a gift, and no one has to worry about what kind of a gift to get. The maximum amount allowed is the equivalent of $10, and it is anonymous. So, no one has to worry about the appropriateness of the gift or how impressive the gift is.

婚礼

参加传统的日本神道教婚礼是十分独特而又难忘的体验。在日本生活的这些年，我参加过很多在教堂举行的婚礼和日式婚宴，但有幸参加传统神道教婚礼的机会则只有一次。

大部分日本人既是神道教徒又是佛教徒，他们的婚礼一般选择按神道教仪式进行，而葬礼则按佛教仪式举行。鲜有国家能在不同宗教之间转换自如，游刃有余，但日本便是如此，上述两种宗教传统的方方面面在日本随处可见。

许多日本人会在家里同时供奉佛教祭台和神道教神龛；许多企业在建造新楼时，不仅会摆放小型神道教神龛，还会请神道教祀官为之祈福；综合借鉴两种宗教，日本家庭会请佛教主持在奥本节期间（八月的一个节日，其间人们把祖先的魂灵请回家）念诵经文，在亲人的祭日举行纪念活动。

传统神道教婚礼十分庄重，极具仪式感。新人身着传统服饰，新郎身着袴裙（一种褶状裤裙）与黑色和服上衣，和服前胸上方左右两边往往缝饰有新郎的家族饰章。

新娘身穿精心绣制的纯白色和服（"白無垢"），袖子长长的，盖过膝盖。穿长袖和服表示新娘单身未嫁；而一旦结婚，则只穿表明已婚身份的短袖和服。

白色和服可以追溯至日本的武士时代，表明当时的妇女愿意顺从于夫家，意思是"我的白色和服可以按照你家庭的意愿及其社会地位染成任何一种颜色"。

新娘除了身着走动时在足畔拖行的和服外，还会化精致的白色妆容并佩戴传统的假发，大多数西方人认为这是艺妓的装扮；新娘还会在假发上佩戴白色丝质发罩，长久以来，这种头饰被用以掩盖新娘的"嫉妒心"。

婚礼由一位神道教祀官主持，两位神道教御神子则会参与协助婚礼的仪式部分。因为神道教历史悠久，信奉万物有灵，敬畏自然，所以婚礼仪式也在很大程度上体现了崇尚自然的宗教传统。

然而，神道教婚礼最重要的部分，是夫妻互敬新婚酒的复杂仪式。在这个仪式中，米酒（日本清酒）寄托了对新人的祝福。在神道教祀官和新婚夫妇身旁的木架上整整齐齐地叠放着三只酒杯，新郎首先拿起最顶端的酒杯，随后御神子优雅地往杯子里倒酒。

新郎小心翼翼地啜三小口，意为"三三九度"，加深夫妻间的关系以形成更加牢固的婚姻纽带。然后，新郎把杯子递给新娘，酒杯再次斟满后，新娘也啜三小口酒。

第二杯酒则由新娘先啜三小口后再递给新郎；同样，两位新人按照第一杯酒的流程，再喝第三杯酒。每位参加婚礼的客人也会喝一点米酒，以进一步巩固两个家庭刚刚建立起来的姻亲关系。

在过去，神道教婚礼都在真正的神社进行，而如今则大多在有仿制得极其逼真的神社的酒店里完成。记得有一次，当我抵达婚礼的指定房间时，我大吃一惊，从外面看，这个房间和普通的宴会厅没什么两样，然而，门打开后，映入眼帘的是一座为婚礼精心设计的木结构神社。

这样的婚礼并不表示新婚夫妇已经成为合法夫妻。只有在市政府（新郎和新娘递交正式结婚文件的机构）进行民事登记才能确定其婚姻的合法性。婚礼本身及随后奢华的婚宴与新郎和新娘是否为合法夫妻没有任何关系，只有当他们递交了结婚申请（結婚届け）、完成登记之后才算合法夫妻，这和在欧洲成为合法夫妻的传统一样。

我的一位朋友，为了满足父母有生之年看到她结婚的心愿，举行一场盛大的婚礼，就像真正的婚礼一样，所有的程序一样不落，只是她没有正式登记结婚。因此，从法律上讲，她并未真正结婚，而只是社会意义上的结婚。朋友的父母对于女儿结婚的场面感到心满意足，但他们绝不会知道他们认为已经结婚了的女儿没和自己的丈夫去市政厅登记结婚。那场婚礼也让那些爱管闲事的邻居和亲戚们不再说长道短：她早过了正常结婚年龄，怎么还没结婚呢？

有趣的是，最近在日本全境出现了一种供外国人在酒店和小教堂举行婚礼的家庭小产业。就如搭设神坛一样，酒店也装修了外观逼真的乡村小教堂，并安排了一位主持婚礼的外国牧师。问题是，大部分主持婚礼的牧师是没有牧师任命书的英语教师。因为婚礼对新婚夫妇并没有法律约束力，多半只是做做样子，所以，在日本扮演牧师的人也就无所谓合不合法。另外，大部分举行"教堂"婚礼的新人甚至都不是基督教徒，而是佛教徒或神道教徒。嗯，也可能既是佛教徒又是神道教徒。

不管是选择传统日式婚礼还是决定在教堂举行由牧师主持的西式婚礼，新婚夫妇都要在婚礼过后举办一场婚宴。

紧随婚礼之后的婚宴往往会在举办婚礼的同一家酒店进行，神道教婚礼和基督教婚礼均是如此。一般而言，人们会严格控制受邀参加婚礼的人数，但出席婚宴的宾客数目则会多得多，包括新人的近亲、远亲、朋友、邻居、同事等。

受邀参加婚宴当然是一种荣幸，但收到明显是装着喜帖的厚信封时，却着实让身为大学教授的我犯难，倒不是自己不想参加过往学生的喜庆婚宴，而是自己在日本教书30年来，收到过太多这样的请帖。

每次收到婚宴请帖，受邀宾客都要支付参加婚宴的费用（お祝い，意为贺礼），费用的多少依据宾客与新婚夫妇的亲疏程度以及宾客自身的社会地位而定。当然，总的来说，东京的婚礼招待费比日本其他地区高出不少。

如果设宴家庭享有相当高的社会地位，婚宴则同样可以成为宾客在席间通过用餐和交谈建立业务关系的有利时机。

因此，在东京参加婚宴的费用人均在500至1,000美元之间。我知道，这听起来挺吓人的，但东京的一切消费都更加昂贵，婚宴也不例外。

在我居住的地方，参加婚宴的费用低廉，大概在200至500美元之间；同样，这也依受邀者与新婚夫妇的关系及其在当地的地位而异。这种"参宴费"作为送给新婚夫妇的礼物，用以支付招待宾客的奢华婚宴的费用。

新婚夫妇随后会给每位宾客送上一份"感谢礼"，感谢他们光临自己的婚宴。最近十分流行的做法是，新婚夫妇向每位宾客发放一份清单，让宾客从中挑选自己喜欢的礼品。清单内附明信片，供宾客在上面按喜爱程度依次填写三件最想要的礼物。之后礼品公司开始处理订单，并在一两周内把礼物送到客人家里。

在过去，新婚夫妇会挑选一件礼物送给客人，这种做法带来的问题是，礼物往往可能并不实用。近来这一新的做法让客人得以挑选自己可能真正心仪或需要的礼物。最近，我在一场婚宴上挑了一个电饭锅，在另一场婚宴上选了一个烤面包机。这些"宾客回礼"的价值一般在50美元左右。

婚宴开始时，新婚夫妇被迎进宴会厅，在此，所有客人都在指定的位子上就坐。安排座位必须极其小心谨慎，以避免冒犯参加婚宴的客人。新郎所在公司的老板和新娘单位的领导，通常被安排坐在大厅前部的上座，接着是安排新婚夫妻大学时代的教授们坐在上座。

之后，则会根据客人的地位及其与新婚夫妇的关系，从宴会厅前部往后部依次安排每位客人的座位——宴会厅前部的座位属于上座，后部的座位则是最不招人喜欢的。新婚夫妇的家人通常总是坐在紧挨着厨房门的末排座位，而酒店工作人员就是进出厨房门给客人们上菜的。把最好的座位留给客人，显得新婚夫妇的家人们很谦卑。

日本婚宴以繁文缛节和沉闷刻板而著称。新郎和新娘依然身着婚礼时的传统服饰，和"仲人"，即"媒人"夫妻坐在宴会厅的前部，媒人夫妻是传统上促成这桩婚事的人。如今，传统意义上的"包办婚姻"相比20年前要罕见，但在婚宴过程中由媒人协助新婚夫妇举办婚礼的风俗依然延续下来。

接下来是婚宴致辞，贵宾、公司老板和大学教授会向新婚夫妇发表冗长的致辞，就他们的未来提出建议并祝他们婚姻幸福，白头偕老。这样的致辞通常有标准的主题，如鼓励他们早生贵子；这个主题总是让我觉得好笑，因为新婚夫妇甚至都还没有度蜜月呢。

致辞一结束，婚宴就可以开始了。席间，新婚夫妇在他人陪同下步出宴会厅，新娘更换数套不同款式的婚宴礼服。首先，新娘可能换下白色和服，穿上红色和服，但依然保留在传统婚礼仪式上的假发和妆容；尔后，新娘通常会换上有裙环的晚礼服，新郎则会换上一件燕尾服；最后，新婚夫妇会在婚礼临近结束时换上西式婚服。

当新婚夫妇离开宴会厅更换服装时，常有朋友唱音乐剧和卡啦OK，或有专业乐队演奏，为宾客们助兴。也有客人手里拿着啤酒瓶走来走去，主动给其他客人倒酒。

在日本，人们没有往自己酒杯里倒酒的习惯，而是等着身旁的客人为你倒酒。如果没人注意到你的酒杯空了，你只需主动给其他人倒酒就行了。对方会做出回应，给你倒酒。同样，走上台往新婚夫妇的酒杯里倒上啤酒，表示你赞同他们的结合，也不失为一种礼貌的举止。

婚宴会持续好几个小时，当婚宴结束，最后算下来，总计要花费大约3万

日式婚礼

至5万美元。当然,请的客人越多,新娘所租用的礼服越多,所需的总费用也就越高。因此,当人们收到婚宴邀请时,请帖上绝不会写着"某某携家人"的字样。一家四口都去赴宴的话,那就得破产了,更不用说会打乱婚宴预定的座位安排。只有受邀者本人会前去赴宴,而其配偶或重要的伴侣则会留在家里。

Weddings

Attending a traditional Japanese Shinto wedding is quite a unique and memorable experience. I have attended a number of church weddings and Japanese-style receptions over the years while living here, but only once have I had the privilege of attending a traditional Shinto wedding ceremony.

Most Japanese consider themselves to be both Shintoists and Buddhists, usually opting for a Shinto wedding and a Buddhist funeral. Few cultures offer the opportunity to glide so easily between religions; but Japanese culture does, and aspects of both religious traditions are everywhere you look in Japan.

Many people maintain both a Buddhist altar and Shinto shrine in their homes. Many businesses will display a small Shinto shrine, as well as invite a Shinto priest to bless the construction of a new building. Families invite Buddhist priests to chant sutras during the Obon season (the August holiday where ancestral spirits are invited back to the home) and to perform ceremonies during the anniversaries of loved ones' deaths—combining and borrowing from both religious traditions.

A traditional Shinto wedding ceremony is beautiful in its solemnity and ritual. The bridal couple wears traditional costumes. The groom wears a hakama (a pleated pant-like garment) with a black kimono jacket. The family crest of the groom is usually emblazoned on each side of the upper front of the chest portion of the kimono.

The bride wears a pure-white, delicately embroidered silk kimono (called a "shiromuku") with long sleeves that reach past her knees. The long sleeves signify she is single; once married, she will only wear short-sleeved kimonos indicating that she is married.

The white color of the kimono dates back to the days of the samurai when a woman would show her submission to the family she was marrying into, conveying, "I submit myself to you to be dyed any color to conform to your family's wishes and social standing."

In addition to her white kimono that drags around her feet as she walks, she wears elaborate white makeup and a traditional wig that most Westerners associate with that of what a geisha might wear. Over her wig, she wears a white silk covering. This headpiece is traditionally used to hide the bride's "horns of jealousy".

The ceremony is performed by a Shinto priest and is attended by two shrine maidens who assist in the ritualistic portion of the ceremony. Since Shintoism is an animistic religion revering nature, dating to time immemorial, the ceremony reflects much symbolism connected to its nature-worship tradition.

The elaborate ritual surrounding the exchanging of nuptial cups of sake, though, is the most important part of a Shinto wedding. Blessings are bestowed upon rice wine (sake), where three cups are stacked neatly on a wooden stand near the Shinto priest and wedding couple. The bridegroom first takes the topmost cup and the shrine maiden delicately pours sake into the cup.

Carefully, the groom takes three small sips signifying "san-san-kudo" or the deepening of the relationship to form a stronger connection between the wedding couple. The groom then hands the cup to his bride and it is re-filled and she repeats the ritual.

This is then reversed for the second cup, with the bride first partaking of the sake in three sips before handing it to the groom. Just as the first cup's ritual, the couple then each partakes of the sake from the third cup. Each guest in attendance also drinks a bit of the rice wine, further solidifying the new union which extends to the families.

Traditionally, Shinto weddings were held in actual shrines, but today most are held in hotels that have recreated exact replicas of shrines on the premises. I remember being awestruck when I arrived at the appointed room that looked to me like an ordinary banquet room from the outside; when the doors opened, however, a beautifully constructed wooden shrine, perfectly designed for wedding ceremonies, was revealed.

This ceremony doesn't necessarily mean the couple is legally married. A secular registration at the city office (where the proper papers are submitted by the bride and groom) actually legalizes the union. The wedding itself, and the lavish reception that follows the ceremony, has no bearing whatsoever on the couple's legal status as husband and wife. It only becomes legal once the marriage notice (konintodoke) is submitted and registered, which is similar to the European tradition and custom of legalizing marriages.

A friend of mine once had a huge wedding party to satisfy her parents' desire that she marry before they died. It had all the makings of an authentic wedding, except she never registered it formally...and hence was not really married in the legal sense, just the social sense. Her parents were satisfied that the "appearance" of a marriage took place. They never knew that she and the man they thought she married never registered it with the city office. It also kept prying neighbors and relatives from gossiping about why she hadn't married even though she was past the normal marrying age.

Interestingly, a cottage industry has recently been created for foreigners to perform weddings in hotel and wedding hall chapels all over Japan. Just like there created shrines, hotels decorated a "church" with an authentic looking country chapel and a foreign minister to perform the ceremony. Most of the ministers who perform the weddings are English teachers with no ordination papers. Because the weddings are not legally binding and are mostly for show, there is nothing illegal about a person impersonating clergy or ministers in Japan. Besides, the majority of the couples who have "Christian" church weddings are not even Christian, but are Buddhist or Shinto...well, probably both.

Whether the couple opts for a traditional Japanese-style wedding or decides to have a western-style wedding in a church with a minister, they always hold a reception following the ceremony.

The reception that immediately follows the wedding ceremony (both Shinto and Christian) is often held in the same hotel where the wedding ceremony took place. Normally, the number of guests invited to the actual ceremony is strictly limited, but the reception guest list is much larger, including close family members, extended family, friends, neighbors and work colleagues.

Being invited to a wedding reception is an honor, of course, but as a university professor, I cringe when the telltale thick envelope arrives in the mail. I don't resist joining in the joyous celebrations of former students, but after 30 years of teaching here I receive a lot of invitations.

With each invitation, then, is the obligatory attendance fee (oiwai) that guests are expected to pay for attending the wedding party. The closer the family member is to the couple, as well as the higher the social position of the guest, dictates the amount of money one should give to attend the reception. Wedding receptions in Tokyo, of course, generally command a much higher fee.

Also, if the status of the family who is hosting the reception is fairly high, the reception can then become an opportunity for the guests to network between meal courses and speeches, making it an opportune time to make business contacts.

So, in Tokyo the fee can be anywhere from $500~1,000 per person. This sounds outrageous I know, but everything in Tokyo is more expensive, and wedding parties are no exception.

Where I live, the cost to attend a wedding party is at the bargain price of around $200~500, again depending upon one's relationship to the couple and one's social status in the community. This "attendance fee" is in lieu of giving a gift to the couple and it goes toward paying for the lavish wedding reception and sumptuous meal served to the guests.

In appreciation, the couple then presents each guest with a "thank you gift" for attending their reception. Recently, it has become quite trendy for the couple to give each guest a catalogue from which to choose a gift of their own liking. A postcard is included that the person fills out with three possible selections in the order of what they want most. The catalogue company then processes the order and the item is delivered to the guest's door within a week or two.

In the past, the couple would select a gift to give the guests. The problem was that often it was something that may or may not be useful in a practical sense. This new system allows guests to choose things that they may really want or need. Recently, I have selected an electric wok from one reception, and a toaster oven from another. The "guest's gift" is usually valued at around $50.

As the wedding reception begins, the bridal couple is ushered into the banquet hall where all the guests are seated in assigned seats. Much care and discernment is taken in making these seating arrangements as not offend those in attendance. The groom's company boss and bride's work supervisor are usually given the seats of honor at the front of the hall; next are the bridal couple's university professors who are seated in seats of honor.

The status and relationship of the guest to the couple are then taken into account as each person is seated from front to back—the front being the choice assignments, and the back being the least preferred. Unfortunately, the families of the couple are normally seated all the way in the back next to the kitchen door that is used by the hotel staff to serve the guests. By offering the choicest seats to the guests, the family demonstrates humility and a sense of humbleness.

Wedding receptions in Japan are notorious for their formality and stuffiness. The bride and groom, still dressed in the traditional costumes from the wedding ceremony are seated on a platform at the font of the hall with the "nakoudo", the "go between" couple who traditionally were the ones that arranged the marriage. Today, "arranged marriages" in the traditional sense are much rarer than they were just 20 years ago, but the custom of having the matchmaker assist the couple during the party endures.

Next are the speeches. The honored guests, company bosses and university professors, make rather long speeches to the couple, giving advice to them about their future and wishing them a lifetime of wedded bliss. The speeches often have standard themes that encourage the couple to have children as quickly as possible. This always amuses me because the couple hasn't even gone on their honeymoon yet!

Once the toast is made, then the party may begin. In between courses, the couple is escorted of the hall where the bride changes into several different wedding outfits. From the white kimono, she may change into a red kimono, leaving her wig and make-up on from the traditional ceremony. Next, she will often change into a formal evening gown with a hoop (the groom change into a tux with a tail). Finally, the wedding couple changes into western-style wedding attire at the end of the party.

While the couple is away changing, often times friends will entertain the guests with musical plays, karaoke, or a professional band will play music. The guests meander about, beer bottle in hand, offering to refill other guests' beer glasses.

In Japan, it is customary not to fill your own glass with a beverage, but to wait for the person next to you to fill it for you. If your own glass is empty, and no one has noticed, all you have to do is to offer to fill the other person's glass. The person will then reciprocate by filling your glass. Also, it is polite to go to the platform and offer to refill the bridal's glasses of beer to show one's approval the union.

The wedding reception lasts several hours, and when it is all said and done the total cost can be around $30,000~50,000 for the wedding reception. Of course, the more guests that are invited, and the more changes the bride makes in and out of the rented gowns, increases the total cost. Hence, when someone is invited to a wedding, the envelope never says "and guest". It would bankrupt a family of four to attend a wedding in Japan, not to mention upseting sitting arrangements. Only the person invited attends the wedding leaving his/her spouse or significant other at home.

葬礼

如今，美国的葬礼习俗在文化层面发生了巨大的变化，这种改变体现在参加葬礼者的着装、祭品的种类等方面，祭品可以是鲜花、绿植及纪念品（送给逝者家属以纪念逝者的物件）。甚至葬礼中"歌颂死者生平"这一程序的风格都发生了极大的变化，不再像过去那样阴郁沉闷。总之，近些年来，美国现代葬礼的正式程度已经大大降低，并让参加葬礼者在礼仪方面享有更多的空间。

而日本却不是这样，日本葬礼仍旧非常正式，严格遵守既定的规矩。比如，日本人在参加守灵、葬礼或火化仪式时的穿着都非常正式。

每个参加葬礼的人从头到脚都是黑色装束。穿燕尾服的男士甚至都打着黑色领带。不管是谁，只要见到有人打着黑色领带，就知道此人要么是去参加葬礼，要么是刚参加完葬礼回来。

相反，如果有人穿着黑色西装，打着白色领带，那么他要么是去参加婚礼，要么是刚参加完婚礼回来。男士参加葬礼和婚礼都穿燕尾服，差别就在于领带的颜色。

女士通常选择穿着十分素净（但很正式）的黑色裙装。这些裙装样式独特，通常毫无时尚感可言，而是显得四四方方，十分单调。在这样的场合穿着过于时尚，是一种不敬的表现。手提包和鞋子同样是黑色的，以便和裙子相配。

女性也会穿黑裙出席婚礼，但裙子的样式时尚，并搭配有五颜六色的饰物。女性在参加葬礼时，除了有时可能佩戴灰色的珍珠以外，不会佩戴其他颜色的饰品。

甚至给守灵者准备的食物也是暗色系的,寿司和刺身(生鱼片)因其色彩鲜艳喜庆,极少出现在斋饭之中。

我仅参加过一次斋饭当中有生鱼片的葬礼。死者是曾经担任过国防部长和农业部长的政界名人,由于有很多重要人物出席,根据社交礼仪要准备最高标准的食物,所以生鱼片是免不了的。制备食物的人解决这一文化难题的方法是用灰色的纸裹住装生鱼片的菜碟,以掩盖其鲜亮的颜色。

给痛失亲人者送花是没有问题的,但必须是颜色素雅且没有香味的花。明亮鲜艳的颜色在葬礼上是不合适的,因此挑选白菊花是合适的。在日本,颜色亮丽、香气浓郁的鲜花只适合幸福喜庆的场合。

在日本,参加葬礼时给逝者家属礼金是一种合乎社交礼节的风俗。这种礼金叫做"香典",数额依你与对方的亲疏程度、你在当地的社会地位以及经济条件而定。礼金金额通常为30~50美元。尤为重要的一点是,钱要装入一个用黑白细绳精心绑扎的香典袋里。另外,香典袋内的纸币应是磨损的旧钞,而不是新钞。如果香典钱是新钞,会让人觉得你早就料到了逝者的亡故,因此有时间提前准备新钞。而给新婚夫妇的礼金正好相反,只能是尚未在市面流通的新钞,这表明你专程去银行换取崭新纸钞,说明你认可这桩婚事。结婚礼金如果是旧钞,那可能意味着你对新婚夫妇的结合不甚满意。

这些文化习俗的微妙之处,使得一个外来者想要在一定程度上避免冒犯他人变得十分困难。这些文化传统具有悠久历史,由一个成分高度单一的民族践行和传承。日本人凭借自身的文化背景和处事准则,能够对这些文化暗示心领神会,见机行事。相反,像我这样的外国人,必须自己摸索,反复尝试,最终学会如何行事。

而美国由千差万别的文化背景相互融合构成,民族成分纷繁复杂,所以美国永远都不会拥有如此隐晦的风俗。

如果有人用一张流通过的100美元旧钞作为贺礼送给一对美国新婚夫妇,他们是不会多想的。其中隐含的意义在日本是显而易见的,但要让美国人理解,却需要通过更加直接的方式(比方说,红包里没放有礼金,美国人才会注意到)。

日本和美国操办葬礼的丧葬费,都十分昂贵。参加葬礼的人给逝者家属的礼金可用来支付这笔费用。反过来,为了还送礼者的人情,逝者家属会给他们每人送份小礼物,对他们的慷慨表示深深的谢意。

这些礼物的价值一般在15~20美元之间,并且用白色、灰色或黑色纸张包起来,礼品袋里通常会放一张表达谢意的便条。这些礼物会在参加葬礼者离开时交到他们手上。

我以往参加葬礼时,收到过电话卡、可以兑换大米的票券、手帕和擦手巾等。根据日本的社交礼仪，人们在收到礼金后应该以某种方式还礼，所以，这就是逝者家属必须在葬礼期间或过后不久送参加葬礼者象征性礼物的原因。

此外，很重要的一点是，参加葬礼者需用浅色甚至灰色的墨汁书写香典袋上的内容。同样，用很浓很黑的墨汁写字，会显得逝者的亡故在预料之中，书写者有充足的时间研磨墨汁。用灰色墨汁写字表明，逝者的亡故让人如此震惊，竟来不及好好研墨，只好匆匆调制墨汁，调出来的墨汁就成暗灰色了。

在我任教的大学，有一位女书法家，她总是乐于帮我写这类毛笔字。她在香典袋上写字时的动作是那么轻盈，书法十分漂亮——简直就是一件艺术品。相比之下，我的日语书法就像一个3岁小孩写的一样。

现如今，商店里提供的各种物件，让这些免不了的事变得更加容易。人们可买一支灰色墨汁的自来水笔。所有的超市和便利店都辟有这样一个区域，售卖此类特定文化活动所需的各式礼袋，就如有各种葬礼用的香典袋，同样也有婚礼用的红包及其他更喜庆的场合用的礼袋，这些礼袋有红色的、白色的和金色的。

扫墓者

礼袋越精致，表明里面装的礼金越多，在装饰华丽的礼袋里只装少量的礼金会显得很怪异。因此，可供选择的礼袋多种多样，从很朴素的到很华丽的，一应俱全，如何选择取决于礼金的多少。

日本的葬礼风俗根植于该国古老的传统，这些传统常常可以追溯到远古时代。当然，日本的葬礼风俗是将逝者火化，并将骨灰放到墓园的家族祭坛里（而不是按美国人的惯常做法，将逝者埋在地下）。这种风俗源于佛教，但也是出于实际的考虑,因为日本可用的土地极少,价格高昂,将逝者葬在私人墓地并不现实。

Funeral Rituals

Today, in America, funeral customs have undergone tremendous cultural changes from the way people dress to attend a funeral, to what types of offerings are made in the form of flowers, plants, and keepsake gifts (things given to the family in memory of the deceased person). Even the styles of services have metamorphosed greatly with "celebrations of the person's life" often taking place instead of morose funeral of yesteryear. All in all, modern American funeral rituals have become much less formal in recent years and offer people attending funerals a lot more leeway in the etiquette department.

Not so in Japan, Japanese funerals are still very formal with a prescribed protocol that is strictly adhered to. For instance, Japanese people dress very formal to attend the wake, funeral, or cremation ceremony.

Each attendee dresses from head to toe in black. Men even don a black tie to wear with their tuxedo-like suits. Anyone who sees a man wearing a black tie knows he is on his way to or has just been to, a funeral.

In contrast, a man wearing a black suit with a white tie is either on his way to or is returning from, a wedding. The tuxedo-like suit doubles for both occasions; the color of the tie is what makes difference.

Women usually opt to wear very plain (but formal) black dresses. These dresses are unique in that usually they are not at all fashionable but are often boxy and drab in appearance. It would be disrespectful to stand out at such an event due to stylish apparel. Matching black handbag and shoes are also worn.

Women will also wear black dresses to weddings, but these are usually stylish with colorful accessories. A woman attending a funeral wears no added color with the exception of maybe pearls, which are sometimes gray in color.

Even the meal that is served to the attendees at a wake is comprised of foods that are muted in color. Sushi and sashimi (raw fish) are rarely served at funeral-related dinners because of their bright and happy colors.

Only once have I attended a funeral where such sashimi was served. It was for a well-known politician who was once the Defence Minister and Agriculture Minister, with so many important people in attendance, social protocol required that the meal be of highest quality which meant sashimi should be served. The way the caters got around this cultural conundrum was to wrap the plate lightly with the gray colored paper to hide the bright color.

It is appropriate to offer flowers to people who have suffered a loss, but the flowers should be subdued in color and have no scent to them at all. Bright garish colors are considered inappropriate at funerals with white chrysanthemums being the flowers of choice. Scented flowers in bright colors are reserved for only happy, joyous occasions in Japan.

In Japan, it is customary and socially correct to make an offering of money to the deceased person's family when attending a funeral. This money is called "koden", with the amount given dependent upon how close you were to the person, your social position in the community, and/or your own financial ability. The usual amount of money offered is around $30~$50. It is extremely important that the money given is put in a special envelop that has black and white cords elaborately tied around it. Also the bills should be old and well-worn—not new. Offering a new bill as a funeral offering could give the appearance that the death was expected and you had time in advance to prepare "new" bills for the occasion. The opposite is true when offering money to a wedding couple; only new yet to be circulated bills, should be given. This shows that you made a special effort to visit the bank in order to prepare crispy new bills which shows you approve of the wedding. Used bills for a wedding could convey that you are not that pleased about the union.

The subtlety involved in these types of cultural practices make it very hard for an outsider not to offend people on some level. These cultural cues are based on a long tradition, practiced amongst a very homogenous group of people. Japanese people intuitively know such implied hints and can read the situation instantly, relying on their own cultural background and knowledge "to do the right thing". Outsiders like me, on the other hand, must fumble around and learn by trial and error.

America, with its patchwork of ethnic groups, could never have such indirect customs due to wide variety of cultural backgrounds that have fused together to make the United States the country it is today.

An American bridal couple would not give it a second thought if someone gave them a $100 bill that had been in circulation; the hidden meaning so apparent in Japan would have to be more direct for Americans to get it (e.g. putting no money in envelope—now that would get an American's attention).

The cost of a funeral in Japan, like in the United States can be exorbitantly expensive. The monetary offering paid by each attendee helps to defray the cost incurred upon the family. In return, in order to cancel out any obligation to the person giving monetary gift, the family then prepares a small gift for attendees as a token of their profound appreciation for their generosity extended to them.

These gifts are usually valued at $15~20, and are wrapped in white, gray or black paper; usually included in the gift-bag is a note of appreciation from the family. The attendees are handed these gifts when they leave the funeral.

In the past, I have received phone cards, coupons to exchange for rice, handkerchiefs and hand towels in such instances. Japanese social etiquette requires that the gift of money be reciprocated, in some way, hence the reason why the family is obliged to offer guests a token gift at the funeral or soon after.

In addition, it is important for the attendees to write on the offering envelope in very light, even gray ink. Again, to use a rich, dark ink would suggest that the death was expected and the person writing had ample time to prepare the ink from an ink-stone. Using gray ink conveys that the death was such a shock that the person had no time to properly concoct the ink, hurriedly mixing it, resulting in a dull, grayish colored ink.

A woman at my university is a master calligrapher and she is always ready and willing to help me with these calligraphy-related duties. When she writes on a funeral envelope, it is ever so light and her writing is so beautiful—a work of art. My Japanese writing, in contrast, looks like it was done by a three-year-old child.

Nowadays, stores offer a huge assortment of items to make these necessary tasks easier. One can purchase a pen that automatically writes in a grayish ink. All supermarkets and convenience stores have a section that sells the various types of envelopes needed for these culture-specific obligations. Just as there is an assortment of envelopes for funerals, there are those for weddings and other happier occasions that come in red, white and gold.

The more elaborate envelopes signify the amount of money placed inside it.

It would be strange to use a highly decorated envelope with only a small amount of money placed inside it. So there are all kinds of envelopes to choose from—the very plain to the ostentatious—depending upon the size of your offering.

Funeral customs in Japan are steeped in tradition that often goes back to ancient times. Of course, the burial custom in Japan is to cremate the deceased and then place the ashes in a family altar at a gravesite (and not bury the person in the ground, like we normally do in the US). This custom has its origins in Buddhism, but is also done out of practicality. The scarcity of available land, and the exorbitant cost of land, makes it impractical to bury people in individual plots.

第六部分
日本节日

Part 6
Japanese Holidays

新年

　　日本的新年和美国的圣诞节十分相似,是家人团聚的节日,这个时候,亲人们会从离家或远或近的地方赶回来,聚在一起庆祝。日本人会在新年前陆续回到老家准备过年,就和美国人在圣诞节前赶回家过圣诞一样。

　　正月,即新年,是日本所有一年一度的节庆活动中最重要也最为隆重的。大部分日本上班族从12月30日到1月3日休假以便在新年假期和家人团聚。

　　但在12月底放假之前,全日本的办公室和学校都会进行一次彻底的大扫除,需要把桌子和书架从墙边搬开以便清扫每个角落和每处缝隙,把闲置的东西扔掉,并确保把一切重新井井有条地摆放好,以迎接新年。许多家庭也会在岁末打扫卫生,把里里外外收拾得干干净净,迎接新年的到来。

　　在日本庆祝新年期间,我养成的一个习惯是日本称为"初诣"(或指在新年首次到神社或寺庙参拜)的传统。在新年的午夜时分,我穿着厚实保暖的衣服,和朋友们一道,冒着严寒,步行前往当地的神道教神社朝拜。

　　神社里总是一派喜气洋洋的氛围,人们兴高采烈地选购破魔箭、护身符,以求接下来的一整年都能有好的运气和健康的身体。

　　当人群走向神社正前方时,大家会依次拍拍手,向神供奉一枚硬币。并不是所有人都会在新年的半夜前往神社朝拜,真是谢天谢地,要不然人群会挤得挪不开步。人们可于1月7日左右正式前往寺庙或神社参拜,祈求来年全年都走好运。

　　多年前,我和朋友一家在东京度过了一个新年。新年当天,我们先搭乘一趟趟巴士,然后转了几趟火车前往全日本最著名的神社——明治神宫。在此之前,我从未见过这么多人挤在如此有限的空间里。人群的冲力把我们往前挤,我们无力地试图投掷硬币。想想真是后怕,要是有人摔倒了,肯定会被活活踩死。

　　我宁愿到家附近的一座寺庙参拜。在那儿,我几乎总能碰到熟人——同事或邻居——这让我们可以当面互致新年问候,"明けまして、おめでとうございます"(恭贺新禧)是日语中祝别人"新年快乐"时的常用语。

　　佛教寺庙里的大钟会从半夜12点开始连续敲击108下,以驱赶过去一年里的晦气。日本全境的公共电视都会播放全日本著名寺庙的住持庄重地敲响新年钟声的画面。

日本的孩子们——从蹒跚学步的幼童到大学生——都热切期盼新年的到来，因为他们可以收到成年的亲戚朋友给的"お年玉"（压岁钱），就是装在小信封里的现金。这一习俗就跟美国孩子在圣诞节收到礼物一样。

很难说给多少钱合适，但我通常是按孩子的年龄给的，就是几岁就给几张100日元。这个习惯是从我侄子生日时我给他钱开始的，他几岁我就给他几美元。当他8岁时，看到从我给他的生日卡里掉出来八张一美元钞票时，兴奋极了。

我这个划算的给钱办法在日本似乎同样管用。其实，100日元还不到1美元，但这是最接近1美元的日元币值。因此，考虑到每年的通货膨胀，我认为逐年多给现金，也许是最合理的。如此一来，孩子长到20岁，就能从我这得到大约20美元。

街坊四邻家家户户都会在门前挂"注连绳"（由秸秆编成的绳索，上面吊着白色的小纸条）。这种装饰不仅表明该户家庭请"年神"或"新年的神灵"于新年之际来家里暂住，也用来驱除鬼怪，不让鬼怪进家门。

典型的日本年菜（御节料理）盛放在可堆叠的漆盒里，里面有各式日本美食。这些特色美食极耐储存，不易腐坏，因此它们在年前就准备好了，这样就省去了新年头几天花很长时间在厨房制作食物的麻烦。

流行的传统美食有炖黑豆、盐渍鲱鱼籽、红烧沙丁鱼干、醋腌牛蒡、火炙鱼酱、方形甜蛋卷、火炙虾、鲷鱼、萝卜沙拉，这些菜品都有颜色鲜艳的蔬菜和水果做配饰，十分讲究。

很多家庭会在当地超市购买现成的御节料理，或者事先从喜欢的餐馆订购盒装菜品，这样就能节省更多准备饭菜的时间。这些菜品都被精致地装在人造漆盒里。

有时候，我会以日本传统的方式招待外地来的客人，以此迎接新年。不过，我的确也会将一些传统的美国新年菜品和传统日本料理搭配在一起招待客人。因为对于一个来自印第安纳州的人而言，盐渍鲱鱼、水煮鱼酱和黑豆无法满足喜欢吃蜜汁火腿、芝士通心面以及咸牛肉配卷心菜的我。

New Year's Day

New Year's Day in Japan most resembles Christmas Day in the United States in that it is a family holiday where relatives travel from near and far to celebrate the holiday together. Before New Year's Eve, Japanese family members begin to arrive at their ancestral home to prepare for the New Year, just like American families do before Christmas.

Shougatsu, or New Year's, is by far the most important and most celebrated of any of Japan's annual events. Most Japanese workers are given from December 30th—January 3rd off from their jobs in order to be with their families during this holiday.

Before leaving work at the end of December, though, offices and schools all over Japan do a thorough and compete cleaning. This "osoji" is a deep cleaning that requires pulling out desks and bookshelves from the walls to clean every nook and cranny, throwing out unused items, and making sure all is arranged back nicely for the New Year. Many families do similar cleaning of homes at the end of the year to make everything fresh and clean to bring in the New Year.

One custom that I have adopted herein Japan during the New Year celebration is the tradition of "hatsu-moude" or the first shrine or temple visit of the New Year. At midnight, on New Year's Eve, I bundle up in warm clothes and traipse out into the bitter cold to the local Shinto shrine with friends to pay my respects.

The atmosphere at the shrine is always jovial and happy; people are excitedly buying lucky arrows, talismans, and amulets to ensure they have good luck and good health throughout the next year.

As the hordes of people make their way to the front of the shrine, everyone takes a turn to clap their hands and offer a coin offering to the "kami" or gods. Not all people visit a shrine at midnight on New Year's Eve, thank goodness, as there would be no space to move. Officially, one can visit a temple or shrine until around January 7th in order to get the full effect of good fortune throughout the next year.

Many years ago, I spent the New Year's holiday in Tokyo with a friend's family. On New Year's Day we took a bus, then a couple of trains, to get to the most famous of all shrines in Japan—Meiji Shrine. I have never in my life seen more people crammed into a finite space. The momentum of the crowd carried us to the front as we feebly tried to toss our coins against the surge of people pushing us by. It was actually scary because if anyone had fallen, surely the person would have been trampled to death.

I prefer visiting the temple near my home. I always run into a number of people I know—colleagues and neighbors which allows us to exchange verbal New Year's greetings to one another. "Akemashite omedetou gozaimasu" is the common Japanese phrase used to wish someone a "Happy New Year".

Huge bells at Buddhist temples are gonged 108 times, starting at midnight, to chase away the evils of the past year. From north to south, famous temples all over Japan are featured on public television, showing the priest of the temple solemnly ringing the bell.

Japanese children—from toddlers to university students—anxiously anticipate New Year's Day because they are given "o-toshidama", a small envelope with money, by adult relatives and friends. This custom is akin to American kids receiving presents on Christmas Day.

It is hard to know how much is appropriate, but I generally give 100 yen for each year of the child's age. This is a custom I started with my nephew giving him $1 for each year of his age on his birthday. When he turned eight, he was quite excited when 8 one-dollar bills tumbled out of his birthday card.

Similarly, my cost-effective system seems to work well here. Actually, 100 yen is a bit less than a dollar, but is the closest denomination to an American buck. So, taking into consideration yearly inflation, I figure this gradual yearly increase of cold, hard cash is probably about as fair as any; when the kids turn 20-year-old, they can expect around $20.

Homes all around my neighborhood display "shimenawa" (a sacred rope of straw with small strips of white paper dangling down) on the front doors. This is to distinguish the home as being one that is a temporary domicile for the "toshigami" or New Year deities that visit the home during this season; it is also used to discourage any malevolent spirits from entering the home.

A typical New Year's Day meal (osechi ryouri) is served in stackable lacquered boxes filled with a variety of Japanese delicacies. These specialty foods are highly preserved, hence prepared well in advance of the day, eliminating the need to spend endless hours in the kitchen cooking during the first few days of the New Year.

Popular and traditional foods include stewed black soybeans, salted herring roe, dried sardines cooked in soy sauce, cooked burdock marinated in vinegar, broiled fish paste, sweet omelet squares, broiled shrimp, sea bream, radish (daikon) salad, and all daintily garnished with brightly colored vegetables and fruits.

Many families purchase ready-made osechi ryouri at their local supermarket, or order the boxed meal in advance from a favorite restaurant, which cuts the preparation time down even more. These are delicately arranged in faux lacquer boxes.

I sometimes bring in the New Year in typical Japanese fashion by entertaining out-of-town guests for the holiday. I do, however, plan to have some traditional American New Year dishes mixed in with the traditional Japanese ones. Salted herring, broiled fish paste, and black soybeans won't satiate this Hoosier's love of honeyed ham, macaroni and cheese, and corn beef and cabbage!

女孩节和男孩节

"雏祭り",又称"女孩节",是每年3月3日在日本举办的玩偶节。庆典上允许出现一切女孩子气的东西,好让女孩们尽显少女情怀。

通常,女孩们会穿上传统和服,用"菱饼"(菱形米饼)这种特别的食品招待朋友,为的是让大家坐下来观赏精心陈列在多层台架上的玩偶。这些玩偶因为太过精致,所以绝不会像一般玩具那样被拿到浴缸或沙箱里玩。

一整套玩偶通常有15个左右。代表皇帝和皇后的两个主要玩偶总是置于台架顶层,身着传统宫廷服饰,其两侧各放置一只微型灯笼,身后则是漂亮的镀金屏风。下面几层摆着皇帝和皇后的随从,包括男女侍者和宫廷乐师。

再往下的几层交替摆放着皇帝和皇后个人物品——箱子、放着食物的桌子、乐器,甚至还有牛车。

母亲们常常把从自己母亲那里获得的玩偶套装送给自己的女儿。这套玩偶往往世代相传,每一位新主人都会为这套玩偶添置新的成员。展出的玩偶套装像极了圣诞树,仅供观赏,而非把玩,在陈列大约两周之后会被撤下台架,之后小心翼翼地包好收起来,等来年再次展出。

女孩节期间,许多百货大楼会出售玩偶套装。购置一整套玩偶需要2000美元以上,这样的高价令人震惊不已。这也就是许多家庭在小女孩出生时将具有感情价值的玩偶和新的玩偶收藏在一起的原因。

我曾受邀到邻居家参加女孩节。这家的小女孩5岁左右,很自豪地向我展示她收藏的玩偶,指着每一件玩偶向我解释它们分别是什么人物和什么物件。当时我们都坐着，一边吃点心，一边观赏她所展示的这些壮观的传统工艺品。

不可不提的是，日本的男孩们同样会在每年5月5日庆祝自己的节日（也叫儿童节）。为了庆祝这个节日，有男孩子的家庭会在屋外用杆子竖起巨大的鲤鱼形条幅，使其迎风飘扬，这些条幅日语叫做"鯉のぼり"，代表男子汉气概，因为鲤鱼是一种坚强勇敢的鱼类。

这一传统其实源自中国，和中国神话中一条鲤鱼逆流而上，最终神奇地化身为龙的故事有关。日本自身的传说一直认为鲤鱼与众不同，这也增添了鲤鱼的魅力。

日本家庭屋外飘扬着的鲤鱼旗的大小及数量，代表了这个家庭里男孩的年龄和人数。当然，最长的条幅代表长子，第二大的条幅代表次子，以此类推。即使住公寓的人家也会根据家中几个儿子的年龄，依次悬挂尺寸短小一些的条幅。

近年来，一些现代日本家庭对这一风俗做了调整，他们为每个孩子分别挂上一面旗幡——不仅是男孩，也包括女孩。当然，正统主义者会恪守性别的差异，用玩偶庆祝女孩节，用鲤鱼旗庆祝男孩节。

两个节日的庆祝方式各异，却同样令人叹为观止。玩偶是精湛手工艺的典范，而在空中高高飘扬的鲤鱼旗也十分壮观。西方人因这两种物件独有的日本韵味而被深深吸引。

很多年前，一个在日本生活的美国朋友觉得，用这些条幅做成浴帘，一定十分独特有趣。但问题是，鲤鱼旗的裁剪和缝制方式独特，要把它们改制成浴帘绝非易事。

女孩节的玩偶

这位美国朋友决定写信给制造鲤鱼旗的公司，要求购买一匹未经裁剪和缝制的鲤鱼旗布料；公司对她的想法很感兴趣，欣然将布料免费赠送给她。现在，每当客人们用过她家点缀得如此漂亮的浴室后，她都会就此津津乐道一番。

Girls' Day and Boys' Day

"Hina Matsuri" or "Girl's Day" is a doll festival held every year on March 3rd in Japan. This celebration recognizes everything girlish, allowing little girls to be little girls.

A common practice is for girls to dress up in traditional kimono to entertain their ends with special treats—"hishimochi" (diamond shaped rice cakes). The idea is to sit and admire the meticulously displayed doll collection arranged on a multi-tiered platform. These dolls are never played within the bathtub or the sandbox. They are much too delicate to be touched routinely.

A complete collection usually has around 15 dolls. The two main dolls, representing the emperor and empress, are always placed on the top tier dressed in traditional court costumes, flanked on both sides by miniature lanterns, with beautiful gold screens behind them. Arranged on the lower levels are their retinues: attendants, handmaidens, and court musicians.

Interspersed on each of the lower levels are accouterments associated with the emperor and empress—chests, tables with food, musical instruments, and even an ox-drawn carriage.

Frequently a little girl's doll set is given to her by her mother, who had hers given to her by her mother. It is often a generational heirloom, with each new owner adding to the collection. It is displayed much like a Christmas tree in that it is only to be admired, not touched, and stays set up for around two weeks before it is taken down. It is then carefully packed away until the next year when the process is repeated.

During this season, many department stores have doll sets for sale. I was shocked at how expensive it is to purchase a compete set. The prices ranged from two-thousand to several-thousand dollars. This is why many families combine older pieces that have sentimental value with newer pieces as little girls are born into the family.

Neighbors once invited me to their home to partake in this celebration. The little girl, around 5-year-old, was so proud to show me her collection. She pointed out each piece explaining who and what it was. We all then sat and had refreshments while gazing at this most spectacular display of craftsmanship and tradition.

Not to be left out, boys also celebrate their own day in Japan on May 5th every year (also called "Children's Day"). To mark this day, families who have boys fly huge carp-shaped streamers on poles outside their homes. These banners are called "koinobori" in Japanese and represent manly virtues, because the carp is such a hardy and gallant fish.

The tradition is actually Chinese in origin and is related to a Chinese myth about a carp that swam upstream and magically became a dragon. Japan had long considered the carp to be special in its own lore, so this just added to its appeal.

The size and number of carp banners tying outside a Japanese home represent the age and number of boys living in the household. Of course, the longest streamer symbolizes the oldest son, the next biggest size, is the second son and so on. Even people who live in apartments will display shorter versions in graduated order according to how many sons the family has.

In recent years, some modern Japanese families have adapted the custom to include all of their children by displaying a fag for each child—not only for sons but also for daughters. Purists, of course, stick to the segregation of the sexes, celebrating Girls' Day with dolls, and Boys' Day with flying carps.

Both events are spectacular in different ways. The dolls are exquisite examples of master craftsmanship and the carp streamers look so majestic blowing in the wind high above the ground. Westerners are attracted to both types of objects because of their "Japaneseness".

Many years ago, an American friend living here thought that the banners would make a unique and interesting shower curtain. The problem was the carp banners were cut and sewn in such a way that made it difficult to convert them into a shower curtain.

She decided to write the company that makes the carp banners and asked to buy a set that hadn't been cut and sewn. The company was so impressed with her idea that they sent her the unsown, uncut cloth of the carps free of charge. She now has quite the conversation piece after guests use her beautifully accented bathroom.

7-5-3

在日本，一年之中我最喜欢的日子是 11 月 15 日。这一天，全日本成千上万的孩子会身着色彩鲜艳的丝质和服和袴裙（一种男孩子穿的褶状裤装）去神道教神社参拜。

这一节日实际上叫做"7-5-3"，用来庆祝日本儿童成长过程中的重要节点。很多育有多个孩子的夫妻，恰逢最大的孩子 7 岁，中间那个 5 岁，最小的 3 岁时，就会庆祝这个节日。当然不可能总是这种情况，但我知道几个家庭，他们的 3 个孩子之间都相差 2 岁。

这一传统可追溯到几百年前，但其真正起源无法确知。我曾读过一篇文章，说庆祝该节日与别的文化习俗中成人礼类似。在日本，孩子被认为是"上帝的礼物"，只有当他们长到 7 岁时才成为真正的人，也许这就是 7 岁这个年龄在日本文化中十分重要的原因。

小女孩长到 3 岁，头发已经长长，才可以扎成马尾；长到 7 岁则会收到人生中的第一条"带"（一种用来系和服的宽带）。而小男孩会在 5 岁时收到人生中第一条"袴裙"。

这个节日最初是随着商业化浪潮的到来，百货公司为了促销而宣传推广开来的。在商店还没对这一特殊节日所穿的和服和袴裙进行广告宣传时，主要是东京地区庆祝这一节日。但在和服制造商和童装店的推动下，庆祝该节日很快就演变成了一项全国性的传统。

近些年来，我发现越来越多的孩子在这一天身着西装去神道教神社参拜。这未免是件憾事，因为孩子们身着精致的日本传统服饰的魅力实在太大了。

面对当前严峻的经济形势，做父母的也变得更加实际了。由于这些传统服装十分昂贵，并且确实就穿那么一次。给孩子们买一些在开学典礼、幼儿园毕业典礼等其他重要场合也能穿的服装更加明智。

带孩子去神社参拜背后的初衷是感谢神道教诸神赐予孩子健康，祈求孩子将来健康成长，吉星高照，学业有成。

可以想象，这个节日对参与其中的祖父母来说，也是难忘的时刻，他们用相机不断地拍照，捕捉孩子们一生一次的仪式。大部分日本人都能拿出这样一张照片给你看，照片中，儿时的他们毕恭毕敬地站在神社前，身旁是他们的父母。

尽管11月15日不是日本的法定节日，但日本人普遍会进行庆祝。对于去神社参拜和照相，父母和孩子们一样十分激动。这让我觉得，这个节日和美国的复活节有几分相似，两者都与宗教有关，孩子们购买特别的服装进行祭拜活动。尽管没有复活节兔子，一大篮一大篮的糖果，或是藏在院子或屋子里待孩子们寻找的彩蛋，但日本孩子在这一天却可以享受特别的糖果。

除了孩子们盛装打扮外，许多母亲也会身着和服，这使得当天的景象更加壮观。日本妇女在十分特别的场合才穿和服，平常很少见她们穿和服。在我居住的地方，只有较年长的、从事传统工作及在日本料理店上班的妇女日常穿着和服。

有一年，在这个特别的节日里，我造访了冲绳。在这个热带岛屿上看到所有孩子都穿着和服和袴裙真是一件赏心悦目的乐事。

7-5-3

One of my favorite days of the year in Japan is November 15. On this day, thousands of little children all over Japan dress in brightly colored silk kimono and hakama (a pleated pant like garment that boys wear) to visit Shinto shrines.

The festival is actually called "shichi-go-san" (literally seven-five-three) which marks milestone ages in a Japanese child's development. Many couples who have more than one child will have them so when the oldest is seven, the middle child is five, and the youngest child is three. Of course this isn't always possible, but I know several families whose three children are spaced with two years between each one.

This tradition goes back hundreds of years, but its true origin isn't exactly known. I read once that these celebrations are similar to rites of passage that other cultures observe; in Japan, children were once regarded as "gifts of God" until they turn seven, at which time they become normal human beings. Perhaps that is why the age of seven is significant in Japanese culture.

The age of three marks the first time that a little girl's hair is long enough to be put into a bun; and the age of seven marks the time a little girl receives her first "obi" (a wide sash worn with kimono). The age of five represents the time when little boys receive their first "hakama".

This festival is an example of one that was promulgated originally by department stores with the advent of commercialization. Traditionally, this festival was mainly centered in the Tokyo area until modern times when stores began advertising kimono and hakama for this special occasion. Quickly, it became a nationwide tradition pushed along by kimono makers and children's clothing stores.

In recent years, I have noticed more and more children wearing Western style clothes to visit the Shinto shrine on this day. It is unfortunate, because the charm of seeing the children dressed in their finest Japanese traditional costumes is quite extraordinary.

Today's parents, in these tough economic times, are being more practical. The outfits are very costly and only worn one time really. It makes more sense to buy the children clothes that they can wear for other important occasions, such as the opening ceremony at school, graduation from kindergarten, etc.

The idea behind taking children to a shrine is to thank the Shinto gods for good health, and to ask for future good health, fortune, and success in school.

As one can imagine, this is a great time for grandparents who also get into the act with cameras rolling, and clicking away to capture this once in a life time ritual. Most Japanese people can show you a photo of themselves at these ages standing stoically in front of the shrine with their parents beside them.

Although November 15th is not a national holiday in Japan, it is widely celebrated and parents get as excited about visiting a shrine to take photos as the children do. It reminds me a little bit like Easter in the United States. Both are religiously based, during which children wear special clothes for attending worship services. Although there is no Easter bunny, big baskets of candy, or colored eggs to find hidden about the yard and house, Japanese children do get spoiled with special treats on this day.

In addition to the children dressing up, many mothers wear kimonos on this day which makes it more spectacular. For very special occasions, Japanese women wear kimono, but it is rare to see women wearing kimono as everyday dress. A number of elderly women from where I live and women who work in traditional jobs or in Japanese-style restaurants still wear kimono, but it isn't an everyday occurrence to see women dressed in this traditional costume.

One year, I visited Okiawa on this special day. It was so nice to see all of the children on this tropical island dressed in their finest kimono and hakama.

成人礼

每年1月的第2个星期一，日本列岛全境的年轻人都会参加一个庆祝自己成年的庆典——"成人の日"。

成人礼当天，在上一个公历年里年满20岁的年轻人会身着盛装：女性身穿精致的和服，而男性则大多身着深色的西装。

男性会在大学毕业之际穿着同一套西装参加求职面试；而选择购置和服及腰带的女性，往往会将其作为自己婚礼当天正式的替换服装之一。

然而，许多女性选择租借而不是花高价购买一套和服参加成人礼。现今，人们极少穿和服，因此许多女性选择在成人礼、毕业典礼及婚礼当天租借和服。尽管为不同场合租借和服的费用累加起来相当高昂，但仍然比自己买一套带刺绣真丝腰带的纯丝质高档和服来得低廉。

全日本的市政府都会通过安排本市达官要人演讲、办招待会和拍集体照的方式，为刚成年的年轻人举行庆典。年轻人会回到家乡，和老同学相聚，一起庆祝自己成年。

近年来，由于人们对上述活动的兴致有所减退，成人礼的仪式也相应做了一些改变，以吸引更多年轻人参加。传统的演讲如同布道，高谈阔论成年的重要性及每个新晋的成年人对社会负有的责任。

几年前，在一个小镇举办的成人礼上，场面糟糕至极，演讲者与听众发生了冲突，这在日本相当罕见。当时，年轻人觉得演讲无聊透顶，就大声聊天或通电话，致使演讲者反复批评年轻人的粗鲁举止，他也因此被轰下台。在另一次成人礼上，一些男孩子在演讲期间竟做出燃放鞭炮的蠢事，爆炸声十分尖厉刺耳。

近年来，日本各地的市政办公室都在努力使庆祝活动跟上时代潮流，通过邀请更受欢迎的演讲者以吸引更多的年轻人参与其中，同时也让成人礼更加趣意盎然。

日本庆祝成人礼的历史大约始于7世纪。最初的成人礼没有具体的年龄规定，男孩子个子长到大约140厘米时，便会留更成熟的成人发式，穿成人的服装，还会起一个成人名字。举办成人礼的时间为10~16岁之间的任意年纪，全凭家人决定。

成人礼过后，男孩就被视为成人社会中的一员，可以参与各种成人事务，比如宗教仪式，甚至结婚。女孩通常在12~16岁之间参加类似的成人礼。

日本人传统的成年年龄是20岁。年满20岁的年轻人可以饮酒、抽烟和赌博（年满18岁的日本年轻人可以合法驾驶和投票）。

在成人礼当天前往神社或寺庙参拜是一项极受欢迎的传统。很多年前，我在东京时适逢这一全国性节日，并造访了位于东京市中心的浅草神社。

成群身着西装的年轻男子及穿和服的女士在狭窄的街道上碎步疾行，朝神庙赶去。街道两旁，传统商铺林立，年轻人正在选购诸如护身符之类的纪念品，作为拜访这一著名神社的纪念。

看到这么多身着盛装的年轻人，在神社嬉闹说笑，为自己完全成为成年人而兴奋不已，真是一种独特的经历。我想，他们的感受和年满18岁从高中毕业、初次体验"长大成人"应承担的责任（至少社会是如此看待的）的美国年轻人没什么两样。

然而，不同之处在于，在美国绝大多数的州，年轻人得再等3年才能合法饮酒，而日本的年轻人在20岁时就能一次享受所有成人权利。

成人礼

Coming of Age Ceremony

Every year, on the second Monday of January, Japanese young people from all over the archipelago attended a ceremony to mark their "coming of age" into adulthood—"sei jin no hi".

On this day, young people (who turned the age of 20 over the past calendar year) dress up in their finest clothes—women in elaborate kimono and men mostly in dark business suits.

The men will wear these same suits to interview for jobs once they graduate from university, and women who choose to purchase kimono and obi (sash) often wear it as one of the formal changes of a bride makes on her wedding day.

Many women, however, opt to rent a kimono for the day instead of incurring the huge expense to buy one for this ceremony. The kimono is worn so seldom nowadays that many women rent kimonos for the day, their graduation day and for their wedding day. Taking into account the entire cost of rental fees for the various occasions, although quite dear, is still cheaper than personally buying a high-grade pure silk kimono with an embroidered silk obi.

Municipalities all over Japan hold celebrations for the new adults with speeches by city dignitaries, receptions, and formal group photos. Young people return to their hometowns for the celebrations, meeting up with old classmates to celebrate their adulthood together.

In recent years, some changes have been made to attract more young people to attend these gatherings because interest in such activities has waned over the years. Traditionally, the speeches were sermon-like, pontificating about the importance of adulthood and the responsibility each new adult had to society.

A number of years ago, the situation was so bad at one ceremony in a small town that a confrontation between the speaker and attendees occurred, which is quite rare in Japan. The young adults were so bored that they began to chat loudly with each other and on their cellphone, causing the speaker to lash out with a tirade against the young adults, chastising them for their rude behavior. They booed him off the stage. At another ceremony, some boys engaged in tom foolery by setting off firecrackers during the speech which caused a huge raucous sound.

Recently, city offices around Japan have tried to update their activities to not only attract a higher number of young people to attend, but to make it more interesting for them by inviting more trendy speakers.

Historically, the Coming of Age ceremony has been observed in Japan since about the 7th century. Originally there was no particular requlation about age, but boys who reached the height of about 140 centimeters would embrace more mature adultlike hairstyles and clothing; also they would receive adult names. These usually occurred anywhere between the age of 10~16 with the ceremony being held at the discretion of the family.

After the ceremony, the boy was considered to be a member of adult society, allowing him to participate in adult affairs including religious ceremony and even marriage. Girls had a similar ceremony usually between the age of 12~16.

Traditionally, adulthood in Japan occurs at the age of 20. At this age, Japanese young adults can drink alcohol, smoke tobacco, and gamble (Japanese young people are eligible to drive at the age of 18 and now they can vote).

A popular tradition on Coming of Age ceremony is to visit a shrine temple. Many years ago, I happened to be in Tokyo on this national holiday and visited Asakusa shrine in central Tokyo.

Groups of young men in suits and kimono clad women were scurrying up and down the narrow street leading to the shrine. Along the street, traditional shops line with both sides. The young adults were buying mementos like amulets and talismans, to commemorate their visit to this well-known shrine.

This was a unique experience to see so many young people in their Sunday finest bantering about the shrine excited at being full-fledged adult. I imagined the feeling is not too much unlike that of a young adult turning 18 and graduating from high school, experiencing for the first time the responsibility of being "grown-up" in the eyes of society.

One difference, though, is that American young adult has to wait another 3 years in most states to be able to have a drink legally—in Japan, all rights and privileges of adulthood are given in one flail of swoop at the age of 20.

睡魔节和盂兰盆节

每逢夏季八月，青森县和我曾居住过的弘前市都会举办睡魔节活动。节日期间，一辆辆巨大的扇形花车由众多身穿传统服装的人拉着，沿主干道行进。全国各地的人都会前来参加这个家喻户晓的节日。

人们还会拉着名为"太鼓"的大鼓，并伴随敲鼓的节奏行进。弘前市的节日活动比青森县的要沉闷得多。在我们弘前市的庆典上，人们会用非常舒缓且有节奏感的声音齐声欢唱"ya-ya-do"。

在青森县，拉花车的人们一边用单脚跳跃，一边尖声叫着"ra-se-ra，ra-se-ra"，一副疯疯癫癫的模样。拉花车的人全身上下挂满了用细绳吊着的铃铛，会向街道两旁观看庆典的人群投掷，而现场观众则会竞相争抢。孩子们特别喜欢收集铃铛，多多益善。

这两个节日庆典上的花车做成了色彩鲜艳、精心构造的巨大纸质传奇人物形象。节日期间会进行"最佳花车"竞赛。公司、学校和各个组织会提前数周夜以继日地忙碌，为的就是让这些美轮美奂的花车栩栩如生。这些花车都是在严格保密的情况下闭门制作完成的，或者用帐篷包裹得严严实实。

这是一个夜间节日，花车里面的灯都点亮，所以花车在黑夜的映衬下熠熠生辉。此情此景十分不可思议。我的一个朋友在主干道上有一家酒吧，长长的花车队伍会从那里经过，所以我总会在酒吧二楼预订一个靠窗的座位，坐在那里，鸟瞰那些花车。

我听说，这个节日最初是为了吓跑威胁这个地区的敌对势力。凶神恶煞、佩有剑的武士模样的巨大花车，加上村民们古怪的跳跃和尖叫，足以让敌人避而远之。由此，这一古老的传统便开始了。

据说，弘前市的睡魔节是为了纪念青森县睡魔节的成功举办而开始的。这儿的彩车虽然很大，但形状不像人，而像大扇子。与其他节日类似，花车一面画着众多武士的形象，而另一面则总是一位女神。

有关"睡魔"节起源的另一种说法则与净化有关，人们将其作为在夏末清洁社区的一种方式。人们相信这可以驱除厄运，迎接日本人慰藉祖先灵魂的盂兰盆节。

在盂兰盆节期间，天刚黑，我所在街区的众多小火堆就会点上火。人们在自家门前燃烧木柴，为即将回家的已故亲人照亮道路。我的隔壁邻居是位寡妇,节日期间,她每晚都会虔诚地点上盂兰盆节之火。

我刚搬来现在的家时,她总是让她的孙子孙女给她帮忙,他们很享受生火的新鲜感。但现在他们都长大了,对延续这一传统不再感兴趣。不过,我觉得这个一年一度的仪式很有趣。当她履行这一基于家庭和宗教的职责时,我经常会坐下来和她聊天。

有趣的是,日本人生火是为了吸引魂魄,而在美国,我们在万圣节制作南瓜灯却是为了把鬼魂吓跑。我想,我们想吓跑的鬼魂是邪恶的;而在日本,他们想帮助那些正在回家的已故亲人的灵魂。

最早遵循这一佛教传统的是中国,是一个十分重视祭祖的国家。日本家庭通常会在家庭的主佛坛前设立"灵坛"。他们在此摆放祭拜逝者的特殊物品,如食物、饮料、鲜花等。

我17岁时作为交换生住在东京的时候,得以亲身体验盂兰盆节的一整套传统风俗。人们会请一位僧侣到家里诵经,之后还会用盛宴和大量清酒招待他。僧侣到来前,寄宿家庭的女主人就准备好了已故公婆最喜欢的食物,并把它们都放在灵坛上。她还用蔬菜制作了微型的牛马(用一次性木筷当作腿和尾巴);牛马被放在灵坛上用来送祖先回家。

在盂兰盆节期间,我们在家族长子家相聚,他是我寄宿家庭女主人的哥哥。这很像是美国的家庭团聚,只是我们要一起步行前往墓地,参加扫墓仪式——每人轮流用水和刷子清洁家族墓碑。

因为在日本,所有逝者都要火化,所以整个大家族会有一块大墓碑;亲人的骨灰常常埋在墓碑之下。我们点香,祈祷,然后回到家中举行庆祝活动。

盂兰盆节和日本新年就像美国的感恩节和圣诞节,无论日本人住的地方离他们的祖居有多远,他们都会在节日期间回家。

Neputa Festival and Obon Season

Every summer during August, both Aomori and Hirosaki, the city where I used to live, host the Neputa Festival. Huge, fan-shaped floats are pulled down the main street by scores of people dressed in traditional costumes. The well-known festival is attended by people from all over the country.

Large drums called "taiko" are also pulled along and the rhythm of the beating drums keep people moving along. The Hirosaki festival is much subdued than the Aomori festival. The people at our festival, in unison, chant "ya-ya-do" in very slow and methodical voices.

In Aomori, the people pulling the float work themselves into a frenzy by hopping on one leg screaming "ra-se-ra, ra-se-ra". The float pullers throw the bells hanging by strings that are pinned all over the summer kimonos they are wearing into the crowds of people watching from the sidelines. The festival attendees scramble for the bells, and kids especially enjoy collecting as many bells as they can.

The floats in both festivals are enormous paper images of legendary characters brightly painted and meticulously constructed. Contests for the best float occur and companies, schools and organizations work night and day for weeks in advance to make these spectacular structures come to life. They are done in great secrecy behind closed doors or are completely shrouded in tents.

This is a night time festival, so the floats are lit from inside which make them glow brilliantly against the darkness of the night. It is quite magical. A friend of mine has a pub on the main street, where the long procession of floats travel, so I always reserve a window seat on the second floor to sit and watch the floats from a bird's eye view.

I was told that this festival originally started as a way to scare away warring factions who threatened this area. The giant ominous looking float of sword-bearing Samurai fighters, coupled with the erratic jumping and screaming of the villagers, were enough to keep the enemy at bay. Hence the start of this early tradition.

In Hirosaki, the festival is said to have started as a celebration festival to honor the Aomori festival for being so effective. The floats here albeit gigantic, are not shaped like people, but as big fans. Similar to the other festival, warrior images are painted on one side and the other side always features a goddess.

Another version of the festival's origin relates to purification, as a way to purify the community at summer's end. It is believed to expel bad fortune and to welcome the Obon Season, the time when Japanese console the spirits of their ancestors.

During the time of Obon, just after dark small fires dot my neighborhood. For the departed relatives who will be making their way home, people burn kindling wood in front of their homes to light the path. My next door neighbor, a widow, faithfully lights her Obon Season Fire every night during this period.

When I first moved to my present home, she always had her grandchildren with her to help. They enjoyed the novelty of stoking the fire. Today they are all grown up and uninterested in continuing this tradition. I however, find this yearly ritual to be fascinating. I will often sit and chat with her while she performs her familial and religiously based duties.

Interestingly, Japanese light fires to attract spirits and in the United States, at Halloween, we make jack-o-lantern to scare the spirits away. I suppose the spirits we intend to scare away are evil, whereas in Japan they want to assist the spirits of departed loved ones who are making their way home.

This Buddhist tradition was originally observed in China, another country that places great emphasis on ancestral worship. Typically in Japan, families set up "spirit altar" in front of the family's main Buddhist altar. Here they place special items, such as foods, flowers and drinks as the offerings for the departed souls.

When I lived in Tokyo as a 17-year-old exchange student, I got to experience firsthand the entire Obon festival traditions. A priest was invited to the house to chant a sutra; afterwards, he was treated to a huge feast with lots of sake. Before he arrived, my host mother prepared the favorite foods of the grandparents who had passed and placed all of it on the altar. She also made miniature oxen and horses out of vegetables (using disposable wooden chopsticks for their legs and tails); these were placed there to help transport the ancestors back home.

During the actual Obon holiday, we gathered at the oldest son's house, my host mother's elder brother. It was very much like an American-style reunion, except at one point we all walked together to the graveyard and participate in a cleansing ritual where everyone took turns cleaning the family gravestone with water and a brush.

Since all Japanese are cremated, there is one large stone for the entire extended family; the ashes of the loved ones are often interred there. We lit incense and prayed, then returned to the festivities at the house.

Just like Thanksgiving and Christmas in the US, the holiday season of Obon and New Year's are the two occasions where Japanese will return home no matter how far from their ancestor home they may live.

第七部分
日本旅游

Part 7
Japanese Tourism

公共交通

日本的公共交通系统十分优秀。基本上，人们总是能够乘坐某一快速、便利且实用的公共交通工具准时到达日本境内的几乎任何地点。

人们每天搭乘火车、飞机、汽车、轮船或是骑自行车往来于日本全境。我在日本一直没有车，说实话，我并非真的需要一辆车。我可以搭乘公共交通或者骑自行车到达任何我想去的地方。

尽管我每年只在美国待一两个月，但我在印第安纳州却有一辆车，还会对它进行维护保养。这并不是为了摆阔，而是现实的需要，因为我需要一辆车开去目的地。

有几次回美国，我确实试过租车出行，但是成本太高了，几年下来，我在美国买一辆旧车开要比租车更实惠。我对汽车的需求仅仅限于其驾驶功能，因此我的车是一辆98年款的别克名使，供我回美国时开。我很少开这辆车，我想，在我将它开到报废之前，它就已经成老古董了。

由于我住在九州的南岛，所以往返此地很不便。每当有朋友恰巧到东京出差，他们经常会发电子邮件告诉我他们的行程，并提议当他们在东京期间大家见见面，吃个午饭或晚餐。

除了我往返东京需要花费大约600美元机票钱以外，这主意还是很吸引人的。乘坐夜间巴士往返的费用比机票便宜些，但是单程就需要好几个钟头。子弹头列车的票价比夜间巴士要贵，但单程仍然需要至少5个小时和大约250美元。

因此，除非有事要去东京，又碰巧赶上朋友到访日本，否则我极少为了和别人匆匆吃个午饭而赶往东京。这同一个到访纽约的外国人要邀请家住印第安纳州人到曼哈顿把酒言欢，是一个道理。

当然，一直以来，我都邀请大家到家里做客，可是，一旦他们了解到九州所需的时间和精力（更别提其中的花费），我们通常只会在电话里进行一次愉快的长谈。

费用高昂是日本公共交通系统的主要缺点，但对于生活在此的人们而言，它是日常生活的一部分。因此，在人们决定是否乘坐飞机、子弹头列车或夜班巴士出行时，费用并不是他们考虑的首要因素。这是日本，生活成本自然很高昂。

话虽这么说，但是日本人确实知道如何让出行变得高效、舒适和便利。比方说，当我需要到东京出差时，我通常会坐飞机前往，因为费用是由邀请我的机构承担的。

我在本县离我家最近的国内机场搭乘飞机，经过一个半小时的飞行到达东京。抵达东京后，我可以乘坐单轨铁路前往东京市区，在那里我可以搭乘任意一条地铁快速、便捷地到达东京市内任何地方。

当我住在日本北部时，冬天，因为大雪可能导致航班延误甚至被取消，我几乎不会冒险坐飞机去东京，而会选择乘坐既时髦又舒适的子弹头列车（新干线）。我尤其喜欢乘坐火车从日本最北部南下东京时沿途的风光。从乡村气息浓厚的地区到国际大都市东京，沿途在地形、景致和环境上的鲜明反差，十分赏心悦目。

日本著名的子弹头列车实际上是由众多单独的列车线路组成的。这些线路不仅在本州岛各地提供服务，甚至还跨海延伸到了九州岛，最终到达福冈市。子弹头列车以难以置信的速度非常平稳地在铁轨上滑行，穿过城镇、乡村和农田，驶往各大城市。

乘坐巴士去东京应该是最经济实惠的，而且选择众多。我的许多学生选择乘坐十分便宜的日间巴士，但这需要几乎一整天才能抵达东京。我偶尔会选择坐夜间巴士，晚上10点从我所在的城市出发，到达东京的时间大约是第二天早上7点。

我经常预订超豪华巴士座位，这种座位能倾斜至水平位置，还有搁脚的空间，你可以完全平躺下来。座位四周挂有帘子，得以营造绝对的私人空间。

服下一片助眠药，乘客就可好好睡上一觉，但是行驶中的巴士难免会前后晃动。巴士后部有洗手间，但是，在汽车行驶过程中，要在漆黑一片、满是睡着的乘客的巴士上，摸索着去洗手间，是件令人沮丧的事。巴士上的厕所逼仄狭小，反倒让飞机上的简易洗手间看上去大了不少。第二天早晨，乘客在下车之前会领到一条擦洗用的热毛巾，以便清醒之后在东京臭名昭著的早高峰时段挤地铁或列车。

从日本各地前往东京或东京以南的地区，乘坐轮船或渡轮是另一种出行方式，这要花更多时间，但是如果不赶时间的话，还是很有趣的。

在本文开头，我提到了自行车。如果你要在日本做长途旅行，自行车并不是最切实可行的交通工具。但许多日本城市确实会为游客提供自行车，供他们免费使用或低价租用，以便到城市各处游览。很多城市都有这样的系统，游客可以在火车站取用自行车，并在用后将其置于市内多个停放点。

总而言之，我对日本在公共交通领域的创新和创造力印象深刻。我甚至可以乘坐当地咔哒作响的火车到我的学校去，这段路坐火车只需5分钟车程。

我也可以坐巴士、出租车或骑自行车,当然,我还可以步行前往。实际上,我对自己在日本没有汽车感到高兴。因为,事实上,从我家步行10分钟就到学校了。我知道,要是我有车的话,我会养成美国人的习惯,这几步路也要开车前往。不管我喜欢与否,不开车确实迫使我保持健康。

拥挤的东京地铁

Public Transportation

Public transportation in Japan is out of this world. Essentially, one can travel to just about anywhere in Japan using some form of public transportation that is quick, convenient, practical and always on time.

Between trains, planes, buses, ships and bicycles, people travel to and from all over Japan, every day. I never own a car in Japan, and frankly, I do not really need one. I can get everywhere I need to go by public transportation or bicycle. Even though I only spend a month or two in the United States each year, I do own and maintain a car in Indiana. It is not for luxury but out of necessity. I need a vehicle to get to the places I need to go.

I did try renting a car on a few trips home, but the cost was so prohibitively expensive that after a few years, it became more economical to purchase an older car to have and use when I am stateside. My need is purely functional, so I have a '98 Buick Le Sabre that I drive around when I visit the US. I use it so little that I figure it will become a classic before I even begin to wear it out.

Since I live on the southern island of Kyushu, getting to and from here can be problematic. When friends happen to be coming to Tokyo on business, they will often e-mail me their itinerary, suggesting we meet for lunch or dinner while they are in town.

That would be nice, except it costs me around $600 round-trip to fly to Tokyo. An overnight bus can get me there and back for less, but it takes many hours each way. The bullet train is more expensive than the night bus but still takes a minimum of 5 hours and costs about $250 one way.

So, unless I am going to be there for another reason that happens to coincide with a friend's visit to Japan, rarely do I make the effort to meet someone for a quick lunch in Tokyo. It would be similar to a foreign visitor traveling to New York asking a Hoosier to meet up for drinks in Manhattan.

Of course, I always extend an invitation for people to visit me, but once they realize how much time and effort it takes (not to mention the cost) to travel to Kyushu, we usually just have a nice, long chat by phone.

That is the primary drawback of the public transportation system in Japan—the cost. For people living here, it becomes a part of daily life, so the cost is not the overriding concern when deciding whether or not to take a trip by plane, bullet train or overnight bus. It's Japan, of course, it's expensive!

With that said, however, Japanese really do know how to make transportation efficient, comfortable and easy. For instance, when I am needed in Tokyo for business, I will usually fly, because the cost is covered by the organization inviting me.

From the nearest domestic airport in my prefecture, I take the one and half hour flight to Tokyo. Once in Tokyo, I can hop on the monorail from the airport to central Tokyo, where I can take one of many train lines to get to anywhere within Tokyo quickly and effortlessly.

When I lived in the northern Japan in the winter, I rarely chanced taking a plane to Tokyo because of the risk that snow would either delay or cancel the flight. Instead, I opted to travel by bullet train (Shinkansen), which was quite sleek and comfortable. I especially enjoyed the scenery while traveling from the extreme north down to Tokyo in the south. It was quite interesting to observe the contrasts, not only in terrain changed but also in the landscape and surroundings, going from a very rural area to ultra-cosmopolitan Tokyo.

The fabled "bullet train" of Japan is actually made up of a number of separate lines that provide transportation all over the Honshu Island, even crossing over to Kyushu Island, terminating in Fukuoka. It glides very smoothly at incredible speeds, passing through cities, towns, villages and farmland as it makes its way to all the major cities.

Going to Tokyo by bus can be the least expensive, offering a variety of options. Many of my students take a day bus that is quite cheap, but it takes nearly all day to get there. One alternative that I resort to on occasion is the night bus. Leaving at 10 p.m. from my city, it arrives at around 7:00 a.m. the next morning in Tokyo.

There is an extra-posh "super seat" that I often reserve. It reclines flat and has a cubbyhole to put your legs, allowing you to lie down completely. It has a curtain that is pulled completely around the seat, allowing for complete privacy.

With a sleep aid, one can get some quality shut-eye, but it is a bus and it does rock back and forth. A toilet is located in the back, but maneuvering through the darkened bus full of sleeping people and using the facilities while it is moving, can be daunting. The restroom is so small that it makes the economical facilities on planes seem big. A hot towel is given to each passenger in the morning to freshen up before disembarking and fighting the infamous Tokyo morning rush hour on the subway and train lines.

Ships or ferries are another way to get around in Japan to Tokyo or even further south. These take much longer, but can be fun if time is not an issue.

At the beginning of the essay, I included bicycles. This is not the most practical way to get around in Japan if one has to travel a long distance, but many cities do offer bicycles for tourists to either use for free or to rent inexpensively to tour the city leisurely. Many cities have this system, and the bicycles can be checked out at the train station and dropped off at a variety of sites around the city.

All in all, I am quite impressed with Japan's innovation and creativity when it comes to public transportation. I can even take a clickety-clackety local train to my school, which takes five minutes. I also have a choice of a bus, taxi, my bicycle and, of course, my legs to get me from one place to another. I am actually glad I don't have a car here, because as it stands I have a mere 10-minute walk from my home to my university. I know if I had a car, I would fall into the American habit of driving this short distance. It does force me to stay fit whether I like it or not.

出租车行业

　　一位朋友曾问我，究竟是什么让我对日本如此着迷。一时间，我的脑海中立刻涌现出了许多事物。当我在心里细数日本极具吸引力的方方面面时，我决定列出一个我心中的日本十佳事物排行榜。

　　毫无疑问，在榜单上名列前茅的是出租车。日本的出租车司机外表格外整洁、动作格外麻利且待人格外礼貌。他们常常穿着精心熨烫的制服、戴帽子、带白手套。我经常乘坐的那家出租车公司要求司机们用最礼貌的日语做自我介绍，而他们都记住了我的名字。

　　为了能在异常激烈的市场竞争中脱颖而出，日本各家出租车公司想尽办法。为了吸引回头客，有的出租车公司会出台折扣、优惠券或其他类似的奖励措施。近来，有一种做法在我居住的城市蔚然成风：出租车公司向顾客提供一张"用户"卡，用以累积顾客每次乘坐出租车产生的积分。这些积分随后可以用来兑换不同的奖品。

　　所有日本出租车的一个基本特征是车上都安装了由司机遥控开启和关闭的自动车门。车门通过操纵杆开启，以便乘客进入；到达目的地之后，再次使用操纵杆打开车门，好让乘客下车。在乘客离开后，车门会自动关闭。

　　这一看似出于礼节的不起眼的小动作，却有非常实用的一面。因为大多数日本人出门时会携带袋子或公文包之类，车门自动开闭的功能让他们十分受用，在上下车时，他们无需手忙脚乱地腾出手开车门或者触碰诸如门把手等别人触碰过的东西。

　　有一次，我从日本到访纽约，下了出租车就径直离开了。这时司机冲着我叫嚷，要我把车门关上。当时我尴尬不已，由于坐惯了日本出租车，竟然忘了只有日本的出租车才安有自动门。

同时，日本的出租车还十分整洁。座椅全都包着白色座套，更便于乘客快速进出。车子里里外外都得到了精心的养护，我从没见过有哪辆出租车被撞坏、车身凹陷或是脏兮兮的。

在日本之外的地方旅行时，我才意识到我被日本出租车公司向乘客提供的高水准服务给惯坏了。美国的出租车常常看起来像要散架似的，座位脏得要命，你会好奇在你上车之前究竟载过什么。与此同时，美国的出租车司机对于毫无戒心的乘客并非总是十分诚实，只是想着多绕路多赚钱，所谓的"拉着客人们去兜兜风"。

日本的出租车司机领的是固定工资，和拉多少客人无关，很少会绕路，拉着乘客漫无目的地瞎转悠。事实上，司机们似乎会想方设法尽快到达目的地。

偶尔，当司机因转错了弯而找不到目的地或是上了一条交通拥堵的车道，他会暂停计程表，只要求乘客支付正常路况下到达目的地所需的费用。瞧，这就是诚实。

日本出租车的另一个独特之处是其所使用的燃料。几乎所有的出租车都使用丙烷而非汽油。这种为避免高昂燃油成本的做法很可能源于20世纪70年代能源危机时期。我确信，考虑到汽油价格受近来石油价格上涨的直接影响，使用天然气作为燃料更加经济节能。日本的出租车在排队等待下一位乘客时经常挂空挡不熄火，因为天然气这种清洁能源对大气层的破坏远没有化石燃料大。

日本人在任何场合排队基本上都井然有序。几乎所有的日本火车站都有出租车等候处，出租车在此等候到站的铁路旅客，搭载他们去往目的地。排队搭乘出租车的旅客从不推搡或插队，人们安静地等待空车把前面的旅客接走。

在许多其他国家，情况绝不会是这样。最近我去了泰国一趟，有些人在出租车等候处插队的行为让我万分沮丧。这些人抱着"人人为己"的心理。厚颜无耻地招呼一辆离另一个等候更久的人几步之遥的出租车或者从别人眼皮底下抢坐出租车等，都是很不礼貌的行为。

这种情况在日本很少发生。当然，彬彬有礼是众所周知的日本文化特征，这样的插队行为在日本有失体面；而且也没必要这么做，因为正常情况下拦一辆出租车是很容易的。日本的人均出租车数量很多，因此，从理论上看，拦一辆出租车几乎不成问题。一大群人在大型体育赛事结束之后或是人们为了在暴雨天气不被淋湿，熙熙攘攘地设法找到一辆出租车，这可能是例外的情况。然而，不消多时，几乎总是会有一辆空车亮着红色显示器沿着街道驶来。

在不知情的人看来，日本的出租车收费确实很高，只要一上车，起步价一般就要六到七美元。总费用取决于目的地的远近，前两公里包含在起步价内，此后每行驶500米,费用就会上涨70至80美分。收费似乎还取决于时间,因为在车辆超时等候时,里程数也会增加。深夜至清晨这段时间还会收取约占里程费20%的额外费用。

当然,要是醉酒的乘客往窗外呕吐,吐到车身上,他就必须额外支付清理车辆的费用。几年前,我听说一位客气的出租车司机给了乘客一桶水,让他自己冲洗车辆,从而免收清洁费。

这显示了日本绝大多数出租车司机的职业态度,在大多数情况下司机们都很有耐心,根据我的亲身经历,他们在工作中展现出了难以置信的诚实。

当乘客下车时,司机总是提醒乘客不要落下东西。然而,万一乘客不小心把东西落在车上,遗失物品几乎都能找得回来。

如果是从杂货店采购回来,司机总会帮我把购物袋送到屋里。我使用的出租车公司可在几分钟之内派遣一辆车到我家接我,我刚放下电话,穿上外套,门铃就响了,说明出租车已经到了。瞧,这就是我所说的一流服务!

Taxi

A friend asked once why I like so much. Immediately, a number of things came to mind. As I started to mentally list the aspects I find especially attractive about Japan, I decided to make "Todd's Top-10 List of Things Japanese".

Certainly, high on the list is taxi. In particular, Japanese taxi drivers are clean, quick, and courteous. Often the drivers wear nicely pressed uniforms, hats and white gloves. The taxi service that I regularly use instructs its drivers to introduce themselves in the most polite form of Japanese, and they nearly always greet me by name.

Competition is quite keen within the taxi industry in Japan, so companies do whatever they can to stand out from the others. Some taxi services offer discounts, coupons or other similar incentives to attract repeat customers. Lately it has become trendy in my city for companies to offer customers a "user" card, whereby points are accrued each time the taxi service is used. These points can then be exchanged for different prizes or products.

One standard feature that all Japanese taxis are equipped with is automatic doors which are opened and shut for the customer remotely by the driver. A lever is used to open the door for the fare to enter, and after arriving at the destination is used again to allow the passenger to exit. The door is then automatically closed after the customer leaves.

This may seem like a frivolous gesture based on courtesy and politeness, but it has a very practical side to it. Since most Japanese people carry some sort of bag or briefcase, it is quite helpful to have the door opened and closed, allowing the passenger to enter and exit the vehicle without having to juggle items awkwardly or to touch anything that others have touched, such as door handles.

Once when I visited New York from Japan, I exited the taxi and just walked away. The driver yelled at me to shut the door. It embarrassed me because I had become so accustomed to Japanese taxis that I had forgotten that this is a custom unique to Japan.

Also, taxis in Japan are squeaky clean. The seats are all covered in white seat covers, making it easier to slide in and out. The inside and outside of the taxis are meticulously maintained. Never do I see a taxicab that is banged up, dented, or dirty.

When traveling outside of Japan, I realize how spoiled I am here with the high level of service the customer receives from the taxi companies. Often American taxis are seemingly on their last legs, with seats so grimy that it makes you wonder what was there before you. Also, drivers are not always the most honest with unsuspecting fares, literally "taking them for a ride".

In Japan, since drivers are paid a regular salary that is not dependent upon how many fares they pick up, rarely is a customer driven around aimlessly in order to pad the meter. In fact, it seems that drivers go out of their way to get to the destination as quickly as possible.

On occasion, when a driver has either made a wrong turn, can't readily find the destination, or has taken a route that ended up in bumper to bumper traffic, he will shut the meter off and ask the customer to pay what would be a fair price for only the distance that was expected to be traveled. Now, that's integrity.

Another unique trait of Japanese taxis is the type of fuel they use. Nearly all taxis use propane gas instead of gasoline. This custom most likely started as a way to avoid high fuel costs during the energy crisis in the 1970s. I am sure that with the recent surge in the price of oil, which directly affects gasoline prices, it is a bit more economical and energy efficient to use natural gas as a fuel source. Japanese taxis often idle in queues waiting for the next fare, because this clean burning fuel is not nearly as damaging to the atmosphere as fossil fuels are.

Japanese people are generally very orderly when waiting in lines of any sort. Train stations nearly always have a taxi stand available for people who need to get to their final destination after taking a train. There is never any pushing, shoving or cutting in these lines. People very calmly wait as each person in front of them is collected by the next available taxi.

This is certainly not the case in many other countries. On a recent trip to Thailand, I was so frustrated at how some people would cut in line at the taxi stand. These types of people have the attitude of "each man for himself". Underhandedly trying to hail a taxi several feet in front of another person who has been waiting longer or grabbing a taxi out from under another person's nose are examples of poor taxi etiquette.

Rarely does this happen in Japan. Of course, politeness is a well-known Japanese cultural trait, and such behavior would be disgrace; but it is also unnecessary, because normally it is so easy to catch a cab. Per capita, there seems to be such an abundance of taxis in Japan that hailing one is nearly a statistical certainty. Exceptions would be after a major sporting event where a barrage of people are clamoring to find a taxi or during a rainy season deluge when people are trying to get out of the weather. Nearly always, however, after hardly any time at all, an empty taxi with its telltale illuminated red meter comes cruising down the street.

Taxi fares in Japan do seem pricey to the uninitiated, typically starting at around $6 to $7 for just entering the cab. The total cost of the ride depends upon how far you need to go. The first two kilometers is included in the base price, and the fare then periodically increases around 70 to 80 cents for each additional 500 meters traveled. It is seemingly based on time as well, because the meter does increase while taxi is sitting idly for an extended period. There also is an additional charge of around 20 percent added to fares from late at night until early morning.

Inebriated passengers who happen to heave out the window and onto the side of the taxi are, of course, charged an additional fee for the cleanup of the taxi. Years ago I heard of a passenger being given a bucket of water to rinse the taxi by a polite driver so the customer wouldn't be charged for the cleanup.

This sums up the professional attitude of the majority of taxi drivers in Japan. They demonstrate a high level of patience (in most instances) and in my experience, display an incredible amount of integrity for their work.

As the customer leaves the taxi, the driver always reminds the person not to forget his or her belongings. However, if an item is mistakenly left in a taxi by a passenger, chances are in the customer's favor of having the item returned.

If I am returning from grocery shopping, the driver always assists me in carrying the bags of groceries into the house. The taxi service I use can have a taxi dispatched to my home in a matter of minutes. I barely get off the phone and put my coat on, when the doorbell rings, announcing the taxi's arrival. Now, that's what I call service!

抵达与入住

我第一次来日本时，一切都是那么新奇。当时我还没有意识到，我就此开启了一场最终将对我的未来生活和职业生涯产生巨大影响的人生冒险之旅。

令人更加兴奋的是，20世纪70年代的迪斯科组合"桃子和草本"和我们同乘一趟飞机，还和我们一起排队过关入境。当然，我们都得到了他们的亲笔签名并照了很多相片，纪念和明星的此次邂逅。

最近，一位读者来信，希望我推荐一些日本值得游览的地点，我当时就想起了这一段经历。这是她第一次出国旅行，肯定会造访日本的"大苹果（纽约的昵称）"——东京。她想了解一些关于在东京出行、住宿、餐饮、观光以及购物的内部信息。

首先，独自一人造访日本令人钦佩，但对于第一次来的人而言绝非易事。当然，现在的情况和1979年时相比已大不一样了，但对初次来的游客来说，依然是不小的挑战。

一到东京成田机场，嘈杂的景象和噪音有时会让游客们目瞪口呆。航站楼里，东来西往的巨大客流产生的噪音可能让从未见过这种阵仗的人难以忍受。

如今，这里已是十分现代化和国际化的机场，有英语指示牌为乘客指引方向。当我第一次来日本时，除了指引旅客通往入境处的标示牌之外，没有罗马字或英文的指示牌。当时有一个绿黑两色的发光指示牌，上面用巨大的字母写着"ALIEN（外国人）"，它看起来十分古怪，我忍不住拍了一张照片。

幸运的是，这些指示牌已经更新换代，现在的样子美观了很多，不至于让游客感觉自己那么不受欢迎或像外星人一样。事实上，从那时候开始，日本在让不懂日语的游客易于理解方向和标志方面，已经做得非常好了。

从机场到东京市区有相当长的一段路。我不建议你搭乘出租车坐上近两个小时，除非你口袋里有200美元闲钱没处花。此外，如果考虑到时间因素，乘坐从机场到东京火车站的特快列车会快捷很多，因为没人知道从机场到东京市区的高速公路上的交通状况。

只需合理的票价，就可以很方便地坐"成田特快"列车去往东京市中心。此外，还有其他更便宜的列车可供选择，但其中一些是停靠多个站点的地方列车，另外一些车次的终点站交通不太方便。

干净、舒适、高效的列车，让旅程变得轻松愉快。同时也有从机场到东京市内及周边很多地方的豪华巴士服务，但需要考虑一点的是，恼人的交通状况有时会让正常情况下90分钟的旅程变成几个小时。

我强烈建议在到达东京前预订好酒店。东京有上千家价格不等的酒店，但是如果在旺季或者碰上在东京举办大型活动时，临时订房可能会十分麻烦。

对于那些经济宽裕的高端游客来说，有皇室待遇般的特别酒店可供选择。但你需要为此支付一大笔钱。

精打细算的游客，可以找到价格公道（对东京而言）的合适住宿，每人每晚60~100美元。在日本，西式酒店和传统风格的旅店是按人头而不是按房间收费的。

所以，当一对夫妇想订房间时，他们需要付"双人价钱"，酒店通常会安排他们住有两张双人床的房间。日本很多平价酒店只有双人间或者单人间。涉外酒店的房间有时设有双人床或大号床，但仍是按人数而不是按房间收费。

我觉得一般的日本夫妇住酒店时更喜欢分床睡，而不是像美国夫妇那样常常喜欢同睡一张大床。当我母亲和继父来日本时，一位朋友帮他们在东京订了酒店。朋友觉得以他们的年龄，会想要两张床的房间（像日本的已婚夫妇那样）。当入住时发现是两张床，而不是在美国更常见的双人床或加大床，他们大吃一惊。

我在东京出差期间经常入住的几家酒店属于"商务酒店"，房间小而紧凑，但很干净。正如它们的名字，这些酒店面向那些主要是想找一个舒适、便捷的地方休息的商务人士，这些人不需要更高价位酒店的额外服务（如行李服务、客房服务、送洗服务）。

对于想要体验传统日本文化的游客来说，传统的日本小旅店或者"日式旅馆"是个不错的选择。价格与西式酒店相近，甚至更高，但通常包括了日式早餐的费用。

旅馆的房间地板通常铺设榻榻米垫子，所以不允许穿鞋子进入，房客睡在放在地板上的"蒲团"（日本床垫）上。房间里通常摆放一张矮桌和一些垫子，但不提供椅子。有时候，房间里只有一个厕所，客人和其他旅客一起用日式公共浴室洗澡。但是，东京大部分的日式旅馆，往往提供两种沐浴方式，在各自房间泡浴，或者在主楼层的公共浴室沐浴。客人们在住店期间可使用酒店提供的棉质浴袍和拖鞋。

Arrival and Hotels

I remember arriving in Tokyo on my first trip and just being absolutely awestruck at everything. I didn't know that I was embarking upon an adventure of a lifetime that would eventually have a great influence upon my future life and career.

Adding to the excitement was the fact that the '70s disco group "Peaches and Herb" were on our plane and happened to be in the immigration line with us. Of course we all got autographs and snapped rolls of film, commemorating this brush with fame.

I was reminded of this experience when a reader recently wrote to ask about what places I recommend visiting while in Japan. This is her first trip abroad, and, definitely, she will be visiting Japan's equivalent of the "Big Apple". She wants some inside information on how to get around, where to stay, eat, tour, and shop in Tokyo.

First and foremost, visiting Japan on your own is admirable, but can be quite daunting for the first-time visitor. Of course, today is a far cry from 1979, but it can still give a first-time visitor a run for his/her money.

Immediately upon arriving at Tokyo's Narita Airport, travelers are met with a cacophony of sights and sounds that sometimes leave them speechless. The immense size and the volume of people coming and going in all directions in the terminal can be jarring to the uninitiated.

Today, it is a very modern and international airport with signs in English to help guide you. When I first came to Japan, there were no Romanized or English signs, except for the sign guiding travelers to immigration. A green and black lighted sign had the word "ALIEN" in huge letters. It seemed so odd to me that I was compelled to snap a photo of it.

Fortunately, those signs have been replaced with more tasteful ones that don't make visitors feel so unwelcome or like creatures from outer space. In fact, since that time, Japan has done remarkably well in incorporating easy to understand directions and signs for visitors with no command of the Japanese language.

From the airport to downtown Tokyo is quite a jaunt. I do not recommend jumping into a taxi for the nearly two-hour trip unless you have $200 burning a hole in your pocket. Besides, if time is a factor, the express train from the airport to Tokyo Station is much faster anyway because one never knows what kind of traffic is waiting on the expressway between the airport and central Tokyo.

For a reasonable fare, it is easy to hop on the "Narita Express" train that takes you to the heart of Tokyo. There are several other train options, which are cheaper, but some are local trains that have many stops and others end at stations that are not as convenient.

The trains are clean, comfortable and efficient, which makes the trip quite enjoyable and hassle-free. There is also a limousine bus service from the airport to a variety of destinations in and around Tokyo, but one has to take into account that pesky traffic that can sometimes make the normally 90-minute trip into one that takes several hours.

I highly recommend arranging hotel accommodations before arriving in Tokyo. There are literally thousands of hotels—in all price ranges—but getting a room on demand can be a bit sticky if it is during high season or coincidentally corresponds with a big event taking place in Tokyo.

For the high-end visitor who is not on a budget, there are exceptional hotels that can make a person feel like royalty. But you need a princely purse to pay for it.

For the discriminating but cash-conscious traveler, one can find suitable accommodations at reasonable rates (for Tokyo) costing $60 to $100 per person per night. In Japan, Western-style and traditional-style hotels charge per person and not per room.

So, if a couple wants to reserve a room, they would pay a "twin-rate" and usually be given a room with two twin beds. Many budget hotels in Japan exclusively have either single rooms or twin rooms. Hotels that cater to foreign guests will sometimes have double or queen-sized beds, but the charge is still per person and not per room.

I think the average Japanese couple prefers separate beds, unlike Americans who often prefer to have one big bed. When my mother and stepfather came to visit, a friend reserved their hotel for them in Tokyo. He assumed, because of their age, they would want to have twin beds (like Japanese married couples). It surprised them to see two twin beds, instead of two double or queen-sized beds, which is more standard in the United States.

I have several hotels that I routinely use when on business in Tokyo. These fall into the category of "business hotel", which means the rooms are small, compact, but clean. These hotels, as the name suggests, cater to businesspeople that basically need a comfortable and convenient place to sleep without the frills of more higher-priced hotels (bellhops, room-service, valet service).

The traditional Japanese inn, or "ryokan", is a nice choice for visitors who want to experience traditional Japan. The prices tend to be as expensive, or more so, as Western-style hotels, but a Japanese breakfast is often included in the price.

The rooms are covered with tatami mats, so no shoes are permitted inside; and guests sleep on futon on the floor. These rooms usually have a low table with cushions, but often no chairs are provided. Sometimes, only a toilet is a part of the room, with guests using a traditional Japanese-style communal bath for bathing. Most ryokan in Tokyo, however, tend to offer both—a full bath in each room and the option of bathing in a communal bath on the main floor. Guests are given cotton "yukatta" (robe) and slippers to use while at the hotel.

在东京游览

虽然我不是很喜欢"跟团游",但对于第一次到东京,并希望在有限的时间里尽可能多游览几个地方的游客,我还是强烈推荐坐汽车跟团游览东京,因为除非你时间充裕且不怕迷路,不然的话还是坐汽车去各大景点更加方便,最终也会更加惬意的。

多年来因工作和休闲往返东京,我已经学会了如何自信从容地在这座庞大的城市穿行,但从一个地点到达另一个地点还是要花许多时间。到达车站,赶上正确的列车而后转车,再转乘地铁,爬楼梯到地面找到正确的出口,再徒步去你想要参观的景点,然后再反方向重复一遍之前的行程。之后,按照同样的流程去下一个地方——你肯定能理解的。

日本的巴士游确实已经做到了尽善尽美,不仅让游客感觉舒适和便捷,还能给游客提供十分有用的信息。提供全方位服务的巴士配有外语导游,让旅游团在景点下车游览,随后又把游客载往下一个景点。

为保证时效,巴士游的线路经过精心设计,以便高效有序地到达各大景点。当我的表兄弟们来东京游玩时,我们报名参加了一个半日游的旅游团。我们随团参观了东京的各大历史文化名胜。我很喜欢这种游览方式,因为它免去了我集东道主、导游及日本通于一身的压力,让我们在充分利用有限时间的同时,增长了见识,愉悦了身心。

一直以来,日本让我印象深刻的一点是,商场的售货员在接待顾客的时候是如此优雅和彬彬有礼。很少有国家能把商场经营得像日本一样出色。这些顶级商场可以用阔气、现代、新潮、时髦等词语来形容。

要是谁运气好,在早上开门时就来到商店,成为一天中最早的一拨顾客,迎接他们的将是一排排身着熨烫整齐的制服和套装的店员们诚挚的深度鞠躬问候。

使日本百货商店与众不同的正是这样的细节。女店员也会就如何与顾客交谈和向其做比划动作接受严格的训练,以使用最礼貌的语言和最优雅的手势。

首次到访东京的游客最好去参观一下东京塔或者东京天空树塔,并不是因为这两座塔的构造独特(巴黎的埃菲尔铁塔更加古色古香),而是因为在塔顶能鸟瞰广阔无垠的东京市。

东京塔明亮的红白色钢架顶多只能算是平淡无奇。但在晴好的天气,登上东京塔能够一览巍峨的富士山的风采,以及塔身四周拥挤的摩天大楼和其他建筑,在新近建成的东京天空树塔上也能饱览同样的风光。

在东京也能体验到传统的日本。我极力推荐去明治神社。漫步在神社内精心维护的地面上,你会忘记在神社大门之外就是熙熙攘攘的东京市区。要是走运的话,还可能碰上一对身着和服的新婚夫妇正在拍摄以神社为背景的正规婚纱照。

另一座有趣的神社是浅草神社,沿着狭窄的街道缓步走向神社正是其中的乐趣所在。街道两侧林立着兜售各类日本食物和饰品的老式摊位和商铺。

日本皇宫因其花园和庭院面积广阔,逛逛也颇为有趣。当然,游客虽然不能接近皇室的住所,但是可以了解足够多在雄伟的石墙和护城河里面皇室生活的信息。这里有好几处地方可以拍摄以皇宫建筑和宫墙为背景的照片。

Touring Tokyo

Although I'm not a big fan of guided "group" tours, I highly recommend taking a bus tour of Tokyo for the first-time visitor who wants to pack as much as possible into a finite amount of time. The reason is that unless you have lots of time and are not afraid of getting terribly lost, it is just easier and in the end, more enjoyable to be driven around to all the major sites.

After years of traveling back and forth to Tokyo for business and pleasure, I have learned to maneuver around this sprawling city with a certain degree of confidence and success. It still takes a lot of time to get from point A to point B, however. Finding the station, catching the right train, changing trains, switching to the subway network, climbing stairs, finding the correct exit, hiking to the site you want to see, then doing it all in reverse...and again to go to the next place—well, you get the picture.

The Japanese have certainly perfected the art of doing "bus tours" by making them not only comfortable and convenient but also quite informative. The full-service bus drops off the group at the exact place of interest, with a foreign language speaking guide, and picks the group up afterward to go to the next site.

The bus route is meticulously laid out to make it time-effective, hitting the major points of interest in a very organized and efficient manner. When my cousins came to visit, we signed up for a half-day tour that took us to all the major places of historic and cultural interest in Tokyo. I loved it because it took the pressure off me to be host, tour guide and Japan expert. It made the best use of our limited amount of time, while being very informative and interesting.

One aspect of Japan that I am regularly impressed with is how elegant and courteous department store clerks are when serving the store's customers. Few countries run department stores as well as Japan. Sleek, modern, trendy and swanky are a few words to describe shopping in one of these state-of-the-art emporiums.

If one is lucky enough to arrive as the doors open in the morning, the first customers of the day are treated to lines of perfectly dressed employees in neatly pressed uniforms and suits greeting shoppers with deep, respectful bows.

It is this type of detail that makes Japanese department stores stand out from the ordinary. Also, women clerks are strictly trained in how to speak and how to gesture toward customers, incorporating only the politest of language while using the most graceful of hand movements.

The first-time visitor to Tokyo would do well to see the Tokyo Tower or Sky Tree Tower for, instead of being as a structure they are so unique (the Eiffel Tower of Paris is much more quaint), they offer a bird's-eye view of how endlessly expansive Tokyo appears to be.

Tokyo Tower's bright red and white steel frame is tacky at best, but on a clear day one can catch a majestic glimpse of Mount Fuji, along with all the skyscrapers and buildings that are packed together in every direction. The same is true for newer Sky Tree Tower.

In Tokyo tourist can indeed experience traditional Japan. I highly recommend a visit to "Meiji Shrine". Strolling through its meticulously kept grounds makes one forget that outside the gates is the hustle and bustle of downtown Tokyo. If you're lucky, a newlywed couple in kimono may be getting a formal wedding photo taken with the shrine as a backdrop.

Another Shinto shrine that is fun to see is "Asakusa Shrine". Slowly making your way to the shrine down the narrow street is the fun part. Lining each side of the street are traditional stalls and shops hawking everything Japanese from food to trinkets.

The Imperial Palace is interesting to see because of its extensive gardens and grounds. Of course, tourists do not get anywhere near the imperial family's quarters, but visitors are shown enough to get an idea of what life must be like behind the imposing stone walls and moats. There are some really great places to get snapshots with buildings and palace walls as background.

在东京就餐与购物

在这个世界上——可能除了纽约之外——没有其他城市像东京这样拥有那么多餐厅和酒吧。人们能在东京找到任何一种食物，从埃塞俄比亚菜到蒙古菜再到南美菜，应有尽有。对于想体验正宗日本饮食文化的游客来说，传统的寿司店是最好的选择，因为你在别处吃不到如此新鲜的鱼。事实上，有的时候，当寿司师傅将餐碟摆在你面前时，餐碟里的鱼还在动。当然，胆小者可见不得这样的场面。

假如你不喜欢吃海鲜或鱼类，还有其他适合西方人口味的美味佳肴，比如"烧き鸟"（烤鸡肉串），"豚カツ"（日式炸猪排）或者"天妇罗"（裹面糊油炸鱼虾）等。

对爱吃肉的人来说，去一趟正宗的烧烤店就能美餐一顿。这些餐馆其实最初是韩式烤肉店，但现今在日本十分流行，数量众多。餐桌中间摆着用来烤肉的"火鉢"（铁板烧）烤架。生肉端上餐桌，每个人根据自己的喜好烤着吃。也可以点一些蔬菜作配菜，和肉一起烤，当然还会就着一扎一扎的啤酒吃下白色的糯米饭。

东京的夜生活举世闻名，尤其是在叫做六本木的地区。东京的这一区域就像磁铁一样吸引着想彻夜换着酒吧逍遥和跳舞的外国游客。这种事对我来说有些不齿，但那些想要见识东京夜生活的人却值得一试。近年来，人们通过新建餐饮和购物等豪华场所，试图一改该地区以往的形象，但是一到晚上，就不好说了。

东京尽管十分安全，但确实有个区域名声不太好，有一点危险，尤其是在晚上，那就是歌舞伎町。该区色情产业遍布，有黑帮出没。过去，有很多大型电影院坐落在此，人们为了看电影不得不冒险前往。如今，更大、更现代、优雅得多的影院遍布东京，民众不是非得去这一区域不可。

东京是个好玩的城市，这儿有很多地方可看，有很多事情可做。

银座因其房价跻身世界之最而闻名于世。二战后，东京的这一地区迅速成为高价商品云集的前沿时尚中心。如果你想买一串人工养殖的珍珠项链，银座便是不二之选。御木本（日本著名珠宝品牌）的旗舰店就坐落于银座的中心地段。

涩谷和原宿是年轻人和时尚人士常去的地方。一位家乡的朋友来日本时，她坚持要在那些地方站几分钟，仅为看看周围的人潮，因为一切时髦流行的东西都可以在这两个地方看到，人们一眼便知什么正在东京的时尚界流行，什么已经过时。日本年轻人非常注重时尚和配饰，任何流行时尚都能在这里见到。

涩谷地铁站外的人行道也值得体验一番。当示意行人通过的交通信号灯变绿时，几乎数以千计的行人朝各个方向交错穿越宽阔的大街，这种场景着实让初来乍到者措手不及，过马路时还得尽力避免被人踩踏。

在原宿，有一条穿过数个街区、名叫"竹下通"的小道。对追求最新潮的服装、鞋包以及其他时尚商品的年轻人来说，这里就是人间天堂。得提醒一句：窄巷里挤满了人，你必须像逆流而上的三文鱼一样拼命往前挤。

在竹下通的另一端，是通往"东京香榭丽舍"的一小段路——表参道。这条林荫大道面向的是富有而时尚的购物者。年长一点的有钱人喜欢去银座购物，而表参道面向的则是25~55岁上下的生意人和职业人士。

这里有一座名叫"表参道山"的购物广场，十分高端优雅。漫步于这家建于地下、设计独特的购物中心是一种享受。相比其他国家的购物中心，这里的实际空间十分狭小，但建筑师和设计者们营造出了一种错觉，让它看上去空间开阔。

我推荐去位于同一条林荫道上的"东方集市"购买纪念品。游客可以在这家店里买到古董、新旧和服、陶瓷和其他任何具有日本特色的物品。

不过，你可以在回家的路上顺道去机场的"东方集市"分店停下来逛逛，这样就无需一路随身携带此前购买的日本小玩意和纪念品。尽管规模要比总店小很多，但这里有很多纪念品供游客选择，且价格和总店一致，并没有因为在机场就抬高价钱。

真正精打细算的旅行者最好去一家名为"100日元商店"的日版"一美元"商店。这样的店铺到处都是，商品种类繁多，令人难以置信。因此给国内的家人和朋友购买日本纪念品很方便。一件纪念品那么便宜，可能你都不好意思说出口，这是日本为数不多的便宜货之一。

预算有限在日本可玩不转,最好带上大把钞票,因为日本的消费可不便宜。精打细算的游客可以玩得很愉快,但大多数游客无论多么节俭,在最初的消费冲动之后,开销最终必定会超出其预算的金额。毕竟,这里可是东京。

Restaurants and Shopping in Tokyo

No city on earth—with the possible exception of New York—has as many restaurants and bars as Tokyo. One can find any type of food, from Ethiopian to Mongolian to South American...and anything and everything in between. For the visitor who wants to experience the real Japan, a traditional sushi bar would be a good choice because you can't get any fresher fish anywhere else. In fact, sometimes the fish is still moving when the master chef sets the plate down in front of you. Not for the fainthearted, for sure.

If seafood or fish isn't your thing, there are other wonderfully delicious delicacies that are quite agreeable to the Western palate. "Yakitori" (skewered chicken), "tonkatsu" (breaded pork tenderloin) or "tempura" are some examples.

For meat lovers, a visit to a typical "yakiniku" restaurant would be a treat. These restaurants are actually Korean in origin but are prevalent and abundant all over Japan. In the center of the table is a "hibachi" grill, where the meat is cooked. The uncooked meat is brought to the table, and each person grills the meat to their liking. Side orders of vegetables can be ordered to be grilled alongside the meat, and of course, white, sticky rice is eaten, along with mugs of beer to wash it all down.

Nightlife in Tokyo is world-renowned, especially the area called "Roppongi". This part of Tokyo seems to be a magnet for foreign tourists wanting to barhop and dance the night away. It is a bit too seedy for my tastes, but it's worth a gander to those who want to see what Tokyo's nightlife has to offer. In recent years, this area has tried to clean up its image by creating tony areas for dining and shopping but at night can still be a bit dicey

Though Tokyo is generally a safe city, one area that does have a reputation for being a tad bit dangerous, especially at night, is Kabuki-cho. It is here that much of the sex-related industry is located, with gangs being visibly present. In the old days, many of the big movie theaters were in this area, making it necessary to venture there. Today, bigger, more modern, and much more elegant theaters dot the city, making it less likely to have to go to this part of town.

Tokyo is a fun city to visit, because there is so much to see and do.

The "Ginza" is internationally notorious for having some of the priciest real estate in the world. After World War II, this area of Tokyo quickly became the center of high fashion and high prices. If you are in the market for a strand of cultured pearls, this is the place to go. Mikimoto's flagship store is located in the heart of the Ginza.

The areas of Shibuya and Harajuku are where the young and fashionable hang out. When my friend visited from my hometown, she insisted upon standing for several minutes just to "watch people" because any and every type of fashion trend can be seen in these two areas. It offers a glimpse into what's hot and what's not in the Tokyo fashion world. Japanese young people take fashion and accessorizing quite seriously; if it's in style, it will be seen here.

Outside Shibuya Station is a crosswalk that is worth experiencing once. When the light turns green for pedestrians, literally thousands of people crisscross the wide avenue in every direction making a newcomer dizzy trying to take it all in, while at the same time, trying to avoid getting trampled.

In Harajuku, a narrow alleyway running a number of blocks called "Takeshita Dori" is heaven on earth for young people trying to find the latest apparel, shoes, bags or other fashion-related goods. A word of warning: It is usually wall-to-wall people, so you must charge forward aggressively to make your way, like salmon swimming upstream.

At the other end of Takeshita Dori, it is a short walk to the Champs-Elysées of Tokyo—Omotesando. This tree lined boulevard caters to the well-heeled and trendiest of shoppers. Where the Ginza attracts older, wealthy shoppers, Omotesando is geared toward the mid-20s to mid-50s business and career minded crowd.

A shopping plaza opened there called "Omotesando Hills" which is very high-end and elegant. It is enjoyable to stroll in its uniquely designed mall that goes deep underground. The actual physical space is quite small in comparison to malls in other countries, but the architects and designers created an illusion of having vast space in an area that is actually quite narrow.

I recommend the "Oriental Bazaar" on this same boulevard for souvenir shopping. One can find antiques, new or used kimono, as well as ceramics, books and just about anything Japanese in this store.

However, instead of carrying your Japanese baubles and mementos throughout the rest of your trip, you can hold off and visit a branch of the Oriental Bazaar at the airport on your way home. Although it's a much more scaled down version of the main store, there are plenty of souvenirs to choose from and for the same price. There is no mark-up even though it's at the airport.

The truly budget-conscious traveler would do well to visit a Japanese version of a "dollar" store called "100-yen Shop". These stores are everywhere and the variety of merchandise is unbelievable. It is very easy to find Japanese-type souvenirs for family and friends back home. It can be your secret that it is so cheap. This is one of the few bargains in Japan.

Visiting Japan on a shoestring budget is not easy. It is best to come with fistfuls of money, because it isn't cheap. A budget traveler can have an enjoyable stay, but most visitors, after the initial sticker-shock, do eventually succumb to spending more than they intended, no matter how frugal they try to be. It's Tokyo, after all.

观赏樱花

在日本，我最喜欢的活动就是一年一度的"花见"（赏樱会）。4月底5月初有一系列的国家法定节假日，即黄金周期间，在我曾居住了20年的地方总能欣赏到美丽的樱花。

从3月份开始，从南到北，全日本的樱花陆续开放，并伴随着一年一度的赏花活动。人们一边赏花，一边在樱花树下野餐和娱乐。

如果要给体现日本精神的风俗习惯列个清单，那赏樱聚会无疑会名列榜首。大中小学的学生，公司的同事，俱乐部的成员，以及其他任何群体都聚集在一起，欣赏那些娇嫩的粉色花朵在头顶摇曳生姿的美景。

赏花当天，公司会指派新进职员在清早去寻找最佳的赏花地点，他们把大张的塑料布铺开并固定在地上以待盛会。随后，年轻的职员则会一整天坚守阵地，直到傍晚时分同事们带来食物及大量酒水。

如赏花者没有自带食物，则通常由众多餐馆或酒吧中的一家提供，这些餐馆、酒吧在樱花季生意很兴隆。除了赏花，最吸引人的莫过于边喝啤酒边吃传统食物了。

夜色渐深，总会有人站起来即兴跳舞或献歌一曲。事实上，有些团体甚至会自带便携式卡啦OK机，这样就能纵情歌唱。

通常，几个小时后人群就会开始"二次会"，或是在事先订好的酒吧里举行第二轮派对。这样的派对通常都是在工作日的晚上举行并持续到黎明，因此赏花者在第二天早上一身疲惫地进办公室时穿戴往往有点邋遢。

我第一次赏花是和我工作的教育单位的教职员工一起去的。组织者考虑到了每个细节，预计到有人会宿醉，他们给了每个人一瓶功能饮品，在日本，这种饮品常用来治疗宿醉者，让他们在酒后的第二天早上彻底清醒。令人吃惊的是，没有人打电话请病假，也没人会抱怨头痛，这些功能饮品里肯定添加了某种成份。

四月份大学开学不久恰好赶上樱花季，大学生们有时难免会饮酒过度，而因此导致酒精中毒已司空见惯，所以赏花现场就停着救护车，随时准备救助那些过度放纵的人，或处理其他突发医疗事件。

每年，市政当局都会在大学校园内外张贴海报，警示学生饮酒过度的危害。毫无疑问，教育工作者反对学生参与名为"一口气，一口气"的游戏，因为这种游戏怂恿学生们一口气吞下整杯酒——这是一种一喝下去当场就醉倒的喝法。

值得注意的是，虽然很多人醉得一塌糊涂，走路都东倒西歪，他们却都依然遵守秩序，极少有斗殴事件发生。通常，各个群体都会照顾好自己的成员，确保他们安然无恙地回到家。

赏樱

观赏樱花的风俗在日本由来已久。早在奈良时代（710~794），赏花集会在上层社会和贵族间就非常流行。最后，赏花的风俗在江户时代（1603~1868）流传到了民间，并一直延续至今。

在这个期盼已久的季节，整个日本都如痴如醉。有趣的是，你会看到记者被派去寻找全日本最佳的赏花地点，采访市民并现场报道樱花的开放情况；晚间新闻还会每天展示樱花的开放进程，通过巧妙地在日本地图上标出粉色区域来告诉人们哪里的樱花已经盛开了。

当樱花在日本南部的花期已过，国境最北端的樱花正准备盛开。幸运的是，我曾居住的弘前市就以有全国最引人入胜的樱花节之一自居。

来自日本各地的人们每年赶赴此地，在弘前城堡所在的公园里漫步，像昔日的武士一样享受着这一年一度的秀丽景色。在这座中世纪古城以及护城河的周围，簇拥着与城市一样古老的数千棵樱花树。

经我多年来对这一无比奇妙而独特的景色细致入微的描述，家乡的一位亲密故友终于决定从印第安纳跋涉来我居住的世界一隅，亲眼看看这一大自然的绝妙景致。

当我们惬意地在两旁盛放着樱花的阡陌小道上徜徉，克里斯突然停了下来，凝视着我们头顶犹如天篷和隧道一般、似乎无限延伸的粉色花海。她说："知道吗，此情此景简直无法用言语形容，真是美得叹为观止。"我只能如此回答她："我早跟你说过了。"

Cherry Blossoms Viewing

My favorite activity in Japan, every year, is "hanami" (cherry blossom viewing). The area where I lived for 20 years always enjoys cherry blossom season around Golden Week, a series of national holidays that occur at the end of April and the beginning of May.

Commencing in March, from south to north, all across Japan, cherry trees blossom, and an annual ritual takes place—the viewing of the blossoms while eating and drinking from beneath their branches.

If there were a list of customs and rituals that—when combined—formed the "soul" of Japan, cherry blossom viewing parties certainly would rank high on the list. Colleagues from universities and schools, coworkers from companies, members of clubs and just any other combination of people gather to enjoy the delicate pink blossoms swaying over their heads.

In companies, the new recruits are sent out early in the morning on the appointed day to scout out the best spots for viewing. Large plastic sheets are spread out and anchored down in preparation for the big event. The young staff members then guard the spot the entire day until nightfall when their coworkers arrive with the food and copious amounts of alcohol.

If the food isn't carried in by the attendees, it is often catered by one of the many restaurants or bars that do a booming business during this season. Besides viewing the blossoms, the main attraction is to drink beer while eating traditional foods.

As the night progresses, inevitably someone will stand up to do an impromptu dance or to sing a song. In fact, some groups even tote portable karaoke machines so they can sing to their hearts' content.

Usually after several hours, the party moves on to a "niji kai" or second party held at a pre-designated bar or pub, allowing everyone to continue their partying until the wee hours of the morning. Often, a viewing party will take place on a work night, so the blossom viewers are often a little worse for wear when they drag into their offices the next morning.

My first blossom viewing party was attended by teachers and staff at the board of education office where I worked. The organizers had thought of every detail. In anticipation of the likely hangovers, they gave everyone an energy drink which is widely used here as a cure-all for the morning after. Amazingly, not one person called in sick, and no one complained about having a headache. There must be something in those energy drinks.

University students can sometimes go overboard with the drinking aspect, because the cherry blossom season occurs shortly after classes begin in April. Too often, excessive drinking leads to alcohol poisoning, so ambulances stand by ready to assist in any over-indulgence that may occur or to assist in other types of medical emergencies.

Every year, city offices place posters in and around university campuses to warn of the dangers of overdrinking. A game which educators certainly discourage students from participating in is called "iki, iki" where students are goaded into drinking their entire drinks in one gulp—a sure way to get drunk really fast to a point of no return.

Remarkably, though, with the high number of really inebriated people stumbling about, everyone is quite orderly and fisticuffs are actually quite rare. Normally, the various groups take good care of those who are in their charge, making sure they get home in one piece.

The custom of cherry blossom viewing has a long history in Japan. During the Nara period (719~794), hanami parties were very popular with upper-class society and the aristocracy. Eventually, the custom spread among the common people during the Edo period (1603~1868), which still continues today.

Japan is a nation obsessed during this well-anticipated season. It is interesting to watch news reporters who are sent out to find the best viewing spots around Japan, interviewing people and then reporting live on the status of the blossoms. Nightly newscasts show the gradual progression of the flowering blossoms each day by delicately shading a map of Japan in pink indicating where the blossoms have begun to flower.

By the time the blossoms have come and gone in the south of Japan, they are about to bloom in the northern-most part of the country. Luckily for me, the city where I lived—Hirosaki—boasts one of the most spectacular cherry blossom festivals in the country.

People from all over Japan make their way here every year to stroll through the park where Hirosaki castle is located, to enjoy this once-a-year spectacle just as the samurai of yesteryear did. Literally, there are thousands of cherry trees around this medieval castle and moat that are as old as the castle itself.

After years of describing in minute detail this most unique and wonderful attraction, an old and dear friend from my hometown finally made the long trek from Indiana to my little corner of the world in order to see for herself this most splendid display of mother nature.

As we leisurely strolled through the many pathways lined with trees in full bloom, Chris paused momentarily to gaze at the sea of pink flowers that made a canopy-like tunnel over our heads that extended for what seemed like an eternity. She said, "You know, there are no words to accurately describe what we are seeing. It's beyond beautiful." All I could say was, "I told you so."